Verge

STUDIES IN GLOBAL ASIAS

Volume 4, Issue 2
Fall 2018

Verge (ISSN 2373-5058) is published twice a year in the spring and fall by the University of Minnesota Press, 111 Third Avenue South, Suite 290, Minneapolis, MN 55401-2520. http://www.upress.umn.edu

Postmaster: Send address changes to *Verge,* University of Minnesota Press, 111 Third Avenue South, Suite 290, Minneapolis, MN 55401-2520.

Essays (between 6,000 and 10,000 words) should be prepared using parenthetical documentation with a list of works cited. Authors' names should not appear on manuscripts; instead, please include a separate document with the author's name and address and the title of the article with your electronic submission. Authors should not refer to themselves in the first person in the submitted text or notes if such references would identify them; any necessary references to the author's previous work, for example, should be in the third person. Submissions and editorial queries should be sent to verge@psu.edu.

Books for review should be addressed to

Verge: Studies in Global Asias
c/o Department of Asian Studies
102 Old Botany
University Park, PA 16802

Address subscription orders, changes of address, and business correspondence (including requests for permission and advertising orders) to *Verge,* University of Minnesota Press, 111 Third Avenue South, Suite 290, Minneapolis, MN 55401-2520.

Subscriptions: Regular rates, U.S.: individual, 1 year, $35; libraries, 1 year, $100. Other countries add $5 for each year's subscription. Checks should be made payable to the University of Minnesota Press. Back issues are $17.50 for individuals, $50 for libraries (plus $6 shipping for the first copy, $1.25 for each additional copy inside the U.S.; $9.50 shipping for the first copy, $6 for each additional copy, outside the U.S.). *Verge* is available online through the JSTOR Current Scholarship Program at http://jstor .org/r/umnpress. A subscription to *Verge* is a benefit of attending Penn State's biennial Global Asias conference.

Verge Studies in Global Asias 4.2

■ INDIGENEITY   FALL 2018

Essays

Editors' Introduction

CHARLOTTE EUBANKS AND PASANG YANGJEE SHERPA

We Are (Are We?) All Indigenous Here, and Other Claims about Space, Place, and Belonging in Asia

WHAT IS INDIGENOUS about Asian Indigeneity?[1] A decade after the adoption of the United Nations Declaration on the Rights of Indigenous Peoples (UNDRIP) by the General Assembly, the UNDRIP notion of Indigeneity has proved quite mobile, interfacing with a wide variety of groups through organizational forums such as the UN Permanent Forum on Indigenous Issues and the International Work Group for Indigenous Affairs and regional interlocutors like the Asia Indigenous Peoples Pact Foundation (AIPP), based in Thailand, and Asian Indigenous and Tribal Peoples Network, based in India. Dominant globally circulating notions pertaining to Indigeneity (perhaps exemplified most strongly in the UNDRIP) constellate around issues of recognition. Assuming a structural condition of oppression vis-à-vis majority ethnic groups and the surrounding state apparatus, this rights-oriented framework assumes (and then advocates on behalf of) tight connections between specific territorial units (lands, rivers, mountains, forests) and specific cultural units (Indigenous Peoples and their distinct social, political, cultural, economic, linguistic, and spiritual systems). Deeply influenced by the legal apologetics of settler colonial states toward displaced Native, First Nations, and Aboriginal peoples, however, this notion of Indigeneity—at once largely modern, Western, and neoliberal—meshes imperfectly with autochthonous conceptions of Indigeneity as articulated in a wide variety of Asian contexts. This special issue presents such articulations to reveal the complicated ways in which peoples have deployed the term *Indigenous* in its various forms.

Indigeneity is "out there" (Karlsson 2003, 416), and like many other social categories, it is a contingent, interactive, and historical product

(Merlan 2009, 319). In Asia since the 1970s and 1980s, concepts of Indigeneity have been "linked to emancipatory political objectives associated with assisting oppressed peoples; not only those colonized by Europeans, but also others subjected to various forms of domination by Asians living in close proximity" have emerged and become popularized rather than linking to the notions of "first peoples" or "original peoples" (Baird 2015, 54). It is also the case that in some situations, as with Tibetans, who have their own historical and political landscape to consider, significant uptake of the term *Indigenous* has not happened (Yeh 2007). More specifically, Tibetans do not currently take part in the international mobilization of Indigenous Peoples (IPs), or what Niezen (2003) calls *indigenism* (Yeh 2007, 71). "For Tibetans in exile, indigeneity is too weak a political claim. Within Tibet, it is too strong under the current political situation" (Yeh 2007, 71).

Indigenous spaces are nevertheless claimed, although many IPs from Asia are not the first peoples in places they currently live (Baird 2016). For example, Morton et al. (2016) show that despite multiple historical experiences of displacement, marginalization, and, more recently, colonization, the Akha minority residing throughout the Upper Mekong Region have maintained their connection with ancestral homeland by way of "intimate place-making cosmographies." Through this form of "mobile indigeneities," the Akha communities recraft "non-Akha" spaces where they cannot lay claim to be the first people as a microcosmic totality of the Akha cosmos (580). The Bunong diaspora from Vietnam, as another example, connects with a growing Cambodian Bunong Indigenous rights movement, displaying translocal articulations of Bunong Indigeneity to build cross-border dialogue in concert with international law regarding the rights of IPs (Keating 2016). Their aim is "a new kind of politics that makes political space for their voices and aspirations to be heard and heeded by states to a meaningful and satisfactory degree" (Keating 2016, 575).

Though no less politically invested than UN terminologies keyed to structural violence and reparations, such regional and local terms provide an inventory of texture and distinctiveness, revealing the economics, identitarian stakes, and legal valences of people–space relations that may disappear under the singular moniker of "Indigenous." In India and other parts of South Asia, for instance, a careful probing of the term *adivāsi* (a twentieth-century Sanskrit neologism meaning, literally, "original inhabitant") reveals a long and complex history of subjugation and "pacification," beginning in the British imperial era and extending well beyond it, in which certain groups were identified with geographical areas (such as forested uplands) and accorded particular legal treatment as Scheduled Tribes in need, so the reasoning goes, of civilizing influence. In contemporary Nepal, the term is doubled: *adivāsi janajāti*, not only indexing "original inhabitance" in a specified locale but also raising issues of caste, ethnicity, and cultural distinctiveness while attempting to reclaim and invert some of the pejorative force of *janajāti*'s secondary connotations of backwardness.

By contrast, East Asian discourse on Indigeneity, broadly speaking, has been more heavily informed by Stalinist models of "minority nationalities" (in Chinese, *shaoshu minzu*). By declaring all citizens to be "heritage residents" (Chinese: *shiju minzu*) of the nation, as *the* social and cultural unit of import, the Chinese state could thus declare that "everyone is indigenous here" and, ipso facto, there simply *are* no IPs in the UNDRIP sense of the word. Largely rejecting international, rights-oriented discourse, then, cultural groups within China specifically, and much of East Asia more generally, have largely relied on the alternate framework of "original ecology" (*yuanshengtai*) to valorize environmental stewardship and cultural distinctiveness while sidestepping problematic rights-based claims that would seem to threaten state stability.

Southeast Asia presents an even more complex layering of terminologies, registering a rich mixture of Stalinist/Maoist "minority nationality" thinking blended with postcolonial and postimperial concerns about "original inhabitance," while also reflecting local political concerns and histories of ethnic relation. Thus, for instance, we see in Myanmar the conceptualization of "ethnic nationalities" (Burmese: *taingyantha*) and the even more insistent doubling of "*local* ethnic nationalities" *(htanay taingyantha)*. And in Malaysia, we see in use the term *bumiputera* (sons of the soil): a category that includes Malays and minority ethnic groups but excludes Chinese and Indian Malaysians who arrived largely during British colonial rule.

Indigeneity in Asia: a messy—and deeply provocative—nexus, to be sure. From the moment we decided to create this special issue, we wanted to invite a wide range of vantage points on, and interventions into, this tangled web of nested vocabularies, contradictory concepts, and contentious claims. As Ian Baird (2016) has noted, while any number of Asian governments may accept the rights-based concept of Indigeneity as comprehensible and even defensible for groups displaced by European settler colonialism, few political leaders in Asia consider it applicable to their own countries—one important exception being Taiwan, which does recognize various Aboriginal peoples and their rights to land restoration. In our initial call for papers, we noted our interest in charting (some of) the interactions between notions of Indigeneity and Asian-ness, as connected to broader conceptual concerns. If UNDRIP-style rubrics of Indigeneity spring largely from the historical ground of settler colonialism, is it a term that can, in fact, function in Asia? What cultural and social work does Indigeneity *do* for specific peoples, and how are they reshaping the term in the context of their own political realities? What does rethinking Indigeneity through the lens of "ethnic" or "minority nationalities" reveal about the (limitations of) colonial underpinnings of Indigeneity as theorized in the Global West?

To help us answer some of these questions, we invited submissions from scholars working on conversations between Asian American and First Nations peoples and tensions between identity, land, and language; Indigenous activism in response to climate change and international development (whether in the Himalayan region, the Gobi Desert, or the littoral zones of Pacific islands); the place of Indigenous cultural production vis-à-vis the/a State (e.g., the circulation or suppression of Chukchee literature in Eastern Siberia, the questions of ownership over cultural property in Vanuatu, the display of native artifacts in national museums); practices of resistance and policies of assimilation, both historical and contemporary (Ainu in Japan and Eastern Russia, Aboriginal groups in Taiwan, the Orang Asli in peninsular Malaysia, designated "national minorities" in the PRC, the Dravidian–Aryan divide in South Asia, etc.); historical encounters of Indigenous groups with expanding states and empires; the many problematics, demographic and otherwise, of categorizing Pacific Islanders with Asian Americans; practices of Indigenous knowledge in Asia and Asian America; the human geography of settler and Indigenous communities (e.g., the displacement of Hawaiians by Asian settlers, the legal rubric and social position of "Asians" in East Africa and "overseas Chinese" in Southeast Asia vis-à-vis "local" communities, claims to biculturalism in Aotearoa New Zealand); the creation of land reservations for IPs (in the Philippines, for instance); the international politics of Indigenous rights; archeology and the deep histories of Indigenous artwork and artifacts; the digitalization of Indigenous "ways of knowing." We cast a wide net, and although we did not bring up fish of every sort (the relative paucity of submissions focused on Asian diasporas in the Americas, for instance, and the glaring absence of anything focused on periods before 1900), we are proud to present what we find to be a thought-provoking set of interrelated discussions.

As always, we open this issue with the **Convergence** section, beginning with *Field Trip,* the ambit of which is to provide a report on the state of a field or subfield from the vantage point of a particular experience (participation in an institute, creation of a museum exhibit, construction of a new course, engagement with interlocutors during field work, and so forth). Lindsay Skog's powerful thought-piece "Thinking *with* Indigeneity: Imperatives and Provocations" provides an important methodological argument and a crucial intervention into existing practices of scholarly discourse. Anchored in moments from her own work in Khumbu, Nepal, Skog's is a crisp and well-written call for a turn away from thinking *about* Indigeneity and IPs to thinking *with* it and *with* them (some of whom are also "us," let us not forget). Indeed, Skog's piece grew out of her participation in the 2017 Asian Studies Summer Institute on Trans-Asian Indigeneity, held at Penn State. This weeklong event brought together eight young scholars representing a range of disciplines, geographical locations, and institutional settings, as well as a variety of relationships to Indigeneity. Several of the participants identify as IPs, and a constant theme in Institute discussions turned around questions of thinking with, rather than about, Indigeneity. A crucial first step in that process involves, of course, thinking *with* Indigenous scholars. If speaking *about* involves a still-colonialist top-down (empirical as imperial) mind-set, then it is imperative to begin with speaking *with*: engaging in open conversation in which one does more listening than talking.

In the spirit of collaboration and polyvocality, our second feature is an *A&Q,* a curated conversation between a handful of scholars around a shared set of questions. This issue's *A&Q,* "Indigeneity at Sea," germinated from a roundtable convened at the Global Asias 4 conference (March 31– April 1, 2017, at Penn State, University Park). Utilizing Lisa Kaholeole Hall's (2015) recent essay "Which of These Things Is Not Like the Other: Hawaiians and Other Pacific Islanders Are Not Asian Americans, and All Pacific Islanders Are Not Hawaiian" as a point of provocation, we asked several scholars—RDK Herman (senior geographer at the Smithsonian Institution, National Museum of the American Indian), Yu-ting Huang (assistant professor of modern Chinese literature at Wesleyan University), Dean Itsuji Saranillio (assistant professor of social and cultural analysis at New York University), and Erin Suzuki (assistant professor of literature at University of California, San Diego)—to reflect on interactions between notions of Indigeneity and Asian-ness in the Pacific Islands and Oceania. We are excited by how this collaborative piece addresses issues surrounding trans-Pacific Asian American and Indigenous studies, exploring various ways in which we might create meaningful alliances in Asian studies and Asian American studies without erasing IPs and Pacific Islanders.

Interface, another polyphonic **Convergence** feature that highlights digital scholarship, continues to engage with questions of Indigeneity and diaspora, shifting to work with IPs from/in the trans-Himalayan region. Two short essays ("What Next for Digital Himalaya? Reflections on Community, Continuity, and Collaboration" and "Orality and Mobility: Documenting Himalayan Voices in New York City"), prefaced by a short introduction, provide snapshots of two web-based digital projects, one nearing its second decade, the other in its second year. Collectively, the feature addresses issues surrounding the co-creation of knowledge and the collaborative nature of linguistic and cultural preservation work both in the Himalayan region and in a North American diasporic setting.

Our final **Convergence** feature is *Codex*, a collaborative book review that focuses this time on Chadwick Allen's groundbreaking study *Trans-Indigenous: Methodologies for Global Native Literary Studies* (2012). In the first response, Hsinya Huang outlines the promise of Allen's approach, which "opens up the possibility of center-to-center conversations among Indigenous Nations," while also calling attention to a critical limitation of Allen's cases, which are limited to Anglophone sources and thus "run the risk of reaffirming settler-state logics." Rob Wilson then provides a deep contextualization of Allen's work within the discipline of comparative literature while also drawing out the ways in which *Trans-Indigenous* extends Allen's earlier work. The final contributor, Alice Te Punga Somerville, provides a crucial counterpoint, limning some necessary qualifications of Allen's methodologies with respect to Pacific Islander communities and pointing out important aspects of the "pushback" between Pacific and Indigenous as conceptual categories—a nice circling back to Skog's opening provocation.

The **Essays** section opens with Yu Luo's "Alternative Indigeneity in China? The Paradox of the Buyi in the Age of Ethnic Branding." While sketching a history of policy and terminology pertaining to Indigeneity in the PRC, Luo's article gives a thought-provoking analysis of "ethnic branding" in late-socialist China. Luo shows how, since the mid-1950s, groups like the Buyi have worked creatively to accommodate ethnic identity with the shifting demands and opportunities of state policy, consumption practices, ethnic tourism, and heritage debates. Luo proposes that groups like the Buyi have creatively blended "original ecology" (*yuanshengtai*) discourse with the language of state policies concerning "minority nationality" (*shaoshu minzu*) status, recognizing in ethnic branding the possibility for a pragmatic, agential strategy that can be negotiated to provide a "safe, legitimate, state-recognized" means of claiming Indigenous space in contemporary China.

Continuing this exploration of "artfully" claimed Indigenous spaces in Asia, Megumi Chibana examines land disputes concerning the Yomitan Airfield in Okinawa. In "An Artful Way of Making Indigenous Space,"

Chibana charts the ways in which local activists have utilized aspects of globally circulating Indigeneity discourse to formulate new accounts of belonging, boundary politics, and exclusion. Importantly, as with Luo, Chibana excavates a crucial shift in the politics of Indigeneity as articulated in East Asia—a shift away from identity and toward agency. That is, the question is not "*who* is Indigenous?" but rather "what can Indigeneity *do*?" for specific people living in a specific, contested space. Chibana thus argues for what she calls micro-Indigeneity, a hybridization of UNDRIP-style conceptualizations with Japanese state-based terminologies and legal realities that center on sub-municipal-level community organizations called *aza*. By viewing contemporary Okinawan micropolitics through the lens of Indigenous organizing, Chibana's essay addresses intriguing questions of land responsibility and the "everyday" actions of self-determination.

The final essay, "Getting Connected: Indigeneity, Information, and Communications Technology Use and Emerging Media Practices in Sarawak," shifts the disciplinary focus from political science to media studies. Christine Horn, Patricia Philip, and Clement Langet Sabang explore the ecology of information and communication technologies (ICTs) among Indigenous groups in the Sarawak region of Malaysia. Whereas critics of globalized technology point out that Western corporate culture continues to dominate digital infrastructure in ways that may not be appropriate to other cultural settings, Horn, Philip, and Sabang argue that many people with Indigenous backgrounds, "as digital natives, are well equipped to unsettle monocultural media landscapes through the production of their own digital content." Horn and her colleagues document Indigenous use of digital media to invent spelling systems for Indigenous languages, document cultural events, and discuss genealogies, among other things. Although such usage does not fundamentally alter power dynamics or redress matters of structural inequality, it does provide, they argue, new models for Indigenous connectivity and identity formation: localization, in other words, rather than homogenization. While "diasporic ruptures and connections—lost homelands, partial returns, relational identities, and world-spanning networks—are fundamental components of indigenous experience today" (Clifford 2007, 217), the internet and other digital technologies play an important role in facilitating those processes.

Our cover image, taken in 2016 in Long Luyang by Horn et al., shows women of different generations looking at pictures on an iPad. These pictures will be shared with other community members when they visit. Even as this cover image can be read as an illustration of how new technologies can easily adapt themselves to new populations, the backdrop of Sarawak's intellectual property (IP) obstacles in working with ICT, as discussed by Horn et al., also encourages us to perceive IP's inventive, adoptive, and productive engagement with such technology. In *thinking with Indigeneity,* then, we invite the readers of this special issue to notice how spaces are claimed, places are made, and connections are maintained—even if not always in the ways we initially imagine.

Charlotte Eubanks is associate professor of comparative literature, Japanese, and Asian studies at the Pennsylvania State University. She is the author of *Buddhist Textual Culture: Miracles of Book and Body in Medieval Japan* (2011) and is completing a book-length study of arts-based activism in twentieth-century Japan.

Pasang Yangjee Sherpa is an anthropologist from Nepal. She is affiliate faculty at Jackson School of International Studies at the University of Washington.

▣ NOTE

1. In this special issue, we use capitalized "Indigeneity" to refer to the concept as in "Asian Indigeneity." We also use capitalized proper noun "Indigenous Peoples" instead of "indigenous peoples." No alteration is made to spellings in in-text citations.

▣ WORKS CITED

Allen, Chadwick. 2012. *Trans-indigenous: Methodologies for Global Native Literary Studies.* Minneapolis: University of Minnesota Press.

Baird, Ian G. 2015. "Translocal Assemblages and the Circulation of the Concept of 'Indigenous Peoples' in Laos." *Political Geography* 46: 54–64.

Baird, Ian G. 2016. "Indigeneity in Asia: Emerging but Contested Concept." *Asian Ethnicity* 17, no. 4: 501–5.

Clifford, James. 2007. "Varieties of Indigenous Experience: Diasporas, Homelands, Sovereignties." In *Indigenous Experience Today,* edited by Marisol de la Cadena and Orin Starn, 197–223. New York: Berg.

Hall, Lisa Kahaleole. 2015. "Which of These Things Is Not Like the Other: Hawaiians and Other Pacific Islanders Are Not Asian Americans, and All Pacific Islanders Are Not Hawaiian." *American Quarterly* 67, no. 3: 727–47.

Karlsson, Bengt G. 2003. "Anthropology and the 'Indigenous Slot' Claims to and Debates about Indigenous Peoples' Status in India." *Critique of Anthropology* 23, no. 4: 403–23.

Keating, Neal B. 2016. "Kites in the Highlands: Articulating Bunong Indigeneity in Cambodia, Vietnam, and Abroad." *Asian Ethnicity* 17, no. 4: 566–79.

Merlan, Francesca. 2009. "Indigeneity: Global and Local." *Current Anthropology* 50, no. 3: 303–33.

Morton, Micah F., Jianhua Wang, and Haiying Li. 2016. "Decolonizing Methods: Akha Articulations of Indigeneity in the Upper Mekong Region." *Asian Ethnicity* 17, no. 4: 580–95.

Niezen, Ronald. 2003. *The Origins of Indigenism: Human Rights and the Politics of Identity*. Berkeley: University of California Press.

Yeh, Emily. 2007. "Tibetan Indigeneity: Translations, Resemblances, and Uptake." In *Indigenous Experience Today*, edited by Marisol de la Cadena and Orin Starn, 69–97. New York: Berg.

Convergence

Field Trip

LINDSAY SKOG

Thinking *with* Indigeneity: Imperatives and Provocations

■ INTRODUCTION

In the past two decades, much scholarship has focused on indigeneity as a globally circulating and rights-bearing concept (Tsing 1999; Li 2000; Niezen 2000; Povinelli 2002; Karlsson 2003; Yeh 2007; Lucero 2008; Fabricant and Gustafson 2011; Keating 2013; Baird 2015). Within this critical scholarship, indigeneity is often traced to the 1957 International Labour Organization's (ILO) Convention 107 on "Indigenous and Tribal Populations," which rendered indigenous peoples legible in international law by categorizing culturally and geographically diverse groups of people as "indigenous" (Shah 2007; Bryan 2009; O'Sullivan 2012; Keating 2013; Yeh and Bryan 2015). Subsequently, the legal definitions of indigenous and the rights guaranteed to indigenous communities were expanded through the adoption of ILO 169 and the United Nations Declaration on the Rights of Indigenous Peoples (UNDRIP). From this framework of international law, a global indigenous political movement has emerged through which some communities articulate their identities to support a variety of claims, including rights to access and control of resources, territorial claims, and inclusion or exclusion from the state.

In 2013, and following this global movement, I set out to untangle why it was Sherpas in Khumbu, Nepal, were *not* mobilizing an indigenous identity in order to claim rights to representation, resources, and territory in the ongoing efforts to draft a new democratic constitution in Nepal (Skog 2015). Through interviews and conversations, I came to understand that there were fundamental questions still to be asked: Are Sherpas, an ethnic group who trace their ancestral homelands to both eastern Tibet and the southern slopes of Chomolungma (Mt. Everest), *adivasi jananati* (indigenous peoples) in Nepal? And, if so, what is at stake in mobilizing with the *adivasi janajati* movement? And more broadly, without a legacy of colonial domination from outside the state, is everyone in Nepal indigenous? Is anyone?

Today, in Nepal, the terms *adivasi* and *janajati*, taken together, are synonymous with *indigenous*, yet both terms are contentious and wrought with ambiguity. *Adivasi* is generally thought to refer to the original people to inhabit a place, whereas *janajati* translates to "peoples' caste," taken to mean "ethnic peoples," with pejorative and derogatory connotations for some. While in some cases, ethnic groups in Nepal may claim both these meanings, in many other situations, they cannot. The joining of the two terms in this way emerged in the 1990s, following *Jana Andolan I*—the first people's movement and uprising, as some of Nepal's marginalized peoples began mobilizing to demand greater social and political inclusion. With the growth of Nepal's people's identity movement, so did use of the term *adivasi janajati*. In 2002, the Government of Nepal officially recognized and defined *adivasi janajati* as "a tribe or community as mentioned in the schedule having its own mother language and traditional rites and customs, distinct cultural identity, distinct social structure and written or unwritten history" (Hangen 2007, 21, citing National Foundation for Development of Indigenous Nationalities). Today, *adivasi janajati*, originally forged in struggle and movement, is a highly politicized identity in Nepal and thus associated with a situated history of marginalization, disenfranchisement, exploitation, and discrimination.

Yet, among my Khumbu Sherpa colleagues, friends, and informants, the understandings and meanings of *adivasi janajati* ranged from confusion over the joining of the two terms and questioning whether Sherpas fit this category, or not, to well-informed explanations of how the term relates to UNDRIP (Skog 2015). Some found the question of whether Khumbu Sherpas were *adivasi janajati* moot, as they saw little at stake in Nepal's current political wranglings and little to gain by mobilizing with the indigenous people's movement. And yet, like those claiming an indigenous identity elsewhere, Sherpas—regardless of where they travel or reside—are rooted by place-based attachments and kinships, have sustainably managed resources in the region for 550 years, identify the region as a sacred landscape, and experience similar discrimination and marginalization by the state and dominant high-caste hill Hindu elites as other ethnic groups claiming an indigenous identity in Nepal (Brower 1991; Sherpa 2008; Skog 2015). This lack of articulation of an indigenous identity among Sherpas in Khumbu exposes the fault lines in our current definitions and mobilizations of indigeneity. Are we asking the right questions? To what ends? Is it time to rethink the ways in which we approach indigeneity?

These same questions surfaced at the 2017 Penn State Asian Studies Summer Institute, which focused on the theme of "Trans-Asian Indigeneity." For five days, seven early-career scholars, including me, and three organizers interested in indigeneity from across the humanities and social sciences, some indigenous, others not, worked to untangle the who, what, where, when, and with what effect of indigeneity in the broadly defined Asian context. We explored the varied meanings, contradictions, and conundrums presented in and by current scholarship on indigeneity through discussions of a shared set of readings and workshopping each other's yet unpublished writings (many of which appear in this volume).

Through our discussions and debates, a couple points became clear. First, the complexities and contradictions of indigeneity, indigenous recognition, and the uptake of an indigenous identity in the Asian context is quickly becoming well-trodden territory (Kingsbury 1998; Li 2000; Yeh 2007; Baird 2016). As opposed to the meanings of indigeneity throughout the Americas, New Zealand, and Australia, where indigeneity is situated in the history and contemporary struggles of settler colonialism (Wolfe 2006), the category of indigeneity in both Asia and Africa is not as clear. While both these world regions certainly have their own histories of colonial and imperial struggles, the concept of indigeneity in Asia and Africa is more closely associated with marginality and exclusion by dominant ethnic and caste groups, as opposed to European and North American colonial domination. This differentiation is further shaped by a generally more recent involvement in the global indigenous rights movement than indigenous peoples in New Zealand, Australia, and the Americas, from where the movement originated. As a result, questions of who is indigenous, why, and with what effects remain at the fore of social and political debates in both Africa and Asia.

The differing, and often entwined, ways in which activists, scholars, states, and those identifying as indigenous invoke indigeneity further complicates its meanings. For some, to identify as indigenous references experiences in place and community, as well as relations to dominant society, cultural worlds, and states. For others, indigeneity takes on an instrumental set of meanings (Clifford 2001; Povinelli 2002; de la Cadena and Starn 2007; Yeh and Bryan 2015). Thinking about and debating who is indigenous and what is indigeneity, however, seems to lead us into questions around what is at stake in claiming an indigenous identity or mobilizing in an indigenous rights movement. For some, resource access and control are at stake; for others, human rights and state representation are at stake.

The second point to emerge from our Summer Institute discussions was that many of those scholars and activists thinking about, writing about, and researching indigeneity, including us, do so because of its emancipatory potential; yet, we seem to be inching ever closer to a limitation in which the multiple definitions, articulations, and mobilizations of indigeneity are undermining that very emancipatory potential. For many, recognition of an indigenous claim by the state offers the possibility of autonomy, control of territory and resources, and a way out of some forms of political, material, and social domination. Activists and scholars, however, have pointed to a number of concerns and injustices in our current approach to indigeneity. First, thinking about indigeneity compels us to define it in place and time. That is to ask, To where are indigenous peoples indigenous? And when were they there, in relation to colonial powers? Both the UNDRIP and the ILO 169 reinforce this fixing of indigenous peoples in time and place by tying together indigenous peoples and their rights to resources and territory. Along these same lines, others have highlighted the ways in which ties between indigenous peoples, the environmental movement, and territory work to problematically eco-incarcerate indigenous peoples (Tsing 1999; Yeh and Bryan 2015). Moreover, when indigenous peoples move beyond those delimitations, they risk challenges to their authenticity (Nadasdy 2005). Finally, beyond the double bind of indigeneity, others have further problematized the emancipatory potential of current indigenous politics by illuminating the "hypermarginality" of those excluded by the identification of an indigenous majority (Bessire 2014).

In recognition of the diverse and situated meanings of indigeneity, as well as the risks, UNDRIP, activists, and scholars emphasize the importance of self-determination and self-recognition of an indigenous identity. Yet, such self-determination may also be accompanied by it own bind, as people requesting recognition by a state as indigenous must conform to the state's definition and expectations of indigenous peoples, which may not align with a group's self-determined identity (Corntassel 2012). Indeed, many of our own scholarly discussions that work to reconcile the who, what, when, and where of indigeneity with the importance of self-determination may inadvertently replicate the very binds we work to break. Others have pointed out that state-centered frameworks for recognizing the rights of indigenous people to resources and territory problematically further extend the authority of the state and enmesh indigenous peoples in the very state politics they seek to resist (Bryan 2012; Corntassel 2012).

Corntassel (2012, 88) writes, "Being Indigenous today means struggling to reclaim and regenerate one's relational, place-based existence by challenging the ongoing, destructive forces of colonization." While I suggest a broader approach to indigeneity, it is important to note that Corntassel pushes us to reconceptualize *indigenous* as an adverb by moving away from *indigenous* as an adjective and *indigeneity* as a noun. To think what, when, and where is indigenous belies the multiple identities, roles, cultural worlds, grounded realities, and ontologies of those identifying as indigenous. Rather than thinking about how *indigeneity* is being used in a particular context, who is identifying as indigenous, on what grounds, who recognizes indigenous claims, and so on, I suggest we explore what it means to think *with* indigeneity. What would it mean to think of indigeneity as a methodology?

To Think With . . .
What I offer here extends from the discussions and debates at the Penn State 2017 Asian Studies Summer Institute as well as the works of indigenous scholars who encourage us to rethink the categories and frameworks upon which we build our inquiries and activisms in indigenous studies and movements (Corntassel 2012, 2014). In what follows, I aim to initiate a conversation around the question of what it may mean to think *with* indigeneity, as opposed to thinking *about* indigeneity. To do this, I offer a set of provocations and imperatives that, taken together, may suggest a way out of the limitations and binds intruding upon our current ways of thinking, writing, and talking about indigeneity.

To think *with,* as opposed to *about,* compels us to think methodologically and philosophically (Jackson and Mazzei 2011). To think *about* a concept asks us to first interrogate and arrive at the meaning of a concept—an exercise that restricts and limits. To think *with* prompts us to position ourselves alongside of, or even within (when possible), a concept; it urges us to shift our gaze across a landscape of possibilities and to take in the various forms of power shaping those possibilities. By thinking with indigeneity, we may begin to untether the concept from its objective questions of what, who, where, and when. We can then trace its subjective contours to better understand what is at stake and for whom in the concept of indigeneity. In doing so, we move past the limitations and constraints imposed by fuzzy definitions and categorizations, while opening up to the emancipatory potential that comes from recognizing interconnection and experience.

I am a cis-gendered white female. As the great great granddaughter of European settlers in the United States, I too am a settler. As I have moved around the United States, I have been complicit in the ongoing colonization of indigenous peoples, including the Odawa, Ojibwe,

Wyandotte, Potawatomi, Arapaho, Cheyenne, Ute, Kalapuya, and Chinook Nations. I have also been a guest, once imposed, then invited, in the Sherpa homeland of SoluKhumbu, Nepal, the *Sherwayul*. It is through my hosts' willingness to share that I have come to ask the questions that have led me here. I cannot speak from an indigenous perspective, but I can challenge others and myself to think closely and slowly with, and to listen to, those around us who identify as indigenous.

In exploring the meanings, mobilizations, limitations, and binds of indigeneity, Yeh and Bryan (2015, 538) suggest, "A route forward takes claims made by indigenous movements at face value, thinking *with* the ideas and resources they mobilize to grasp the ontological differences that inform differing epistemologies" (italics added). Decentering indigeneity by taking seriously self-determination "at face value," as opposed to self-determination as it is legible to the state or at the international scale, is a first step toward thinking *with* indigeneity. From here, I outline pushbacks, questions, and tensions to provoke conversation. This set of imperatives and provocations is not meant to be complete or distinct; rather, it is designed to invite expansion, contestation, and thought.

▓ IMPERATIVES AND PROVOCATIONS

Attention to Power...
Perhaps the most apparent invocation that comes to mind when thinking with indigeneity is the necessary attention to multiple forms of power indexed through indigeneity: state power, colonial power, epistemic and ontological power, structural power, violence, resistance, resurgence, and so on. Indeed, much of the social science research with indigenous peoples works through a postcolonial theoretical framework (Yeh and Bryan 2015). Yet, such a framework privileges an analysis of state–indigenous peoples relations. Recalling that the state is as much a constructed framework as indigeneity, how can we rethink power in these relations through, or with, indigeneity? Along these lines, Corntassel (2012, 89) challenges us to focus on processes of decolonization that center power with the everyday acts of resurgence and to "have the courage and imagination to envision life beyond the state." Thinking with indigeneity refocuses us on the ways in which colonialism and decolonization work in and through everyday acts. What might inquiries look like if we decenter the state as the loci of power? How may thinking with indigeneity move us "beyond the state" (system)?

Multiverses, Pluriverses, Multiple Cultural Worlds . . .

Thinking with indigeneity begins with recognizing the plural and inter-connected cultural worlds within which people identifying as indigenous dwell and between which they navigate. It compels a reorientation of perspective to illuminate the ways in which different cultural identities and lifeways come into contact, interact, and must be negotiated at a range of scales. It requires recognizing that as researchers, indigenous or otherwise, our knowledge will only ever be partial and is always positioned (Haraway 1988). We must be able to acknowledge our own privileges and positionings to conceptualize the everyday experiences of those negotiating multiple and entwined cultural worlds.

In addition, thinking with indigeneity encourages recognition of the ontological status of the beings inhabiting multiple cultural and lifeworlds. It recognizes the *tirakuna,* the earth beings residing in the Andes (de le Cadena 2015), and the *yul lha,* territory gods, and *lu,* water spirits, dwelling in the Himalaya (Skog 2017) as material beings capable of shaping lifeworlds. De la Cadena (2010) points out that the presence of such beings in material and political worlds challenges the separation of society and nature, a separation fundamental to the problematic double bind of indigeneity itself (Yeh and Bryan 2015). Yet, how do we take multiple cultural worlds seriously without reduction?

Space, Place, Movement, and Networks . . .

Indigeneity implies indigenous *to somewhere.* Indeed, in its use in the Americas, New Zealand, and Australia, the term refers to those people inhabiting a region prior to European colonization. As the term came to circulate and take on meaning in both the political realm and through international social movements, indigeneity became tied to territorial claims (Yeh and Bryan 2015), yet the tethering of indigeneity to place and territory binds those claiming an indigenous identity to specific places and territories. Thinking with indigeneity may overcome these binds by seeing the ways in which indigenous peoples circulate and migrate across scales. For instance, tracing forms of "mobile indigeneity" (Morton, Wang, and Li 2016) as Sherpas circulate between Himalayan ancestral homes, Nepal's urban centers, India, and the United States both challenges the assumptions of indigenous connections to place (and, by extension, eco-incarcerating assumptions) and reveals the ways in which connections are established, revived, remade, and broken. This is not to bring into question indigenous peoples' connections to place; rather, I call here for attention to the ways in which thinking with indigeneity compels us to ask how connections to place are renewed, performed, and experienced.

Expression . . .

Among critical scholars, indigeneity today is often treated as instrumental, with attention given to the ways it is mobilized, taken up or not, and under what conditions (Yeh 2007; Skog 2015). This narrowing, however, risks missing the diverse ways in which indigeneity is expressed. Thinking with indigeneity does not delimit indigeneity to those who self-identify by referencing the specific characteristics, histories, and expressions that have been tied to the word; rather, thinking with indigeneity calls on us to engage language, art, music, performance, literature, and storytelling as modes and mediums through which power is contested and resisted and through which connections to place and territory are established and reshaped (Morton, Wang, and Li 2016).

By extension, we are driven to ask, What may thinking with indigeneity reveal about be(com)ing indigenous? What does it mean to translate indigenous postionings into one's own experience? And what is at stake in such positionings? In what ways are the experiential and instrumental approaches to indigeneity entwined with and productive of an indigenous identity, and how is this expressed?

Scale . . .

Baird (2015) points out that indigeneity is at once intimately local through ties to place and territory and global as indigenous groups mobilize to connect across space. To think with indigeneity means to think across and between scales, to ask how the everyday lives of the family, the household, and the community are shaped by and are shaping the experience *and* the instrumental mobilizations of indigeneity. To think with scale drives us to ask questions about the relationships between the local, the state, and the global articulations of indigeneity and, more importantly, to ask how those scales limit what we see and ask.

Thinking with indigeneity invokes a longer timescale. It requires a temporal context tracing connections between people, other-than-human beings, and places, including those that may not fit on a Cartesian plane, into the past and the future. Once we take seriously indigenous ontologies and epistemologies, how must we think differently about spatial and temporal scales themselves?

Slowing Down . . .

As Yeh and Bryan (2015) point out, thinking with indigeneity takes seriously epistemic differences and the ontological divergences shaping those differences. While ontological differences in material worlds may at times be quite apparent, observing the subtle and often intimate ontological differences in lifeworlds requires time and patience. It requires observing, participating, acknowledging, listening, waiting for an invitation, and a recognition and subsequent release of one's own frameworks, boundaries, and expectations. Yet, this slowing down (de la Cadena 2015) of our social science inquiries is often at odds with the demands of the North American academy. We are then left with the question, How to reconcile this conflict? What may thinking with indigeneity reveal to us about *how* to slow down as scholars, advocates, activists, comrades, and colleagues? What might we see, learn, and experience when we slow down? This, indeed, may be the most vital act in realizing the emancipatory potential of thinking with indigeneity.

■ CONCLUSION

In bringing together these imperatives and provocations, I do not intend to close off others. Moreover, I recognize that many activists and scholars, both indigenous and not, are already working through and grappling with many of the provocations and questions I include here. I am alert to the potential risks of reframing indigeneity in the way I have suggested. For one, if we move away from an instrumental claim of indigeneity, we may indeed threaten its political potential. On the other hand, thinking *with* indigeneity, as opposed to *about* indigeneity, may offer a way out of the binds that often undermine its political and emancipatory potential. My purpose here is to suggest a subtle, but crucial, shift in our approaches. I propose that thinking with indigeneity may more usefully position activists and scholars, especially those who do not identify as indigenous, to work through the binds that complicate and muddle our current conversations about indigeneity.

Lindsay Skog is a geography instructor at Portland State University and Portland Community College.

■ NOTE

I would like to thank my Sherpa hosts, friends, and colleagues; Neal Keating; Micah Morton; Suchismita Das; Megumi Chibana; Christine Horn; Budhaditya Das; and Yu Luo. I am indebted to Pasang Sherpa, Charlotte Eubanks, Tina Chen, and two anonymous reviewers.

■ WORKS CITED

Baird, Ian. 2015. "Translocal Assemblages and the Circulation of the Concept of 'Indigenous Peoples' in Laos." *Political Geography* 46: 54–64.

Baird, Ian. 2016. "Indigeneity in Asia: An Emerging but Contested Concept." *Asian Ethnicity* 17, no. 4: 501–5.

Bessire, Lucas. 2014. "The Rise of Indigenous Hypermarginality: Native Culture as a Neoliberal Politics of Life." *Current Anthropology* 55, no. 3: 276–95.

Brower, Barbara. 1991. *Sherpa of Khumbu: People, Livestock, and Landscape.* Oxford: Oxford University Press.

Bryan, Joe. 2009. "Where Would We Be without Them? Knowledge, Space and Power in Indigenous Politics." *Futures* 41, no. 1: 24–32.

Bryan, Joe. 2012. "Rethinking Territory: Social Justice and Neoliberalism in Latin America's Territorial Turn." *Geography Compass* 6, no. 4: 215–26.

Clifford, James. 2001. "Indigenous Articulations." *The Contemporary Pacific* 13, no. 2: 467–90.

Corntassel, Jeff. 2012. "Re-envisioning Resurgence: Indigenous Pathways to Decolonization and Sustainable Self-Determination." *Decolonization: Indigeneity, Education, and Society* 1, no. 1: 86–101.

Corntassel, Jeff. 2014. "Unsettling Settler Colonialism: The Discourse and Politics of Settlers, and Solidarity with Indigenous Nations." *Decolonization: Indigeneity, Education, and Society* 3, no. 2: 1–32.

de la Cadena, Marisol. 2010. "Indigenous Cosmopolitics in the Andes: Conceptual Reflections beyond 'Politics.'" *Cultural Anthropology* 25, no. 2: 334–70.

de la Cadena, Marisol. 2015. *Earth Beings: Ecologies of Practice across Andean Worlds.* Durham, N.C.: Duke University Press.

de la Cadena, Marisol, and Orin Starn, eds. 2007. *Indigenous Experience Today.* Oxford: Berg.

Fabricant, Nicole, and Bret Darin Gustafson, eds. 2011. *Remapping Bolivia: Resources, Territory, and Indigeneity in a Plurinational State.* Santa Fe, N.M.: School for Advanced Research Press.

Hangen, Susan. 2007. *Creating a "New Nepal": The Ethnic Dimension.* Washington, D.C.: East-West Center.

Haraway, Donna. 1988. "Situated Knowledges: The Science Question in Feminism and the Privilege of the Partial Perspective." *Feminist Studies* 14, no. 3: 575–99.

Jackson, Alecia Youngblood, and Lisa A. Mazzei. 2011. *Thinking with Theory in Qualitative Research: Viewing Data across Multiple Perspectives.* New York: Routledge.

Karlsson, Bengt G. 2003. "Anthropology and the 'Indigenous Slot': Claims to and Debates about Indigenous Peoples' Status in India." *Critique of Anthropology* 23, no. 4: 403–23.

Keating, Neal B. 2013. "Kuy Alterities: The Struggle to Conceptualise and Claim Indigenous Land Rights in Neoliberal Cambodia." *Asia Pacific Viewpoint* 54, no. 3: 309–22.

Kingsbury, Benedict. 1998. "'Indigenous Peoples' in International Law: A Constructivist Approach to the Asian Controversy." *American Journal of International Law* 92, no. 3: 414–57.

Li, Tania. 2000. "Articulating Indigenous Identity in Indonesia: Resource Politics and the Tribal Slot." *Comparative Studies in Society and History* 42, no. 1: 149–79.

Lucero, Jose Antonio. 2008. *Struggles of Voice: The Politics of Indigenous Representation in the Andes*. Pittsburgh, Pa.: University of Pittsburgh Press.

Morton, Micah F., Jianhua Wang (Aryoeq Nyawrbyeivq), and Haiying Li (Miqsawr Pyawqganr). 2016. "Decolonizing Methods: Akha Articulations of Indigeneity in the Upper Mekong Region." *Asian Ethnicity* 17, no. 4: 580–95.

Nadasdy, Paul. 2005. "Transcending the Debate over the Ecologically Noble Indian: Indigenous Peoples and Environmentalism." *Ethnohistory* 52, no. 2: 291–331.

Niezen, Ronald. 2000. "Recognizing Indigenism: Canadian Unity and the International Movement of Indigenous Peoples." *Comparative Studies in Society and History* 42, no. 1: 119–48.

O'Sullivan, Dominic. 2012. "Globalization and the Politics of Indigeneity." *Globalizations* 9, no. 5: 637–50.

Povinelli, Elizabeth A. 2002. *The Cunning of Recognition: Indigenous Alterities and the Making of Australian Multiculturalism*. Durham, N.C.: Duke University Press.

Shah, Alpa. 2007. "The Dark Side of Indigeneity? Indigenous People, Rights and Development in India." *History Compass* 5, no. 6: 1806–32.

Sherpa, Lhakpa N. 2008. *Through a Sherpa Window*. Kathmandu, Nepal: Vajra.

Skog, Lindsay. 2015. "The Beyul Campaign: Spatial Articulations of Territory and Religion in Khumbu, Nepal." PhD diss., University of Colorado at Boulder.

Skog, Lindsay. 2017. "*Khumbi Yullha* and the *Beyul*: Sacred Space and the Cultural Politics of Religion in Khumbu, Nepal." *Annals of the American Association of Geographers* 107, no. 2: 546–54.

Tsing, Anna Lowenhaupt. 1999. "Becoming a Tribal Elder and Other Green Development Fantasies." In *Transforming the Indonesian Uplands: Marginality, Power, and Production*, edited by Tania Li, 159–202. Amsterdam, Netherlands: Harwood Academic.

Wolfe, Patrick. 2006. "Settler Colonialism and the Elimination of the Native." *Journal of Genocide Research* 8, no. 4: 387–409.

Yeh, Emily T. 2007. "Tibetan Indigeneity: Translations, Resemblances, and Uptake." In *Indigenous Experience Today,* edited by Marisol de la Cadena and Orin Starn, 69–97. Oxford: Berg.

Yeh, Emily T., and Joe Bryan. 2015. "Indigeneity." In *The Routledge Handbook of Political Ecology,* edited by Tom Perreault, Gavin Bridge, and James McCarthy, 531–44. London: Routledge.

A&Q

___

Indigeneity at Sea

The sea was open to anyone who would navigate a way through. . . . Oceania is vast, Oceania is expanding, Oceania is hospitable and generous, Oceania is humanity rising from the depths of brine and regions of fire deeper still.
   —Epeli Hauʻofa, "Our Sea of Islands"

In a context where representation (as "Asian American") simultaneously takes place with nonrepresentation (the specificities of being Korean, Hmong, Pakistani, etc.), Pacific Islanders become another un(der)represented Asian American constituency to them that just needs more inclusion within the larger project. The problem with this, however, is that Pacific Islanders are not another underrepresented Asian constituency that fits uneasily into the Asian American coalition; they are not Asian American *at all,* and the political coalition that linked the two different pan-ethnic groups in the political and bureaucratic imaginary was the product of a moment that is long over, though its conceptual categories live on, much to the detriment of Pacific Islanders in general and Hawaiians specifically.
   —Lisa Kahaleole Hall, "Which of These Things Is Not Like the Other:
      Hawaiians and Other Pacific Islanders Are Not Asian Americans,
      and All Pacific Islanders Are Not Hawaiian"

AS ALWAYS, this issue's *A&Q* is a polyvocal feature, this time growing out of a panel organized by Charlotte Eubanks for the Global Asias 4 conference, convened at Penn State on March 31 through April 1, 2017. Each of the panelists was invited to respond to a set of questions (provided in edited form herein), reflecting on them from the specific vantage point of their own particularly institutional and disciplinary setting. The goal of the roundtable was to chart some of the interactions between notions of indigeneity and Asian-ness by focusing especially on Pacific Islanders and Oceania and attending to the particular histories, ideas, and epistemologies that such targeted attention might highlight.

1. What might a truly trans-Pacific Asian, Asian American, and/or Indigenous studies look like? If we set Asian studies and Asian American studies "adrift," (how) can we craft meaningful alliances without erasing indigenous peoples and Pacific Islanders?
2. What is at stake—demographically, aesthetically, legally, socially—in the categorization of Pacific Islanders with Asian Americans? With the categorization of Pacific Islanders with Indigenous peoples?
3. How might we approach the relations between settler and indigenous communities without expunging difference and locality? What third terms are available, and how might these open crucial, nonbinary space?
4. How is your understanding of indigeneity shaped by, and how does it seek to shape, the institutions and disciplines in which you work?

Pacific Worlds: Indigeneity, Hybridity, and Globalization

RDK HERMAN

The title of this essay today draws on my web-based indigenous-geography project Pacific Worlds (http://www.pacificworlds.com/). Created in 2000, this project works to portray Pacific Island communities through the words of community members themselves. The premise is that, despite climatic, linguistic, and material-culture similarities, each Pacific Island culture presents a complete and distinct worldview. And these worldviews developed in situ, through generations of interactions between the people and the environment.

This kind of locally developed human–environment knowledge is the cornerstone of what I call "indigeneity." By this term, I am not referring to Indigenous Peoples as defined by the United Nations or other scholars or bodies. As I have stated elsewhere, all of our ancestors were Indigenous once, somewhere. Rather, my focus here is on a way of being in the world: being indigenous to a place means having a depth of knowledge, understanding, and connection to that place (Herman 2008). Indigeneity also includes a sense of stewardship and responsibility for managing that place and working respectfully with its nonhuman inhabitants. This included holistic and spiritual engagement—both an extraordinary awareness of environmental conditions and, through that, a sense of consciousness and connectivity with the natural world and all its inhabitants. Prior to the onset of modernity, most people on this planet retained some degree of Indigeneity under this definition.

I contrast *indigeneity* with *modernity,* the mode of human–environment interaction based on industrial capitalism and characterized by commodification and exploitation of the environment. Capitalism fosters individual gain blind to consequences for other people, animals, and the natural world. And this approach has been spread across the planet through globalization.

So today, we do not see unadulterated Indigeneity. The forces of modernity have penetrated nearly every corner of the globe to one degree or another. But we must acknowledge that cultural change does not equate with culture loss. To the extent that Pacific Islanders appropriated aspects of, shall we call them, the "visitor cultures" results in a hybridity still rooted in place, to greater and lesser extents. And that transfer went both ways.

The conflation of Asians with Pacific Islanders has been a clumsy and heavy-handed tool for people and institutions that are not willing to allow Pacific Islanders their own distinct cultural sphere. At the Smithsonian Institution, where I work, there is no distinct place for Pacific Islanders among the peoples represented. The National Museum of the American Indian covers the Hawaiian Islands, but none of the other U.S. Pacific Island territories (Guam, CNMI, American Samoa, at the least). The Asian Pacific American Center covers only Pacific Islander *Americans,* which does cover these entities but not the rest of the Pacific Islands. And as in other such units, the focus on Asian Americans far outweighs that on Pacific Islanders. There are two Pacific Island–focused scholars in the anthropology department at the National Museum of Natural History. The Smithsonian has a number of physical scientists working in Hawai'i (and, to a far lesser extent, the rest of the Pacific) and recently looked into establishing a small center there, but to date, Pacific Island studies at the institution remains scattered and fragmented.

A major feature of the Pacific Island cultural sphere—one that distinctly contrasts with the less clumsy but still heavy-handed "Asian identity"—is that these peoples live on remote islands, remote enough that regular intercourse between them and the peoples of the greater Asian region (or any other continent, for that matter) did not exist. True, there are plenty of Island peoples within Asia itself, including all of Indonesia and the Philippines. But these have, to varying degrees, been in regular commerce and communication with each other and with peoples of the Asian continent. And true, some Pacific Islanders have had regular contact with their neighbors. But the severance from Asian roots was otherwise pretty complete. As Crocombe states, "Pacific Islanders evolved and diversified their Asian-derived cultures and controlled their own destinies. Their early origins from Asia were of no significance to Asia/Pacific Islands relations, for the vast majority had no further contact with Asia" (Crocombe 2007, 4).

Instead, we are talking about peoples occupying an ocean that covers at least one-third of the planet, and whose cultures developed in increasing isolation the further one moves from Southeast Asia. Not giving Pacific Islanders their due apart from Asia is based on the relatively small size of the Pacific Islander population and the composite land area, not the spatial extent of the realm (again, one-third the surface of the Earth) and the cultural diversity of the region.

The geographic context of Oceania leads to the evolution of cultural forms quite distinct from Asia. In the first place, throughout most of Oceania, there is no usable metal, so they constitute what might be called a Neolithic culture realm. Second, the biological resources are different and more limited due to distance decay from the continents. Hence Oceanic peoples brought their most important plants with them, thereby also ensuring a certain material culture base shared across the region. Third, the mostly small size of the islands means that all resources are limited and need to be managed carefully to ensure survival. Fourth, most of these islands share tropical climates, while the climates of Asia are far more varied. Finally, the legacy of voyaging is shared among those Pacific Islanders who ventured beyond the continent-hugging islands of Melanesia, and this too has had profound cultural ramifications.

But across these shared characteristics there is also extensive diversity. The various migrations of peoples into Oceania—first into the island of New Guinea and the nearer Melanesian islands, some forty thousand years ago, and then a second wave out of Asia starting about four thousand years ago—produced culture realms that Western science has divided into three regions: Melanesia, closest to Asia and Australia; Micronesia, in the north Pacific but remote from Asia; and Polynesia, the great triangle of the remote central Pacific from Aotearoa/New Zealand to Rapanui (or Easter Island) and the Hawaiian Islands, along with some outliers near Melanesia. These are the Indigenous Peoples of Oceania. It has been said that if we were to use the fifty United States to represent cultural diversity across Oceania, it would look like this: Polynesian would be the state of Maine, Micronesia would be the rest of the New England states, and Melanesia would be the rest of the country.

Then there is what we might call the second colonization of the Pacific: the peoples of modernity. These also came in waves, and from different directions at different times, but all within a period of the past five hundred years. Colonial forces from Europe, Japan, and the United States swept over the islands, sometimes in sequence, and brought about a new division of the region: the French Pacific, the Australian Pacific, the New Zealand Pacific, and the American Pacific—most of which was formerly the Spanish, then the German, and then the Japanese Pacific.

And then with each of these, we get other migrations into and around the region, including Asian merchants and plantation workers. Through these migrations and colonizations, the formerly remote islands of Oceania were brought into the global system. And with the introduction of new ideas, technologies, and social and political forms, island cultures have been changed. So now we have a tension of sorts between indigeneity, hybridity, and globalization. And these play out differently in different places. Three places where I have seen quite different outcomes include Guam, the Hawaiian Islands, and Palau.

When the rest of the German Pacific went to the Japanese at the outbreak of World War I, Guam had been seized by the United States at the beginning of the Spanish–American War in 1898. Guam and the Mariana Islands had been conquered by the Spanish in the seventeenth century, and all the islanders were brought to Guam and located in new villages under the watchful eyes of Catholic priests. As a result, they lost their millennia-old connections to the land and its stories. The Chamorro language is said to consist about 55 percent of borrowed Spanish terms. These terms, however, were reshaped into the Chamorro sound system, and Chamorro grammar remains intact (see Topping 1980, 6–7).

So here, when I went to work with community members to explore and document Indigenous culture, the first answer I got was about the church. The second answer was about funerals and cemeteries, and the third was about marriages. All of these are conducted within the framework of Catholicism. Yet, in each of these, my Chamorro guides saw their distinct island culture manifesting. Each of these embodied important Chamorro values, such the *chenchule'* reciprocity system, or *inafa'maolek*, the need to have respect and balance.[1]

American rule on Guam, unsurprisingly, has done little to uplift the indigenous culture over the past century. As Camacho (2005, 45) notes, American loyalty in Guam was cultivated through American colonial education, health policies, and economic projects attempting to earn the loyalties of Chamorros. "The American Naval government specifically sponsored various activities, such as speech contests and village parades, to acculturate Chamorros to American overseas rule" (Camacho 2005, 45). Yet, as I have discussed elsewhere (Herman 2015), there is a long tradition of the United States framing Guam as "American-yet-not," leaving this island in political limbo as one of the remaining non-self-governing territories left in the world (Herman 2008). The proximity of Guam to the Philippines (another former U.S. colony, briefly) and Guam's role as the major U.S. territory in that part of Micronesia have led to significant in-migration from those countries. Today the population is 37.3 percent Chamorro and 26.3 percent Filipino, with whites, Chuukese, Koreans, Chinese, Japanese, Palauans, Pohnpeians, and other Pacific Islanders and Asians composing small minorities (Central Intelligence Agency 2017).

Then there are the Hawaiian Islands, an independent nation from 1810 to 1893 and afterward a U.S. occupied territory. Hawaiian monarchs had appropriated ideas, technologies, and governmental forms from outside—mostly the United States—but remained distinctly Hawaiian. They embraced a degree of hybridity that suited their needs. At the same time, the huge influx of Asian plantation workers in the nineteenth and twentieth centuries also influenced the culture. In 1854, Prince Liholiho spoke favorably of bringing in Chinese as a desirable admixture with Native Hawaiians, whose numbers had been decimated by epidemics. My own mentor and then head of Hawaiian studies, Abraham Piʻianaiʻa, was part Chinese.

And with the later arrival of Japanese, Koreans, and Filipinos mixing with Chinese and Hawaiians, a plantation culture emerged speaking a new language: Pidgin, or Hawaiian Creole English. This is a language using mostly English words but also words from Asian languages. The grammar, however, is comparable to Hawaiian.[2] And at least until recently, native speakers could distinguish the ethnicity of the speaker by his or her accent and use of Pidgin. For Hawaiians in particular, who nearly lost their language under American rule, Pidgin became a badge of identity in the face of American culture.

Here also foodways and other cultural habits, such as taking off one's shoes before entering a house, were adopted from Asian immigrants, who make up 56 percent of the population.[3] But at its core, Hawaiian culture remains distinctly Hawaiian. And that is rooted to the place itself. Unlike the Chamorros, they never lost all their stories and place-names. In fact, their highly literate ancestors wrote them down.[4]

Palau had been nominally under the Spanish and then the Germans before Japan took Germany's Pacific possessions with the First World War, though Japanese had been settling there since the 1830s.[5] The subsequent settlement of Japanese in the islands was mostly merchants, farmers, and fishermen looking for new opportunities. By 1935, Japanese people constituted at least 60 percent of Palau's population. Despite a segregated school system[6] and a paternalist approach by the Japanese empire toward islanders (Leibowitz 1996, 14),[7] Japanese and Palauans lived side by side and had regular interactions (Matsumoto and Britain 2003, 329).[8] A great number of mixed families evolved. A 2005 study estimated that about 25 percent of Palau's populace has some Japanese ancestry (Fujita 2005). Palauans make up 73 percent of the population, with 25 percent being Asian, plus tiny smatterings of others (Central Intelligence Agency 2017).

Postwar, many Japanese Palauans became prominent businessmen and politicians. In Palau especially, economic success is linked to the Japanese Palauan community.[9] The persistence of Japanese language skills also plays a role (see Kai 2012). One study found that among younger Japanese Palauan women, the use of Japanese is highly valued in the economy as essential for the promotion of tourism and trade (Matsumoto and Britain 2001, 80). Norms of living, eating, and drinking vigorously incorporated Japanese practices, and these remain part of island culture. But it is *island* culture, not Japanese culture.

The two-way cultural appropriation is seen in the story of Chief Uong of Ngiwal village, who returned from a cultural tour of Japan and created a Japanese-style "Ginza road" in his village. He was praised—and secretly mocked—by the Japanese as a successful assimilation but is seen differently by Palauans even today. As Iitaka (2011, 97) writes, "their narratives about the Ginza Road recover the agency of Chief Uong and reverse the hierarchical relationship between Japanese and Palauans. . . . Chief Uong is remembered as a man of vigorous action, who wisely appropriated civilization and minimized the powers of Japanese administration. He is regarded as a prominent leader, rather than as a passive, obedient, amusing, or provincial figure. . . . People in Ngiwal are proud that chief Uong guided villagers with strong leadership and constructed the most beautiful and well organized village in Palau."[10]

Susan Falgout argues that for the aging Micronesian, stories of the war and of the Japanese era are often told as morality tales, "meant to teach younger generations important lessons learned from working together, overcoming hardship, and living through an era far less marked by materialism and individual freedom and more devoted to community service and honor to chiefs than the present day. . . . While these stories are ostensibly about the past, for those who tell them they also bear direct relevance to the current day, and particularly to new directions regarded as unsuitable by the elders who learned valuable lessons from the World War II era" (Falgout 2007, 34; see also Poyer et al. 2001).

Palauan Rubak Ubal Tellei stated that "the best thing about education during the Japanese time was that it gave weight to good morals. Honesty was valued above all. Punctuality and industriousness were also emphasized. . . . Some Japanese customs were similar to Palauan customs; for example, respect for elders." He went on to say, "I think that the American way of democracy does not fit the Palauan way. Now, people will not work for the community, but only work for money" (Mita 2009, 88–89). Other elders shared similar sentiments. For many of them, the Japanese period was the "good old days," a golden era of prosperity and possibility, when traditional values remained intact and in operation.

These are three stories of hybridity—of borrowing from introduced cultures and making things one's own. But in the end, island culture remains island culture. The indigeneity that developed in situ has not gone away or been eradicated. It has simply taken new forms in response to all that has come in on the tide.

Today, the impacts of modernity are manifesting in a different way: climate change and environmental degradation. These crises ask us to reconsider the path that the dominant society took away from its indigenous roots. Pacific Islands—small and highly vulnerable to environmental changes—are on the frontline. And here is where indigeneity—in all its contemporary forms—offers an alternative. Indigeneity is rooted in the Earth itself. And from what I have seen, indigenous cultural resurgence is linked with protecting local environments. This can be done using the tools of modernity: science, technology, research. These are merely tools. What matters is how we use them, and toward what end.

Where modernity fosters selfishness, Indigeneity—especially the forms found on small remote islands—fosters collectivity. Just like the voyaging canoe itself, we are all in the same boat. It's called an island, and our ancestors taught us how to take care of it and ensure that we survive and flourish within its parameters. The lessons of those voyagers, and those cultures that taught us how to live sustainably on small islands, are what we need now to survive on Island Earth.

So I return to Pacific Worlds: my small role in all of this is to document traditional island culture and knowledge, as told by the people themselves, and to help promote education for them—and for us—that keeps those worlds alive and informative of how we may better walk softly on this planet.

RDK Herman is senior geographer for the Smithsonian National Museum of the American Indian. He holds a doctorate in geography from the University of Hawai'i, and in addition to his work at NMAI, he is the director of Pacific Worlds, a web-based Indigenous-geography education project for Hawai'i and the American Pacific. He serves on the board of the journal *IK: Other Ways of Knowing*.

■ NOTES

1. See Pacific Worlds: Guam-Inarajan, "Church," http://www.pacificworlds.com/guam/native/native3.cfm; "Cemetery," http://www.pacificworlds.com/guam/native/native4.cfm; "Weddings," http://www.pacificworlds.com/guam/stories/story4.cfm; "Chenchule." http://www.pacificworlds.com/guam/stories/story5.cfm.

2. See Tamura (1996) for a discussion of the politics of Hawaiian Creole English. For a discussion of the various linguistic influences on Pidgin, see Siegel (2000).

3. Native Hawaiians and Other Pacific Islanders make up 26 percent, and whites about the same, with a great deal of mixed-ethnicity people across all groups (State of Hawaii 2015).

4. See Nogelmeier's (2010) work on this topic.

5. See Ballendorf (1998, 24) for a review of Japanese settlement in Palau.

6. Peattie (1998, 90) called the educational system for the islanders "education for dependence"—aimed "to perpetuate Japanese rule and to keep the indigenous population in a state of perpetual dependence."

7. Ballendorf (2011, 22) states that for the village chiefs and headmen, "their positions in the Japanese political system were no more than as minor, subordinate officials of the government. In the case where these appointed councilmen were also traditional native chiefs, their power was much reduced under the Japanese. When the Japanese administration wanted to mobilize laborers for public works projects, they would explain to the village councils what was needed, and then leave it to the islanders to carry out the work. This method was seen by the Japanese as smooth 'indirect rule.' In fact, it undermined and weakened the traditional Micronesian systems."

8. Yoo and Steckel (2010) and Peattie (1998) state that Indigenous land rights and ownership were largely protected and maintained, at least in principle.

9. Yuping (2012, 87) states that "the rise of entrepreneurship in Palau is related to the Japanese colonial legacy and to those biracial people whose fathers are Japanese, Okinawan, or Chinese who came to Palau during the war."

10. See the rest of Iitaka's (2011) article for a discussion of Japanese Culture Tours for Micronesians.

■ **WORKS CITED**

Ballendorf, Dirk Anthony. 1998. "Some Positive Aspects of the Japanese Colonial Period in Micronesia, 1914 to 1935." *Japan Studies Association Journal* 2: 24–28.

Ballendorf, Dirk Anthony. 2011. "The Japanese Era." In *The Northern Mariana Islands Judiciary: A Historical Overview,* 19–26. Sapain: Northern Marianas Judiciary Historical Society.

Camacho, Keith. 2005. "Cultures of Commemoration: The Politics of War, Memory and History in the Mariana Islands." PhD diss., University of Hawai'i at Manoa.

Central Intelligence Agency. 2017. "CIA World Factbook." https://www.cia.gov/library/publications/the-world-factbook/.

Crocombe, Ron. 2007. *Asia in the Pacific Islands: Replacing the West.* Melbourne: IPS.

Falgout, Suzanne. 2007. *Memories of War: Micronesians in the Pacific War.* Honolulu: University of Hawai'i Press.

Fujita, Kimio. 2005. *Economic Development and Policy Issues: Pacific Island Countries.* Tokyo: Foundation for Advanced Studies in International Development. https://web.archive.org/web/20110722121419/http://www.fasid.or.jp/daigakuin/sien/kaisetsu/gaiyo17/data/02/Kimio_Fujita_Economic_Development_and_Policy_Issues.ppt

Herman, RDK. 2008. "Inscribing Empire: Guam and the War in the Pacific National Historical Park." *Political Geography* 27, no. 6: 630–51.

Herman, RDK. 2015. "Traditional Knowledge in a Time of Crisis: Climate Change, Culture and Communication." *Sustainability Science* 11, no. 1: 163–76.

Iitaka, Shingo. 2011. "Conflicting Discourses on Colonial Assimilation: A Palauan Cultural Tour to Japan, 1915." *Pacific Asia Inquiry* 2, no. 1: 85–102.

Kai, Masumi. 2012. "Elderly Palauans' Japanese Competence: Observations from Their Predicate Forms." *Language and Linguistics in Oceania* 4: 59–90.

Leibowitz, Arnold H. 1996. *Embattled Island: Palau's Struggle for Independence.* Santa Barbara, Calif.: Praeger.

Liholiho, Alexander. 1854. "Report on Labor and Population." *Transactions of the Royal Hawaiian Agricultural Society* 2, no. 1: 101–5.

Matsumoto, Kazuko, and David Britain. 2001. "Conservative and Innovative Behaviour by Female Speakers in a Multilingual Micronesian Society." *Essex Research Reports in Linguistics* 38: 80–106.

Matsumoto, Kazuko, and David Britain. 2003. "Language Choice and Cultural Hegemony in the Western Pacific: Linguistic Symbols of Domination and Resistance in the Republic of Palau." In *At War with Words*, edited by Daniel Nelson and Mirjana Dedaic, 315–58. Berlin: Mouton.

Mita, Maki. 2009. *Palauan Children under Japanese Rule: Their Oral Histories*. Senri Ethnological Reports 87. Osaka, Japan: National Museum of Ethnology.

Nogelmeier, M. Puakea. 2010. *Mai Pa'a I Ka Leo: Historical Voices in Hawaiian Primary Materials, Looking Forward and Listening Back*. Honolulu: Bishop Museum Press.

Peattie, Mark. 1998. *Nan'yō: The Rise and Fall of the Japanese in Micronesia, 1885–1945*. Honolulu: University of Hawai'i Press.

Poyer, Lin, Suzanne Falgout, and Laurence Marshall Carucci. 2001. *The Typhoon of War: Micronesian Experiences of the Pacific War*. Honolulu: University of Hawai'i Press.

Siegel, Jeff. 2000. "Hawaiian Substrate Influence in Hawai'i Creole English." *Language in Society* 29: 197–236.

State of Hawaii. 2015. "Hawaii Population Characteristics." http://census.hawaii.gov/.

Tamura, Eileen H. 1996. "Power, Status, and Hawai'i Creole English: An Example of Linguistic Intolerance in American History." *The Pacific Historical Review* 65, no. 3: 431–54.

Topping, Donald. 1980. *Chamorro–English Dictionary*. Honolulu: University of Hawai'i Press.

Yoo, Donwoo, and Richard H. Steckel. 2010. "Property Rights and Financial Development: The Legacy of Japanese Colonial Institutions." National Bureau of Economic Research Working Paper 16551. http://www.nber.org/papers/w16551.

Yuping, C. 2012. "The Emergence of Local Entrepreneurs in Palau." *Pacific Asia Inquiry* 3, no. 1: 87–101. http://www.uog.edu/admin/assetmanager/images/pai3/09yuping_87-101.pdf.

Writing Settlement: Locating Asian–Indigenous Relations in the Pacific

YU-TING HUANG

I

In June 1978, in a weekly column in the *New York Times,* Chinese American author Maxine Hong Kingston described buying her first house with husband Earll Kingston in Hawai'i. The essay was later reprinted in her 1999 essay collection *Hawai'i One Summer* as the opening chapter to the volume of various reflections about life on the islands. But the essay was not a celebration of ownership or homecoming; instead, Kingston's account featured her unrelenting anxiety about settlement—about settlement pure and simple and about settlement on land stolen from the indigenous peoples.

Kingston began the essay reminiscing about her former commitment to a sort of radical nomadism, when she was actively participating in antiwar activism in the Bay Area in the late 1960s and early 1970s. "In politics, the householder doesn't say, 'Burn it down to the ground.' I had never become a housewife. I didn't need to own land to belong on this planet" (Kingston 1999, 3). Ownership compromises, declared Kingston. But when political activism failed to dissuade the government from war, Kingston escaped from California to Hawai'i "to have a place for meeting when the bombs fall and to write in a garret" (5). Ownership became more tolerable in political pessimism, and she reasoned, "If we owned a vacant lot somewhere, when the world ends, we can go there to sleep or sit" (5).

As it turned out, it was not possible for Kingston to escape the demands on her political convictions so easily. At the escrow office, the Kingstons received papers detailing the history of the land, reminding them that the supposedly "vacant lot" in Kingston's defeated political dream was once Native Hawaiian land[1]—land that was parceled out, severed, and sold as private titles to American settlers in the 1840s, when King Kamehameha III adopted private ownership in the face of increasing U.S. and other foreign encroachments, in the hope that such measures could help preserve territorial and national sovereignty among Native Hawaiians.[2] But as Lilikalā Kameʻeleihiwa (1992), Noenoe K. Silva (2004), and others have shown, the partition of Hawaiian land into private titles led to more steady erosion of Hawaiian sovereignty throughout the nineteenth century, leading up to the 1893 illegal overthrow of Queen Lili'uokalani, the 1898 annexation, and the 1959 incorporation of Hawai'i into the Union, shortly before a United Nations resolution could have created a pathway for Hawaiian independence—all amid vigorous Native Hawaiian protests.[3] So today, Native Hawaiians are a demographic minority on their ancestral land by official counting, whereas Asians and whites have come to overwhelm them in numbers.[4] In other words, the land that the Kingstons purchased was anything but vacant. Its title as private property was implicated in the history of settler colonialism in Hawai'i, the living testimony of U.S. imperialism that Kingston had so fervently protested back in the Mainland.

"We don't belong on it," Earll Kingston declared, while Maxine Hong Kingston attempted to reason her way through the purchase: "I rationalized, isn't all land Israel? No matter what year you claim it, the property belongs to a former owner who has good moral reason for a claim? We, for example, have right to go to China and say we own our farm, the one piece of property in the world that has belonged to our family since unrecorded history? Ridiculous, isn't it?" (Kingston 1999, 8). Punctuated with question marks, these musings were never confirmed or rejected in the essay. The questions of belonging on stolen indigenous land lingered, as the essay continued to describe Kingston setting up her writing desk and laying down mattresses in the empty house with her husband and son. The ensuing essays in the column and in *Hawai'i One Summer* go on to record Kingston's encounter with the spirited land of Hawai'i and her sense of being an outsider vis-à-vis the Native and Local communities in Hawai'i.[5]

II

The lingering questions signal to me that Kingston was not certain of the comparisons that she drew, that as readers we must notice the difficulty in comparing Kingston's family lot in China with Hawaiian homeland and in comparing either with the seemingly ever-expanding territory of modern-day Israel. In ethically and historically important ways, the homeland left behind in migration is not the same as the homeland invaded and taken, nor are they the same as a homeland that is now supposedly returned amid unending conflicts with those who also call it home. But even if we do compare these various losses, could one's original loss really justify taking the place of another's lost homeland? And can this place making be done without addressing the others' prior loss? Kingston's discomforts echo the more explicit questions asked by Sherene Razack, Malinda Smith, and Sunera Thobani (2010, 2) about theorizing race and gender in the settler colonial space of Canada: "How can we theorize our 'place,' when the place itself is stolen?"

Kingston's invocation of her Chinese ancestral land as rationalization for her settlement on expropriated Native Hawaiian land thus demands consideration about the troubled waters between racialized labor migration from Asia and invaded indigenous lands and communities across the Pacific. Particularly with Haunani-Kay Trask's (1999) critiques of Asian cultural, economic, and political hegemony in Hawai'i and the ensuing discussions about Asian settler colonialism in the same context in 1999 and onward, scholars of both indigenous articulations and Asian immigrant experiences have started to theorize the structural, historical, and activist relations between indigenous peoples and peoples with migratory routes from Asia, finding a particularly ambivalent role that Asians have played in settler colonies' political and economic structures (Fujikane and Okamura 2008; Saranillio 2013).[6] Jodi Byrd (2011), for example, includes Asian Americans in the category of the "arrivants"—a term she uses to signify "those people forced into the Americas through the violence of European and Anglo-American colonialism and imperialism around the globe, but who have functioned within and have resisted the project of colonizing the 'New World'" (xix). Coolie labor and indentured contract workers from Asia, in Byrd's formulation, are forced into participating in the appropriation of indigenous American land by colonial machinations, but they may play either a complicit or resistive role in settler colonial projects. Lisa Lowe (2015) remarks with broader strokes on global dynamics that connect Chinese labor with settler violence against Native Americans as well as transatlantic slave trade; and Iyko Day (2016) has similarly demonstrated that Asian racialization as unsovereign abstract labor in North America—or "alien labor," as her book title names them—is a product of settler colonial capitalist logic. These findings echo the theorizations of settler colonialism by scholars such as Patrick Wolfe (2001) and Lorenzo Veracini (2010, 16–32), who recognize that settler colonies require the presence of racialized labor to extract value out of expropriated indigenous land, and Asians across the Pacific have wittingly or unwittingly participated in such processes of indigenous dispossession.

These structural mappings reveal the ambivalent positions occupied by Asians in settler colonies where they are not dominant and where they are both alien and necessary labor. Asians come to reside on and assist in occupying indigenous lands across the Pacific by different trajectories from those of British and Anglo-American settlers, and like other arrivants in Byrd's theorization, their settlements and local belonging are marked by decades of exclusions and ongoing discrimination. However, these clarifications of historical processes and colonial logic do not yet guarantee the rewriting of relational scripts that is required in decolonization. They do not readily resolve the questions of belonging confronted by the Kingstons and those raised by Razack, Smith, and Thobani, and Asians at these colonized spaces must still grapple with the possible ways to proceed as they continue to relate to indigenous places and peoples. As Karen J. Leong and Myla Vicenti Carpio (2016, ix) argue, rephrasing Razack, Smith, and Thobani's question, "the only way to accurately theorize one's 'place' is by acknowledging that this place has been stolen." We still must ask how such acknowledgment would change the way Asian arrivants live, learn, and write.

My own ongoing research analyzes contemporary literature by Asian settlers and arrivants at several locales across the Pacific as discursive constructions that may either adhere to or resist settler colonial logic vis-à-vis indigenous articulations of sovereignty. With texts like the one that opens this essay, I try to foreground issues of settlement in its political sense as integral to Asian narratives across the Pacific Ocean, where Asian authors inevitably comment on indigenous sovereignty whether they neglect or acknowledge it. Yet, my project has been most productive at those moments when I encounter emerging forms of literary relations aimed at decolonizing communities among Asians, indigenous peoples, and other arrivants and settlers, which are various and still forming. One such attempt comes from Hawai'i, where writers of several generations have together begun writing for genuine decolonization, keeping in mind and speaking through each other's indigenous, migratory, or settler genealogies. At the annual conference of the American Comparative Literature Association in 2015, I got to listen to the poet and scholar Aiko Yamashiro speak about her involvement in a community-based teach-in and poetry performance, "Nā Hua Ea: Words of Genuine Security and Sovereignty," taking place in Kaneohe, Hawai'i, in July 2014. Sharing poetry and stories from the monthlong gathering that preceded the event, Yamashiro described for us a long and conscious process of kinship building among indigenous and settler poets and all those identifying in between or otherwise, as they learned about *ea*—Native Hawaiian understanding of sovereignty and life—in the island environment by praticing Native Hawaiian epistemologies, working with traditional farming knowledge, composing poems, and sharing stories together. She later wrote about the need to recall the hurtful settler history of devastating the land for profit and to invoke at the same time the connecting memories of Asians and other settlers pledging loyalty to the Kingdom of Hawai'i and of striking, struggling, and mourning together with their Native kin and friends (Yamashiro 2016). Yamashiro considered these the "radical genealogies of kuleana that we must remember in order for ea to flow strongly again" and described how the gatherings have brought forth words of joy, surprise, and wonder that were both new and very ancient and rooted. Amid all, Yamashiro emphasized vigilance and vulnerability as the inevitable groundworks of decolonizing collaborations shared by all participants. If colonialism works by separating imported labor from the indigenous communities and their local knowledge system, collaborative processes such as the one leading up to "Nā Hua Ea" have created openings for Asians and other arrivants or settlers to approach their place as necessarily layered with indigenous meanings and offer one possible venue for decolonizing relations.

III

"One possible venue for decolonizing relations"—I put down "one" at the end of the last section not only because there would be multiple ways to imagine and implement decolonizing relations, depending on the genealogies and cultural knowledge of those involved, but also because, in other parts of the Pacific, Asian–indigenous relation could take very different forms.

For instance, if, in Hawai'i, scholars and authors are striving to ensure that Local Asians' contemporary economic, political, and cultural advantages do not submerge indigenous histories and sovereignty struggles, a different set of political and historical realities determines Asians' position in Aotearoa New Zealand and their relation to indigenous Māori sovereignty. Whereas by census data, Asians are the largest population group in the state of Hawai'i,[7] in Aotearoa New Zealand, Asians are a smaller minority (12 percent) than the Māori (15 percent), and both are dwarfed by the overwhelming majority of New Zealanders of European descent (74 percent).[8] But more importantly than their demographic disadvantage, Asians also seem oddly incompatible with the nation's postcolonizing political identity. Rather than ethnic Asian narratives submerging indigenous politics—as many feared in the context of Hawai'i—in Aotearoa New Zealand in the 1990s and early 2000s, it was partially the political rhetoric of indigenous Māori sovereignty that fed the fire of xenophobic anti-Asian sentiments. While Asians' structural participation in settler colonialism remains true in the context of Aotearoa New Zealand, the political reality demands that we also examine how conversations on indigenous decolonization interact with racial discourses concerning those outside of the dominant white settler population.

Aotearoa New Zealand is officially bicultural, and Māori language, cultures, and political authority are incorporated in the nation's educational and governmental systems so that, at least formally, Māori act as equal partners with European settlers. Since the mid-1970s, as a result of unrelenting Māori activism, the nation retroactively upholds the Treaty of Waitangi as its founding document, thereby reinstalling the 1840 agreement of parity between more than five hundred Māori chiefs and British authority as the foundational principle of the national collective (Orange 2004).[9] While many critics of the New Zealand settler colonial regime caution that the implementation of bicultural partnership is not sufficiently substantial or that it does not yet amount to genuine decolonization (O'Sullivan 2007; Fleras and Spoonley 1999), the official status of bicultural partnership does at least manage to create a political climate in which Māori's indigenous sovereignty is central to the national consciousness.

Then, as Māori sovereignty is becoming increasingly significant in public awareness after more than a century of constant struggle and protest, Asian immigrants in turn appear to have no fixed place in the bicultural arrangement. This situation came to a head throughout the 1990s and 2000s, when far right Māori politician Winston Peters led a populist political campaign that pitted Asian immigration against Māori sovereignty. His party, New Zealand First, stoked fear of so-called Asian Invasion among its Māori supporters, to the extent that more Māori opposed immigration from Asia than the national average (Chang 2009). But even outside of Peters's nationalist and populist campaign, the respected Māori scholar Ranginui J. Walker (1993) had also opposed immigration from Asia on the legal grounds that, if the Treaty of Waitangi is the country's first immigration document, it only sets the terms for immigration from Europe, Australia, and the United Kingdom. As several scholars have pointed out, these objections should be scrutinized against the historical reality that Chinese have long composed the third largest ethnic group in the nation (Kukutai and Didham 2009) and that we have records of Chinese presence in Aotearoa as early as the signing of the Treaty of Waitangi (Ip 2003; Williams 2009). Contrasting sharply with the situations in the United States and Hawai'i, the national focus on settler–indigenous relations in Aotearoa New Zealand had in effect prevented serious considerations of Asian presence—settler or otherwise—in the national community.

The ways by which Asians can and must negotiate their place in the bicultural nation thus differ markedly from those in the Hawaiian context. Asian New Zealand literature and other artistic expressions have emerged much more recently than similar expressions have from Hawai'i, and they have done so largely after the treaty had been reinstalled as the nation's founding document. As such, emergent Asian New Zealand authors inevitably engage with Māori sovereign histories with much more deliberation and self-awareness, and some explicitly address the legal discourse around the Treaty of Waitangi. For example, author and activist Tze Ming Mok composed political polemics during a 2004 political controversy over Māori territories while engaging in literary experimentation in response to minority immigrants' uncertain status in the bicultural nation. In an exemplary and award-winning 2014 essay, she urged nonwhite immigrants to recognize their position as settlers with relation to Māori and the Treaty of Waitangi: "People of South, East, and Central Asia, of the Pacific, Africa, and the Middle East: We have to take on the reality of our legal (if not ethnic) role as 'Pākehā' and reject the long-standing fallacy that the Treaty is 'not our business'" (24). Here, Mok demands a change in how "Pākehā" signifies and therefore requests an opening for non-European settlers and arrivants to participate in the nation's decolonizing project. While "Pākehā" has historically been a racialized designation for European New Zealanders, for Mok to urge all immigrants to comprehend their role as "Pākehā" is to negotiate a place for nonwhite minority settlers in the nation's ongoing negotiation with Māori authority about the nation's future.

As Mok seeks conversation, one can observe shared aspirations for alternative relations in the emergent discourses of Asian New Zealand and in the efforts in Hawai'i, as Asian authors across the Pacific come to acknowledge their settler position on the indigenous lands of their residency. Similar conversations and literary endeavors are occurring in Australia and Canada. The larger point here would be that attentions to indigenous political presence in different places across the Pacific have increasingly propelled Asian settler authors to address their settler position, alongside more familiar resistance against exclusion and marginalization. The balance of power may look different from Hawai'i to New Zealand, but the growing critical awareness among writers has begun to resonate across the ocean.

IV

My title promises to sketch out Asian–indigenous relations across the Pacific, but as I close this essay, I also want to raise a question of categorization that problematically assumes a separation between "Asians" and "indigenous," particularly pertaining to Indigenous Asias or the numerous groups of people who may identify or be identified as indigenous *in* Asia. In lieu of a conclusion, I thus now turn to a brief note on this problem.

Throughout this short essay, I have used "Asian" to name a group of settlers' or arrivants' ancestral roots and to mark their differences from either European settlers or Native Hawaiians and Māori. But in using the term "Asia," I have also glossed over the immensely complex population that comes to assume the "Asian designation" by vastly different historical processes. As Greg Dvorak and Miyume Tanji (2015, ix–x) argue in the introduction to their *Amerasia* special issue on Indigenous Asias, indigenous peoples in Asia have been subjected to various state mechanisms that marginalize or valorize their indigeneity for purposes of resource exploitation, cultural assimilation, or postcolonial nationalism. Furthermore, contributors to the special issue also demonstrate how recent articulations from indigenous peoples in Asia have actively contested these mechanisms of state containment. In the context of these emerging conversations, it becomes necessary to wonder where indigenous peoples in and from Asia fit, or not, in the Asian–indigenous relation I have been mapping on Pacific Islands and Oceania so far. How do we think about indigenous networks and their management under local empires and modern nation-states as constitutive elements of Asia as we know it today? How does their marginalization in Asia inform Asian–indigenous encounters elsewhere? How do we consider Asian indigenous peoples' interactions with other indigenous communities in Asia, across the Pacific, and elsewhere? To the extent that an attention to indigenous lives and histories in the Pacific has called on us to rethink the ethical responsibilities of Asian arrivants in the region, our increasing understanding of Indigenous Asias would necessarily move us into new questions and, one hopes, new forms of relations.

In my new institutional home in the College of East Asian Studies at Wesleyan University, I am experimenting with undergraduate teaching that thinks about Asia, Asian America, and the Pacific together through questions of colonization, indigeneity, militarization, and ecological futures. The blessing and the predicament for a new faculty member are my current inability to know how such a course will fare and whether or how, at the end of these critical inquiries, students may come away with the tools they need to cultivate decolonizing relation and to imagine alternative futures. I suspect that we will need something more than critical awareness, that we will need new practices of ethics and care, but an expanded view about these interweaving histories and challenging realities may just provide a step forward.

Yu-ting Huang is an assistant professor of modern Chinese literature at Wesleyan University. Her book project examines Asian–indigenous relations in both Sinophone and Anglophone literatures, mapping Asian settlers' encounter with indigenous communities and lands across the Pacific Ocean.

1. In the essay, Kingston (1999, 6) describes the discovery thus: "this land had been given to E. H. Rogers by Royal Hawaiian Land Grant." I was able to find records of a printer named E. H. Rogers among a group of missionaries that arrived in Hawai'i in 1832, supposedly the fifth company of the American Board of Commissioners for Foreign Missions from Massachusetts. For reference to Rogers's arrival, see Kamahau (1992, 306–7).

2. The event is what is known as the Great Māhele. For the land reform and its lasting effect on Native Hawaiian sovereignty, see Kame'eleihiwa (1992).

3. For conditions of Hawai'i statehood plebiscite in relation to UN Resolution 741, see Trask (2008).

4. According to a 2010 census by the state of Hawai'i and its population data of 1,360,301 people by "race alone or in combination," Native Hawaiians and other Pacific Islanders are the third largest racial group in the state at 26.2 percent, with Asians composing 57.4 percent and whites 41.5 percent of the population. However, it should be noted that, while the census is based on self-reporting, the way that Native Hawaiians are counted here still may diverge from Native Hawaiian methods of self-identification. J. Kēhaulani Kauanui (2008) has demonstrated that Native Hawaiian identity is located socially and genealogically by the invocation of kinship relations that are "always contextual, political, and specific" (37), and as such, it cannot always be conveyed adequately by census data.

5. I capitalize "Local" here to designate the specific multiethnic place-based identity among island-born residents of the Hawaiian Islands, as articulated prominently in the 1970s and beyond. See Yamamoto (1979) for one of the earliest studies of Local identity in Hawai'i.

6. See also Saranillio's contribution to this forum and Erin Suzuki's (2010) work on Local Asian literature in Hawai'i.

7. See note 4.

8. The data presented here are from the most recent census (2013) where ethnicity is self-reported by people either as their only ethnicity or one of several (Stats NZ 2014). One thing to note here is that ethnic relation in Aotearoa is more complex than the triangulation between Māori, European settlers, and Asian New Zealanders; it is also complicated by the immigration of peoples from the Pacific Islands, the fourth largest ethnic group in the nation, making up 7 percent of the nation's population according to the same census. For the fluctuating ethnic landscape of Aotearoa New Zealand, see essays in Spoonley, MacPherson, and Pearson (2004).

9. The treaty is not in itself a transparent document about sovereign

parity, and much bicultural conversation occurs around its interpretation and translation. For a historically situated study on the complexity involved in interpreting the treaty and its bilingual texts, see Ross (1972).

■ WORKS CITED

Byrd, Jodi A. 2011. *The Transit of Empire: Indigenous Critiques of Colonialism.* Minneapolis: University of Minnesota Press.

Chang, James. 2009. "Māori View on Contemporary Immigration: Implications for Māori-Chinese Interactions." In *The Dragon and the Taniwha: Maori and Chinese in New Zealand,* edited by Manying Ip, 185–208. Auckland: Auckland University Press.

Day, Iyko. 2016. *Alien Capital: Asian Racialization and the Logic of Settler Colonial Capitalism.* Durham, N.C.: Duke University Press.

Dvorak, Greg, and Miyume Tanji. 2015. "Indigenous Asias." *Amerasia* 41, no. 1: ix–xxvi.

Fleras, Augie, and Paul Spoonley. 1999. *Recalling Aotearoa: Indigenous Politics and Ethnic Relations in New Zealand.* Auckland: Oxford University Press.

Fujikane, Candace, and Jonathan Y. Okamura, eds. 2008. *Asian Settler Colonialism: From Local Governance to the Habits of Everyday Life in Hawai'i.* Honolulu: University of Hawai'i Press.

Ip, Manying. 2003. "Maori–Chinese Encounters: Indigene–Immigrant Interaction in New Zealand." *Asian Studies Review* 27, no. 2: 227–52.

Kamahau, Samuel Mānaiakalani. 1992. *Ruling Chiefs of Hawai'i.* Revised ed. Honolulu: Kamehameha Schools.

Kame'eleihiwa, Lilikalā. 1992. *Native Land and Foreign Desires.* Honolulu: Bishop Museum Press.

Kauanui, J. Kēhaulani. 2008. *Hawaiian Blood: Colonialism and the Politics of Sovereignty and Indigeneity.* Durham, N.C.: Duke University Press.

Kingston, Maxine Hong. 1978. "Hers." *New York Times.* June 1.

Kingston, Maxine Hong. 1999. *Hawai'i One Summer.* Honolulu: University of Hawai'i Press.

Kukutai, Tahu H., and Robert Didham. 2009. "In Search of Ethnic New Zealanders: National Naming in the 2006 Census." *Social Policy Journal of New Zealand* 36: 46–62.

Leong, Karen J., and Myla Vicenti Carpio. 2016. "Carceral States: Converging Indigenous and Asian Experiences in the Americas." *Amerasia* 42, no. 1: vii–xviii.

Lowe, Lisa. 2015. *The Intimacies of Four Continents.* Durham, N.C.: Duke University Press.

Mok, Tze Ming. 2004. "Race You There." *Landfall* 208: 142–49.

Orange, Claudia. 2004. *The Illustrated History of the Treaty of Waitangi.* Wellington: Bridget Williams.

O'Sullivan, Dominic. 2007. *Beyond Biculturalism: The Politics of an Indigenous Minority.* Wellington: Huia Press.

Razack, Sherene, Malinda Smith, and Sunera Thobani. 2010. "Introduction: States of Race: Critical Race Feminism for the 21st Century." In *States of Race: Critical Race Feminism for the 21st Century,* edited by Sherene Razack, Malinda Smith, and Sunera Thobani, 1–19. Toronto: Between the Lines.

Ross, Ruth M. 1972. "Te Tiriti O Waitangi: Texts and Translations." *New Zealand Journal of History* 6, no. 2: 129–57.

Saranillio, Dean Itsuji. 2013. "Why Asian Settler Colonialism Matters: A Thought Piece on Critiques, Debates, and Indigenous Difference." *Settler Colonial Studies* 3, no. 3–4: 280–94.

Silva, Noenoe K. 2004. *Aloha Betrayed: Native Hawaiian Resistance to American Colonialism.* Durham, N.C.: Duke University Press.

Spoonley, Paul, Cluny MacPherson, and David Pearson, eds. 2004. *Tangata Tangata: The Changing Ethnic Contours of New Zealand.* Palmerston North, New Zealand: Dunmore.

State of Hawaii. 2010. *Population by Major Race Categories Alone or in Combination by County and Census Tract, State of Hawaii: 2010.* Department of Business, Economic Development, and Tourism. http://hawaii.gov/dbedt/info/census/Census_2010/PL94–171/index_html.

Stats NZ. 2014. "2013 Census QuickStats about Culture and Identity." http://archive.stats.govt.nz/Census/2013-census/profile-and-summary-reports/quickstats-culture-identity/ethnic-groups-NZ.aspx.

Suzuki, Erin. 2010. "Haunted Homelands: Negotiating Locality in Father of the Four Passages." *MFS Modern Fiction Studies* 56, no. 1: 160–82.

Trask, Haunani-Kay. 1999. "Decolonizing Hawaiian Literature." In *Inside Out: Literature, Cultural Politics, and Identity in the New Pacific,* edited by Vilsoni Hereniko and Rob Wilson, 167–82. Lanham, Md.: Rowman and Littlefield.

Trask, Mililani B. 2008. "Hawai'i and the United Nations." In *Asian Settler Colonialism: From Local Governance to the Habits of Everyday Life in Hawai'i,* edited by Candace Fujikane and Jonathan Y. Okamura, 67–70. Honolulu: University of Hawai'i Press.

Veracini, Lorenzo. 2010. *Settler Colonialism: A Theoretical Overview.* New York: Palgrave Macmillan.

Walker, Ranginui J. 1993. "New Zealand Immigration and the Political Economy: Indigenous Decry Switch from Biculturalism to Multiculturalism: Claim Right to Restrict." *The Social Contract* 4, no. 2: 86–95.

Williams, Mark. 2009. "The Other from Elsewhere: Arrested Encounters in Bicultural New Zealand." In *The Dragon and the Taniwha: Maori and Chinese in New Zealand,* edited by Manying Ip, 300–318. Auckland: Auckland University Press.

Wolfe, Patrick. 2001. "Land, Labor, and Difference: Elementary Structures of Race." *The American Historical Review* 106, no. 3: 866–905.

Yamamoto, Eric. 1979. "The Significance of 'Local.'" *Social Process in Hawaii* 27: 101–15.

Yamashiro, Aiko. 2016. "Writing Decolonial Poetry for Ea." *Ke Kaʻupu Hehi ʻAle.* July 11. https://hehiale.wordpress.com/2016/07/11/writing-decolonial-poetry-for-ea/.

Haunani-Kay Trask and Settler Colonial and Relational Critique: Alternatives to Binary Analyses of Power

DEAN ITSUJI SARANILLIO

Scholar, activist, and poet Haunani-Kay Trask's article "Settlers of Color and 'Immigrant' Hegemony: 'Locals' in Hawaiʻi" has been the starting point for much of the work on settler colonialism in Hawaiʻi.[1] Arguments that an analysis of settler colonialism emerges, instead, from non-Native scholars are erroneous, at least in the context of Hawaiʻi.[2] Trask's work and mentorship have helped many to think of settler colonialism as pedagogical, as offering us bits and pieces about the historical moment within which we find ourselves. At the same time, the political subjectivities that we historically inherit require political mediation to address new historical understandings and possibilities for resistance. This calls for critiquing and redefining the terms of identity within which we are born. It challenges us to become literate in other histories and struggles besides our own, which then helps us to understand how current identifications come at the expense of other marginalized groups. Such challenges for more robust forms of affinity use an analysis of settler colonialism not for a politics of blame and accusation but rather to open our worlds to a plurality of possibilities outside of the constrained realities defined by the settler state.

Theorizing settler colonialism thus goes beyond telling a simple story about complicity, offering instead new pedagogies for—different ways of knowing, being, and responding to—the living force of the colonial past in the present. Pushing beyond binary conceptions of power—oppressor-victim, white–nonwhite, settler–Indigenous, settler–migrant—the intricate relationality of power relations shows how multiple binaries organize and layer differences within the settler state, which itself constrains what is imagined as politically and economically possible.[3] Differential locations relative to white supremacy and its ongoing effects unsettle supposedly natural or inevitable alliances between historically oppressed groups.

In her essay, Trask catalyzes such thinking by getting at the ways that one can be simultaneously oppressed while participating in the oppression of another. In this, she highlights the imperial violence and labor exploitation suffered by various non-Native peoples but also shows how current framings often normalize the specific forms of settler colonialism that target Native peoples. This kind of relational thinking—an opposition to binary analyses of power where one is either oppressed or oppressive—requires examining processes of settler colonialism, which often leads to difficult and uncomfortable questions.

In this way, Trask's use of the term *settler of color* is meant to unsettle the entrenched identities comfortably used in Hawai'i—Local and American—and especially the paradigms of colonial thought and structures of feeling that uphold them. Local is not only a geographical marker in Hawai'i but a working-class cultural identity formed in the plantations and set in direct opposition to *haole* (white) racism. But the limitation of Local as a category for solidarity, which is how it's often invoked, is that it is premised around a shared victimization from *haole* supremacy, which flattens critical distinctions between Kānaka 'Ōiwi and non-Native groups (Trask 2008). Kānaka 'Ōiwi face distinct forms of colonial oppression within which non-Natives are given every opportunity to participate. While the binary—framed within the configuration of haole versus Local (collapsing Asian and Kānaka 'Ōiwi together), where *haole* are oppressive and Locals are oppressed—flattens Indigenous differences between Hawaiians and non-Hawaiians, it is also a common Local Asian saying that it is better not to get involved in "Hawaiian issues" or that "it's the *haole* who overthrew their nation, not us." Indeed, because of this commonly held belief that it was them and "not us," most cannot get past Trask's use of the term *settler of color* to refer to Asian groups in Hawai'i and argue that she is reinscribing a binarism of Native and Settler. Again, given that Trask does not argue that Asians are white folks, such criticisms of alleged binaries replicate binary analyses of power. Trask's use of the term *settlers of color,* in fact, challenges an either/or analysis where one is either oppressed or oppressive, revealing how such framings allow for what Eve Tuck and Wayne Yang critique as an ever constant "settler move to innocence."[4]

Asian groups, particularly East Asian groups in Hawai'i, hold political and economic power distinct from most of the continental United States. This is not to argue that there do not exist particular forms of unequal power targeting Asian groups; rather, it is to suggest that the Local category can often obscure the complex power relations occurring in the islands. Seemingly in opposition to all forms of *haole* supremacy, the Local category serves an important liberal component in facilitating multicultural forms of settler colonialism in Hawai'i while denying the fact that Locals benefit from and many times facilitate forms of settler colonialism at the expense of Kānaka ʻŌiwi.

A problem with the articulation of Asian settler colonialism, however, is that it leaves no political space for people who want nothing to do with the term settler.[5] Although I critically identify as a Filipino and Japanese settler, one's identification is one's own personal choice. Current debates around settler colonialism often take the form of positivist questions or arguments that pivot around categories of identity: Is this is a settler? Is this an arrivant? Such framings adjudicate these arguments through a kind of moral hierarchy of competing identities that can elide the very structure of settler colonialism, which remains the same regardless of what term one uses. Thus, how is it beneficial to us all, regardless of how one self-identifies, to question the political and pedagogical work that intersectional analyses of settler colonialism do to open one's political imagination to the genocidal consequences of aligning oneself with the settler state? As such, wrestling with one's unique position within the structure of settler colonialism might have more efficacy by questioning what one is doing rather than how one identifies.

Indeed, positivist discussions over who is and is not a "settler" often dissolve into arguments where one cites one's oppression like a badge of honor to shield oneself from having to contend with settler colonialism. Recent scholarship arguing that Asian Americans are "arrivants" voice the important differences between Asian arrivants and white settlers, while remaining oddly silent on the relationship of Asian arrivants to Native peoples. Such analyses take us everywhere but ultimately nowhere, sanitizing the critique of settler colonialism while sidestepping the important questions posed by scholars like Trask. This is not to be mistaken as a dismissal of the term *arrivant* but rather to challenge those who invoke this term so as not to mistake *arrivant* as an invitation to "innocence" (Tuck and Yang 2012). While an arrivant subjectivity has traveled in such circles, it is a phrasing tied to what Chickasaw scholar Jodi A. Byrd (2011) argues as "arrivant colonialism," a relational component to Byrd's overall argument that is often conveniently absent. For this reason, in a Hawaiʻi context, I find it difficult to distinguish how *arrivant* functions differently from *Local*.

Trask argues that this preoccupation with identity is most often a concern for non-Native peoples, while Kānaka ʻŌiwi concerns are grounded in contestations over land and governance. As Trask contends, "the distinction here between the personal and the national is critical. Hawaiians are not engaged in identity politics, any more than the Irish of Northern Ireland or the Palestinians of occupied Palestine are engaged in identity politics" (Trask 2008, 50). Regardless of what terms one finds useful in deploying to identify oneself, such forms of decolonial justice and affinity might be better grounded in the Native histories and struggles beneath one's feet. Taking into account Native epistemes, histories, and knowledges can transform ways of knowing with implications for ways of observing the material force of settler colonialism, particularly injustices that are often obfuscated or ideologically invisible to non-Natives, the particular groups who seemingly stand to benefit. My belief is that, ultimately, settler colonialism comes at the expense of all of us.

Whereas Haunani-Kay Trask begins by revealing the forms of knowledge and subjectivities that uphold Asian settler colonialism in Hawaiʻi, the work of Noelani Goodyear-Kaʻōpua marks a turn in this field by offering a plurality of possibilities that might emerge when Asian settlers work in land-based affinity with Kānaka ʻŌiwi. In urban Honolulu, a school named Hālau Kū Māna uses Indigenous knowledge to structure its secondary student curriculum. Noelani Goodyear-Kaʻōpua, a parent, an educator, and one of the founders of this school, illustrates in her book *The Seeds We Planted* just how Native movements and educational work address current problems by creating and imagining alternative power relations to settler colonialism by rebuilding Maoli governance, foodways, and economies (Goodyear-Kaʻōpua 2013, 127):

> The marginalization and suppression of Indigenous knowledges has gone hand in hand with the transformation and degradation of Indigenous economic systems and the ecosytems that nourish us. Conversely, settler-colonial relations might be transformed by rebuilding, in new ways, the Indigenous structures that have historically sustained our societies.

Goodyear-Kaʻōpua theorizes a Native and Pacific studies inflection to articulation theory, the rearticulation of settler colonial relations "in the face of the fragmenting and harmful forces of racism and settler colonialism" (127). Through such framings, much of Goodyear-Kaʻōpua's work aims for nonstatist forms of decolonization, setting the conditions for cultivating mutual respect by setting the conditions of possibility to be determined by the land, urgently critical in a moment of climate crisis.

I want to end this discussion by invoking genealogy to make more material what it is that I believe is at stake or possible with this set of politics. While Indigenous resurgence of land-based economies is considered unthinkable, if not romantic and idealistic, I turn briefly to alternative histories of Hawai'i's plantations, particularly those set on the margins of the state, to illuminate that alternative land-based economies were, in fact, central to many of the victories in Hawai'i's labor movement. In 1951, on the island of Lāna'i, primarily Filipino laborers organized a strike. The pineapple industry refused a raise for their workers, and all Hawaiian Pine ILWU units, except those from the island of Lāna'i, ratified the contract. Deciding to go out on strike alone, Lāna'i strikers were openly mocked by ILWU leaders and were said to be as uncontrollable as "wildcats." Lou Goldblatt, the ILWU international secretary-treasurer, pointed out that the 1947 strike had the entire support of the ILWU and failed after only five days (Zalburg 1979, 312–13). The 1951 Lāna'i pineapple strike was, according to Jack Hall—a key labor organizer and political insider—doomed to failure because it went against the major strategy of the ILWU, forming unified strikes across plantations that could then pressure planters to negotiate. The strike, in total, lasted far beyond what was imaginable to ILWU leaders, totaling not 5 days but 201 days. There are stories on Maui where I grew up, an island near Lāna'i, that the unharvested and rotting pineapple could be smelled all the way from Lahaina (Noboru Oyama, pers. comm., Lāna'i City, August 5, 2013).

Indeed, the Lāna'i workers were deliberately quiet about their strategy for waiting out the plantation. At the first meeting after voting to go out on strike, the chairman of the Strike Strategizing Committee, Pedro de la Cruz, began by asking those in attendance to divide themselves according to those who knew how to fish, hunt, and plant, and these three committees were charged with feeding the strikers. Furthermore, according to Noboru Oyama, a Hawaiian Pineapple Company manager at the time, Filipino laborers by the 1930s had already established the Federation Camp, a fishing village with homes made entirely out of driftwood and scrapped lumber but, more importantly, capable of subsisting entirely through fishing and planting (Noboru Oyama, pers. comm., Lāna'i City, August 5, 2013). My great grandparents, Sabas and Crispine Bibilone, were a part of establishing this camp, which I believe is akin to the maroon societies talked about in the Black Radical Tradition.

Because Filipino laborers were able to anticipate the tactics of management and create a land-based economy, they were not vulnerable to plantation managers who alienated them from their wages. Ultimately, the Lānaʻi strike managed to gain a pay increase higher than their original demand and secured industry-wide bargaining with all pineapple workers receiving the same benefits as the Lānaʻi strikers. One interviewee remembered this moment as a "happy strike." While some of this might be attributed to a kind of nostalgic "memory without pain," workers were not living according to capitalist time and had, in fact, built a large bamboo structure where more than three hundred were able to share their meals communally.

Such alternative histories not only articulate Indigenous and labor aims together but build on past struggles in ways that allow non-Native peoples to be accountable to present Kanaka ʻŌiwi movements that engage in the alternative worlds that are often disqualified as nonsensical. In this way, Candace Fujikane has powerfully theorized the term *settler ally*: "the term 'settler' roots us in the settler colonialism that we seek to rearticulate so that we never lose sight of those conditions or our own positionality or the privileges we derive from it. At the same time, however, the term encompasses the imaginative possibilities for our collaborative work on ea and land-based decolonial nation-building. For there is joy, too, in these practices of growing ea."[6] I end this piece with an attempt to reconsider what is possible in place-based struggles that take a capacious non-human-centric and nonstatist view of a politics of affinity. Ways of seeing are often guided intimately by ways of knowing, which are themselves shaped by a pedagogy of history, culture, and one's position within the cultural politics of the everyday. I gesture away from an analysis of settler colonialism that morally adjudicates competing identities without addressing the structure of settler colonialism and toward a kind of relational thinking that moves from a politics of identity to a politics of affinity.

Dean Itsuji Saranillio is an assistant professor of Asian/Pacific/American studies and American studies in the Department of Social and Cultural Analysis at New York University. His teaching and research interests are in settler colonialism and critical Indigenous studies, Asian American and Pacific Island histories, and cultural studies. His book on the admission of Hawaiʻi as a U.S. state, titled *Unsustainable Empire: Alternative Histories of Hawaiʻi Statehood* (2018), that examines the complex interplay between different Asian American groups, Native Hawaiians, and whites within historical flashpoints of interaction shaped by opposing versions of history.

1. Trask (2000) makes this argument earlier than the extended article "Settler of Color," which is based on her keynote at the 1997 Multi-Ethnic Literature of the United States conference.

2. J. Kēhaulani Kauanui intervenes in common genealogies of settler colonialism that begin with Patrick Wolfe (2013) and Lorenzo Veracini (2010). Kauanui argues that there are different genealogies of settler colonialism, including those that originate in Palestinian activism and scholarship and, for Hawai'i, the work of Haunani-Kay Trask. Trask often explained that she was herself informed by the same scholarship and activism in Palestine. Kauanui argues that the *Amerasia Journal* and the later anthology *Asian Settler Colonialism: From Local Governance to the Habits of Everyday Life in Hawai'i* (Fujikane and Okamura 2008) "took up Trask's challenge by documenting the role of Asian locals in Hawai'i in relation to Kanaka Maoli" (Kauanui 2016). Studies that narrate the critique of settler colonialism without acknowledging Haunani-Kay Trask not only decenter a Native feminist scholar but actively erase her numerous contributions. Examples of such work include Rohrer (2016) and Snelgrove, Dhamoon, and Corntassel (2014).

3. The use of *relationality* has long been a framing in scholarship analyzing settler colonialism in Hawai'i (see Trask 2008; Fujikane 2008; Saranillio 2008, 2010a, 2010b, 2013, 2014). Recently scholars outside of Hawai'i have also been this using this framework to think through other aspects of settler colonialism (see Vimalassery, Pegues, and Goldstein 2016, 2017; Young 2017).

4. Tuck and Yang (2012, 10) argue that "settler moves to innocence are those strategies or positionings that attempt to relieve the settler of feelings of guilt or responsibility without giving up land or power or privilege, without having to change much at all."

5. I am informed by the conversations taking place in critical disability studies around the use of the term *crip*. See Kafer (2013, 14).

6. Candace Fujikane's Facebook page; see also Candace Fujikane (2016, 63).

■ **WORKS CITED**

Byrd, Jodi A. 2011. *The Transit of Empire: Indigenous Critiques of Colonialism.* Minneapolis: University of Minnesota Press.

Fujikane, Candace. 2008. Introduction to *Asian Settler Colonialism: From Local Governance to the Habits of Everyday Life in Hawai'i.* Honolulu: University of Hawai'i Press.

Fujikane, Candace. 2016. "Mapping Wonder in the Māui Mo'olelo on the

Mo'o'āina: Growing Aloha 'Āina through Indigenous and Settler Affinity Activism." *Marvels and Tales* 30, no. 1: 45–69.

Fujikane, Candace, and Jonathan Y. Okamura, eds. 2008. *Asian Settler Colonialism: From Local Governance to the Habits of Everyday Life in Hawai'i*. Honolulu: University of Hawai'i Press.

Goodyear-Ka'ōpua, Noelani. 2013. *The Seeds We Planted: Portraits of a Native Hawaiian Charter School*. Minneapolis: University of Minnesota Press.

Kafer, Alison. 2013. *Feminist, Queer, Crip*. Bloomington: Indiana University Press.

Kauanui, J. Kēhaulani. 2016. "'A Structure, Not an Event': Settler Colonialism and Enduring Indigeneity." *Lateral: Journal of the Cultural Studies Association* 5, no. 1.

Rohrer, Judy. 2016. *Staking Claim: Settler Colonialism and Racialization in Hawai'i*. Tuscon: University of Arizona Press.

Saranillio, Dean Itsuji. 2008. "Colonial Amnesia: Rethinking Filipino 'American' Settler Empowerment in the US Colony of Hawai'i." In *Asian Settler Colonialism: From Local Governance to the Habits of Everyday Life in Hawai'i*, edited by Candace Fujikane and Jonathan Okamura, 256–78. Honolulu: University of Hawai'i Press.

Saranillio, Dean Itsuji. 2010a. "Colliding Histories: Hawai'i Statehood at the Intersections of Asians 'Ineligible to Citizenship' and Hawaiians 'Unfit for Self-Government.'" *Journal of Asian American Studies* 13, no. 3: 283–309.

Saranillio, Dean Itsuji. 2010b. "Kēwaikaliko's *Benocide*: Reversing the Imperial Gaze of *Rice v. Cayetano* and Its Legal Progeny." *American Quarterly* 62, no. 3: 457–76.

Saranillio, Dean Itsuji. 2013. "Why Asian Settler Colonialism Matters: A Thought Piece on Critiques, Debates, and Indigenous Difference." *Settler Colonial Studies* 3, no. 4: 280–94.

Saranillio, Dean Itsuji. 2014. "The Kēpaniwai (Damming of the Water) Heritage Gardens: Alterative Futures beyond the Settler State." In *Formations of United States Colonialism*, 233–64. Durham, N.C.: Duke University Press.

Snelgrove, Corey, Rita Dhamoon, and Jeff Corntassel. 2014. "Unsettling Settler Colonialism: The Discourse and Politics of Settlers, and Solidarity with Indigenous Nations." *Decolonization: Indigeneity, Education, and Society* 3, no. 2: 8, 11–12.

Trask, Haunani-Kay. 2000. "Writing in Captivity: Poetry in a Time of De-colonization." *Literary Studies East and West* 17: 41–42.

Trask, Haunani-Kay. 2008. "Settlers of Color and 'Immigrant' Hegemony: 'Locals' in Hawai'i." In *Asian Settler Colonialism: From Local Governance*

to the *Habits of Everyday Life in Hawai'i,* edited by Candace Fujikane
  and Jonathan Okamura, 45–65. Honolulu: University of Hawai'i Press.
Tuck, Eve, and Wayne Yang. 2012. "Decolonization Is Not a Metaphor."
  Decolonization: Indigeneity, Education, and Society 1, no. 1: 1–39.
Veracini, Lorenzo. 2010. *Settler Colonialism: A Theoretical Overview.* New
  York: Palgrave Macmillan.
Vimalassery, Manu, Juliana Hu Pegues, and Alyosha Goldstein. 2016. "On
  Colonial Unknowing." *Theory and Event* 19, no. 4.
Vimalassery, Manu, Juliana Hu Pegues, and Alyosha Goldstein. 2017.
  "Colonial Unknowing and Relations of Study." *Theory and Event* 20,
  no. 4: 1042–54.
Wolfe, Patrick. 2013. "Recuperating Binarism: A Heretical Introduction."
  Settler Colonial Studies 3, no. 3–4: 1–24.
Young, Alex Trimble. 2017. "A Response to 'On Colonial Unknowing.'"
  Theory and Event 20, no. 4: 1035–41.
Zalburg, Sanford. 1979. *A Spark Is Struck! Jack Hall and the ILWU in Hawaii.*
  Honolulu: University Press of Hawai'i.

And the View from the Ship: Setting Asian American Studies Asail

ERIN SUZUKI

While the title of this *A&Q* is "Indigeneity at Sea," in this response, I would
like to think through what it might mean to reverse those terms, that is,
to place the (unspoken, yet framing) concept of Asian and Asian American
studies "at sea" and to ground the work of Pacific studies in a constella-
tion of sites from which we might critically interrogate both fields. By
rehearsing these positional distinctions between Asian/American and
Pacific Island studies, I seek to build upon the recent calls of Pacific studies
and Kanaka Maoli (Native Hawaiian) scholars—including Lisa Kahaleole
Hall (2015), Teresia Teaiwa (2010), and J. Kēhaulani Kauanui (2005)—to
distinguish Pacific studies from Asian Pacific, Asian American, and/or
transpacific models and consider their respective fields in a *comparative*
rather than *integrated* framework.

The creation and negotiation of frameworks for comparison between
Pacific Island and Asian/American studies have been discussed and de-
bated for well over a decade by Asian American and Pacific Island scholars
alike.[1] Yet the trend for many institutions and organizations has increasingly been to promote visibility through inclusion and integration under

terms like *Asian Pacific Islander* (API) or *Asian Pacific Islander American* (APIA).[2] While such inclusion may work to boost the visibility of Pacific Islanders, it also runs the risk of overlooking many historical and cultural differences between Asian American and Pacific Island groups as well as needs and services that might be more specific to the demographics of individual Pacific Island communities (Hall 2015; Kauanui 2005). It is in the context of this push toward institutional coalition that the development of critical and comparative frameworks becomes increasingly necessary to ensure that such inclusion does not subordinate Pacific Island experiences to Asian American ones. Transpacific and Asian Americanist scholars should to be able to clearly foreground and articulate the ways that Pacific Islands and Asian American histories, cultures, and epistemologies—taken as distinct yet historically interconnected experiences—interact with one another in ways that can highlight potential sites of conflict and co-optation as well as expanded possibilities for informed allyship and coalition. In practice, this kind of work might involve greater outreach to Pacific Island students and communities; a more robust incorporation of Pacific Island histories, cultures, and literatures into the academic curriculum; and more scholarly work that—like the essay by Lisa Kahaleole Hall cited earlier—reflects critically and clearly on the very processes of institutionalization. It is to this end that I would like to briefly explore the implications of Lea Lani Kinikini Kauvaka's recent reflections on the complex relationship between Pacific Islands studies, institutions, and academia at large, in which she argues for a return to the "landedness signified by berths, anchors, and anchorages" (Kauvaka 2016, 137) as a way of interrogating the images of the canoe and the ocean as they are deployed both within and without Pacific studies as metaphors for "Pacific" epistemologies and practices. These literal and metaphorical berths and anchorages—which include local communities as well as spaces and places like universities and other institutions—remain important in Pacific studies not only because of the role they play in the experiences and activities of Pacific studies scholars but also "because of the ways place is obscured by the rest of the world when they look at Oceania as a region or . . . a discipline encapsulated by the floating canoe" (Kauvaka 2016, 133). Without denying the ongoing importance that the figure of the canoe and the voyaging history it represents continues to have for many Pacific Island communities, cultures, and the field of Pacific studies more generally, Kauvaka argues that a Pacific studies paradigm organized around the idea of a canoe that is "perpetually at sea" has a tendency to "drift" (133) within the academy, giving way to a certain type of scholarly and—as recently illustrated by Disney's *Moana* (2016)—popular discourse that focuses on or fetishizes indigenous epistemologies in isolation from the way that they dynamically interact with local communities, conditions, and institutions.[3] In particular, focusing on these "landed" sites helps to once more emphasize how the idealized mobility represented by the figure of the canoe may not, as Margaret Jolly (2001, 422–23) has observed, prove to be a "compelling vision for all islanders and especially for peoples of the Southwest Pacific who, because of border patrols by nation states, the exclusionary policies of migration, and sheer poverty, are not able, even if they so desired, to move from their newly independent states to other parts of the Pacific, or to North America, Australia, or Aotearoa New Zealand." A Pacific studies that foregrounds the material impacts and formal manifestations that these transpacific military, economic, technological, and political infrastructures take on at the local level before "scaling up" (Aikau 2015, 85) to regional or global analysis connects neatly with other Pacific studies scholars' calls for a more rigorously comparative work that seeks out alliances based on a robust relationality that respects rather than elides historical and cultural difference.[4]

A similar call to think through a more relational and comparative methodology has accompanied the transpacific turn of Asian American studies. Originally invoked to assert the presence and contributions of Asian Americans in the history of the United States and its island territories, since the mid-1990s, the field has largely turned its attention to critical frameworks and methods that are much more transnational in scope. If the sugar plantations and the internment camps were important sites for early assertions of Asian American civil rights and subjecthood within the U.S. nation-state, by the end of the twentieth century, representations of Asian American identity had become much more fluid. The so-called transnational turn of Asian American studies in the 1990s refocused Asian Americanist scholarship on questions of circulation alongside settlement and also sought to interrogate the field's focus on the achievement of political subjectivity within the context of the nation-state. By the late 1990s and 2000s, the emerging field of Asia-Pacific and transpacific studies sought to recognize the ways in which the transpacific operates as a cultural contact zone as well as to think critically think about methodologies of comparison across Asian, Pacific, and American histories, cultures, and literary productions.[5] Such work has drawn attention to the ways that the diverse communities that fall under the broad category of "Asian American" (or "Asian Pacific American") often remain excluded from, or are rendered illegible by, extant legal and narrative frameworks. Yet as Yu-ting Huang notes in her essay in this feature, a number of Asian Americanist and Indigenous scholars—including Candace Fujikane, Jonathan

Okamura, Jodi Byrd, Iyko Day, and Dean Saranillio—have challenged the field to address these frameworks and "theorize the structural, historical, and activist relations between indigenous peoples and peoples with migratory routes from Asia, finding a particularly ambivalent role that Asians have played in settler colonies' political and economic structures." The resulting discussion of Asian settler colonialism has required Asian Americanists more generally to consider their own subject positions vis-à-vis both indigenous populations at "home," diasporic communities abroad, and the ways in which they are yoked together through U.S. imperial ambitions. As Saranillio points out in his contribution here, while such discussions can be profoundly uncomfortable for Asian Americanist scholars, they can in fact serve as an opportunity for the development of "more robust forms of affinity" that lead to "a plurality of possibilities outside of the constrained realities defined by the settler state." Saranillio suggests that Asian Americanists might adopt a politics of affinity rather than identity, one that is open to a "non-human-centric and nonstatist" articulation of being-in-the-world that foregrounds Indigenous histories and epistemologies rather than relying upon and/or reproducing state-driven hierarchies. An Asian American studies thus unsettled by the ethical priority of Indigenous claims and epistemologies might in this context turn to a more broadly "oceanic," entangled framework to articulate its methods, goals, and aims.

In practice, however, what might such a framework look like? And how might we adopt such an oceanic politics of affinity into our daily practice as scholars, teachers, and administrators? Likewise, how might we ensure that our institutions can operate as "berths" for an inclusive and rigorously comparative transpacific studies—to operate as a space that does not seek to delimit or suppress Indigenous experiences or epistemologies but instead welcomes them as experts and participants in the process of creating knowledge? The responses collected here give a number of intriguing suggestions. Doug Herman's web-based project Pacific Worlds operates as an online "berth" of this type that seeks to "portray Pacific Island communities through the words of community members themselves"; by focusing on a range of Indigenous Pacific communities and a variety of voices within those communities, the project emphasizes the "extensive diversity" of the Pacific Islands as well as the site-specific histories that have shaped each community's ways of exploring, mapping, and interpreting the region as a whole. Focusing on Hawai'i, Saranillio addresses the ways that the emergence of primary and secondary educational institutions that use Indigenous knowledges to structure and organize their curricula, noting that such institutions encourage Indigenous peoples and settlers alike to learn how to become more attentive to ways of relating and respecting the land through the structures and practices that emerge from Kanaka Maoli (Native Hawaiian) culture and epistemology. Similarly, Huang explores the ways that knowledge production and dissemination might operate beyond the formal academic classroom by more firmly grounding itself in local landscapes and practices: she cites the monthlong experience of Indigenous and settler poets working and sharing stories together in advance of a community teach-in and poetry performance in Kāneʻohe, Hawaiʻi, as a possible model for the way that Asians and other settlers might learn from—and share responsibility for sustaining—Indigenous knowledge systems that teach sustainable ways of living on and learning from the land. However, Huang also notes that the dynamics of settler–Indigenous relations vary significantly across the region, and the relationships between local and settler experiences present different challenges and opportunities based on their specific local histories and conditions.

In my own research and teaching in the field of literary studies, I seek to accommodate an "oceanic," relational perspective by illustrating the ways that the process of reading, engaging, and learning from Pacific Island texts and aesthetics can operate as one way of opening oneself to "otherness" without fetishizing or foreclosing upon the knowledges and possibilities that they provide. As David Palumbo-Liu has argued, literature works not only to let us imagine the lives of others but can also help us to interrogate the very methods or modes in which we come to think of the "other" as being like, or unlike, our selves; that is, it can draw critical attention to difference as well as similarity (see Palumbo-Liu 2012). A close reading of literature may likewise show us the choices an author makes as he or she seeks to make an "other"—a character, figure, or speaker—either legible to us as readers or not. So, for example, when an author presents us with a character who is inscrutable or unsympathetic or otherwise does not really register as a "full" or "round" figure in the Western realist sense, it forces us to confront a kind of "otherness" that does not conform to our expectations of what a protagonist should or should not be. Because our reading practices are so intimately intertwined with the complex processes of subject making, our choice to either engage with or disengage from such a character provides a useful way to begin to think through how to empathize or ally oneself with a person or persons whose difference cannot be assimilated into our own worldview.

As an example of how such a reading practice might operate, I would like to conclude this essay with a brief reading of Māori novelist Patricia

Grace's most recent novel, *Chappy*. "Chappy" is the nickname given to a Japanese stowaway who is discovered at sea by a Māori sailor, Aki, who is working on a transpacific ship traveling from San Francisco to New Zealand in the late 1930s. Aki brings Chappy home with him, where Chappy is welcomed by the family; Chappy chooses to stay with Aki's family and eventually gets married to Aki's cousin Oriwia. Yet, after hearing about the bombing of Pearl Harbor, he runs away, afraid that his daughters will be identified as half Japanese and interned. After the war, Aki finds Chappy in Tokyo: he cannot convince him to return to Aotearoa but gets him to move to Hawai'i, where he is reunited with his wife and daughters. However, even they cannot convince him to move back to their family land because he wants to first be able to claim full legal citizenship and a sense of personhood under the law. As a result, the family lives apart for many years; in Aotearoa, Oriwia starts up her own business, and her daughters grow up and start families of their own before Chappy is able to move back and take his place with the family. Many years after his passing, his grandson Daniel comes to learn about his history, and the story concludes with Daniel's determination to go to Japan and learn more about his grandfather.

The story ends, as it begins, with Chappy operating essentially as a mystery—a figure of otherness that refuses to be made transparent. While the novel is narrated through multiple points of view, Chappy's voice is never heard directly; it is only reported secondhand. Throughout, his motives are only guessed at by the other characters in the novel, and his stubborn resolve not to return home, even after many years, comes to seem both quixotic and ultimately kind of frustrating. When I taught this novel to students at the University of California, San Diego, many expressed frustrations with the text—particularly about the way that Chappy's unknowability seemed to play into extant stereotypes of Asians as the unassimilable alien. Adding insult to injury, many of them pointed out that the name "Chappy" is, in the novel itself, explicitly identified as a diminutive version of the word "Jap," which carries a particularly bitter sting in the context of U.S. racial discourse.

While these are certainly problematic elements of this novel, I think that another way to approach the book is to read not so much for its representation of Asianness as an identity marked by "otherness" as for the way it imagines an alternate method of relating to Asianness that accepts rather than minimizes or brackets this sense of alterity. Chappy's story is ultimately left untold by Oriwia, Aki, and Daniel because none of them really feel that they have the knowledge or authority to presume to speak for him: although at one point Oriwia attempts to imagine an omniscient third-person narrative of Chappy's experiences, she ultimately confesses to her grandson that while it was "immensely satisfying to write down the story of Chappy on the run," upon rereading it, she felt some doubts about its accuracy (Grace 2015, chapter 12):

> I'm wondering if I got carried away. Let me try to explain. If I had married someone I'd known all my life . . . I'd have understood almost everything about him. But the man I married was exotic. The unfathomable core, the unknown of him, was what made my heart beat. What I did know was that he loved his daughters and me, that he knew how to work hard and that he had a clever mind and clever hands. That was enough.

While Oriwia's confession might seem to reproduce the exoticization and object fetishism that Asian Americanist discourse has long sought to dismantle, her admission of the limits to her knowledge of her husband's "unfathomable core" emphasizes the way that she and her family have been able to incorporate Chappy into their family, their lives, and their very genealogy in the full light of his difference, even if it is never ultimately resolved into similarity. This stands in a notable, if only implied, contrast with the legibility and transparency demanded by Western forms of subjectivity. To be accepted as Americans during the period in which Chappy is set, Japanese Americans had to undergo tests of loyalty intended to demonstrate beyond a shadow of a doubt that they were more similar to their fellow Americans than they were to the imperial Japanese to whom they were ancestrally related. To claim American citizenship then—and perhaps even now—there was no room for reticence, doubt, or difference: one had to perform total transparency or risk imprisonment, deportation, or worse.

Chappy provides a useful way to start thinking through the potential relationships and alliances between Asian diaspora and Pacific Island studies at least partly because of the way that it remixes Asian-slash-American and Pacific Island tropes. Chappy, the Asian immigrant, is the figure who is perhaps most closely aligned to the formless freedom of the sea: he is discovered at sea, spends most of the novel out at sea or on the move, and describes himself as feeling perpetually adrift, a "stowaway." By contrast, Oriwia, his wife, is firmly grounded in her family's land and essentially takes on the task of acting as the head of household in the absence of her male cousin, who was in line to take on that responsibility. When Oriwia and Chappy are finally reunited at the end of the novel, Chappy is able to feel that he has found an anchorage, a place where he can truly belong—but it is an anchorage that is dependent upon a sense of relationality, responsibility, and genealogy rather than the more abstract concepts of nationality and citizenship that he has pursued throughout the novel. Ultimately, what Chappy asks us to do is to explore a specific experience of Asian diaspora through a localized Māori framework. Being able to think through this and other alternate forms of diasporic subjectivity and subject formation might be one way that a comparative Oceanic Asian and Pacific Island studies might help us to reimagine the foundations and flows of contemporary transpacific critique.

Erin Suzuki is an assistant professor of literature at the University of California, San Diego. Her current book project addresses the intersections of Asian American and Pacific Islander literatures.

■ NOTES

1. For earlier debates about the ways that Pacific Island and/or Native Hawaiian studies may or may not fit into an Asian American studies paradigm, see Diaz (2004), Stillman (2004), McGregor (2004), and Kauanui (2005). Other Americanist and Asian Americanist scholars, including Wilson (2000) and Okihiro (2001), have attempted to address these connections by foregrounding the role that Hawai'i, in particular, has played in the shaping of "Asian America."

2. One notable exception is the Association for Asian American Studies (AAAS), which in 2003–4 dropped a motion to change its name to include "Pacific Islander," in part due to concerns about misrepresentation. For more on this, see Peffer (2004).

3. A number of substantive critiques of the film *Moana* have emerged in interviews, online and social media; they are currently archived in the Facebook group Mana Moana: We Are Moana, We Are Maui (https://www .facebook.com/manamoanawearemoanawearemaui/).

4. For other scholarship that addresses the complexities and contradictions of comparative Pacific work, see Deloughrey (2007), Keown (2007), Teaiwa (2010), Somerville (2012), and Hall (2015).

5. Such comparative scholarship includes work by Wilson and Dirlik (1995), Huang (2008), Sakai and Yoo (2012), and Nguyen and Hoskins (2013), among others.

■ WORKS CITED

Aikau, Hokulani. 2015. "Following the Alaloa Kīpapa of Our Ancestors: A Trans-Indigenous Futurity without the State (United States or Otherwise)." *American Quarterly* 67, no. 3: 653–61.

Grace, Patricia. 2015. *Chappy*. Auckland, New Zealand: Penguin.

Hall, Lisa Kahaleole. 2015. "Which of These Things Is Not Like the Other: Hawaiians and Other Pacific Islanders Are Not Asian Americans, and All Pacific Islanders Are Not Hawaiian." *American Quarterly* 67, no. 3: 727–47.

Huang, Yunte. 2008. *Transpacific Imaginations: History, Literature, Counterpoetics*. Cambridge, Mass.: Harvard University Press.

DeLoughrey, Elizabeth. 2007. *Routes and Roots: Navigating Caribbean and Pacific Island Literatures*. Honolulu: University of Hawai'i Press.

Diaz, Vicente. 2004. "To 'P' or Not to 'P'? Marking the Territory between Pacific Islander and Asian American Studies." *Journal of Asian American Studies* 7, no. 3: 183–208.

Jolly, Margaret. 2001. "On the Edge? Deserts, Oceans, Islands." *The Contemporary Pacific* 13, no. 2: 422–23.

Kauanui, J. Kēhaulani. 2005. "Asian American Studies and the 'Pacific Question.'" In *Asian American Studies after Critical Mass,* edited by Kent A. Ono, 121–43. Hoboken, N.J.: John Wiley.

Kauvaka, Lea Lani Kinikini. 2016. "Berths and Anchorages: Pacific Cultural Studies for Oceania." *The Contemporary Pacific* 28, no. 1: 130–51.

Keown, Michelle. 2007. *Pacific Islands Writing: The Postcolonial Literatures of Aotearoa/New Zealand and Oceania*. New York: Oxford University Press.

McGregor, Davianna. 2004. "Weaving Together Strands of Pacific Islander, Asian, and American Interactions." *Journal of Asian American Studies* 7, no. 3: vii–xii.

Nguyen, Viet, and Janet Hoskins, eds. 2013. *Transpacific Studies: Framing an Emerging Field*. Honolulu: University of Hawai'i Press.

Okihiro, Gary. 2001. *The Columbia Guide to Asian American History*. New York: Columbia University Press.

Palumbo-Liu, David. 2012. *The Deliverance of Others: Reading Literature in a Global Age*. Durham, N.C.: Duke University Press.

Peffer, Tony. 2004. "Editor's Preface." *Journal of Asian American Studies* 7, no. 3: v–vi.

Sakai, Naoki, and Hyon Joo Yoo, eds. 2012. *The Trans-Pacific Imagination: Rethinking Boundary, Culture, and Society*. Singapore: World Scientific.

Somerville, Alice Te Punga. 2012. *Once Were Pacific: Māori Connections to Oceania*. Minneapolis: University of Minnesota Press.

Stillman, Amy Ku'uleialoha. 2004. "Pacific-ing Asian Pacific American History." *Journal of Asian American Studies* 7, no. 3: 241–70.

Teaiwa, Teresia. 2010. "For or Before an Asian Studies Agenda? Specifying Pacific Studies." In *Remaking Area Studies: Teaching and Learning across Asia and the Pacific,* edited by Terence Wesley-Smith and Jon Goss, 110–24. Honolulu: University of Hawai'i Press.

Wilson, Rob. 2000. *Reimagining the American Pacific: From South Pacific to Bamboo Ridge and Beyond.* Durham, N.C.: Duke University Press.

Wilson, Rob, and Arif Dirlik, eds. 1995. *Asia/Pacific as Space of Cultural Production.* Durham, N.C.: Duke University Press.

Interface

PASANG YANGJEE SHERPA

Introduction: Continuing Community Collaborations and the Transient Digital

INTERFACE provides "a space to highlight digital humanities projects that span both Asian American and Asian studies" (Koh 2015, 98). Specifically, *Interface* prioritizes digital cultural production and research about and by Asian and Asian diasporic scholars to showcase the extensive work currently being undertaken in this field (98). For this special issue of *Verge*, we explore digital humanities projects within Himalayan studies through Digital Himalaya and Voices of the Himalaya. In the following essays, team members from these projects share their experiences.

In his essay on Digital Himalaya, Mark Turin reflects on community, continuity, and collaboration. Digital Himalaya is a web portal for historical multimedia collections relating to the Himalayan region. Turin discusses changing user demographics, constructive community responses, shifting expectations about the portal's services and role, and the future of this collaborative partnership. According to Google Analytics records, since 2005, the Digital Himalaya website has had more than five hundred thousand unique "sessions." Google (2017) defines a session as "a group of user interactions with [the] website that take place within a given time frame." A single session can contain multiple page views, events, social interactions, and e-commerce transactions. Users of the Digital Himalaya website have been from Nepal (19 percent), the United States (16 percent), India (10 percent), and the United Kingdom (8 percent).

In their essay on the project titled Voices of the Himalaya, Nawang Gurung, Ross Perlin, Daniel Kaufman, Mark Turin, and Sienna R. Craig describe their collaborative process of documenting Himalayan voices in New York City. Their project recognizes the challenges of migration and the assimilation of thousands of Himalayan individuals from specific ethnic communities who have settled in New York City. The project is guided by the questions of how Himalayan New Yorkers are finding a sense of community as they navigate new transnational and intergenerational cultural dynamics and respond to the shifting relationships between "home" and being "over here" in New York. Connections between language, culture, and migration are central to this project. In the essay, the authors discuss how their work at once coheres with and departs from traditional language documentation efforts. Instead of focusing on one marginalized speech or valorizing language endangerment, the project showcases compelling stories of everyday life that capture aspects of happiness and suffering as well as those that are sensitive to politics of self-representation. This novel approach makes its contributions to understanding transnational Himalayan lives today invaluable. In little more than a year, this project has produced twenty-five short videos and made them available to the public through YouTube and social media sites. As of November 2017, the Voices of the Himalaya videos have been viewed on YouTube more than seventy thousand times. Their viewership includes approximately 33 percent from the United States, 15 percent from Bhutan, 14 percent from India, and 6 percent each from Nepal, Switzerland, and Canada.

In both essays, common themes of collaborative effort, community engagement, and "creative exploration of the potential" surface. The Digital Himalaya Project was initiated by a group of four anthropologists and historians at the University of Cambridge to explore ways that would widen access to the Himalayan multimedia materials through emerging digital platforms. Similarly, a team of five anthropologists, activists, and linguists started Voices of the Himalaya to reach a wider audience through newer platforms. The *Interface* contributions presented herein also bring out the question of sustainability that lurks amid the progress and promise the programs represent. Whether it is the seventeen-year-old Digital Himalaya or the one-year-old Voices of the Himalaya, they inevitably have to deal with the financial and technical challenges of keeping the programs running.

In *Himalayan Anthropology: The Indo-Tibetan Interface,* James Fisher (1978, 2) remarked on the need for clearing ethnographic provincialism and to make scholarly communication possible for the vast majority, who tended to work on one side of the mountain more than the other. Fisher was referring to those working with communities living on the southern, northern, eastern or western side of the Himalayas. He was also responding to the scholarly scene of forty years ago, before electricity had reached many of these Himalayan places. The internet and associated digital spaces were nonexistent. The themes of crossing boundaries and reaching the vast majority, however, remain as relevant in 2017 as they were in the 1970s, or in 2000, when Digital Himalaya was initiated. In a previously unimaginable way, Digital Himalaya and Voices of the Himalaya have allowed users across generational, cultural, geographic, national, academic, and disciplinary boundaries to interact through digital domains. However, Digital Himalaya and Voices of the Himalaya team members remind us that engaging the transient digital requires continuous community collaboration. The digital has to be generative, reborn and renewed continually, just as with any medium.

Pasang Yangjee Sherpa, PhD, is a cultural anthropologist from Nepal. Her research areas include human dimensions of climate change, Indigeneity, and development in the Himalayas. She earned her doctoral degree in anthropology from Washington State University in 2012. She was a lecturer in the Department of Anthropology at Penn State University from 2013 until 2015, before taking a postdoctoral fellowship at the New School in fall 2015. She is affiliated with the South Asia Center of University of Washington.

■ WORKS CITED

Fisher, James, ed. 1978. *Himalayan Anthropology: The Indo-Tibetan Interface.* Paris: Mouton.

Google. 2017. "How a Web Session Is Defined in Analytics." https://support
.google.com/analytics/answer/2731565?hl=en.

Koh, Adeline. 2015. "Introduction to Interface 1:1." *Verge: Studies in Global Asias* 1, no. 1: 98–99.

Interface

MARK TURIN

What Next for Digital Himalaya? Reflections on Community, Continuity, and Collaboration

SEVENTEEN YEARS AGO, in December 2000, a group of four anthropologists and historians at the University of Cambridge set out to explore new methods for collecting, protecting, and connecting historical multimedia collections relating to the Himalayan region in ways that would widen access to the materials through emerging digital platforms. Sarah Harrison, Alan Macfarlane, Sara Shneiderman, and I named this pilot project "Digital Himalaya." We began by digitizing older sets of ethnographic data held in university and personal collections across Europe to protect them from obsolescence and decay, forward migrate them as new standards emerged, and share them back with originating communities in the Himalayan region and with scholars everywhere through the web and other digital media, as appropriate.[1]

The process, challenges, early successes, and ethical quandaries—not to mention the steps involved in selecting the original collections for digitization, the process of curation, the frequency of updates, and the necessary international collaboration that ensued—have been the topic of a number of academic and popular articles (cf. Shneiderman and Turin 2002; Turin 2011, 2012, 2015) and are beyond the scope of this contribution. In this short piece, appropriately framed within the *Interface* feature, I wish to explore the changing demographic of our users, the constructive criticism and welcome attention that we have received for the work in which we are engaged, the shifting expectations about what services and role we provide, and some reflections around the future of this collaborative partnership. The analytical backdrop to this article is my growing sense of unease about the sustainability of digital projects, an unease shared by other commentators working with new media in the digital realm. In their important 2014 volume *Re-collection: Art, New Media, and Social Memory,* museum professionals Richard Rinehart and Jon Ippolito ask readers to reflect on how increasingly digital forms of civilization will persist beyond our lifetimes and argue that the vulnerability of new media art illustrates a larger crisis for social memory. Rinehart and Ippolito's proposed "variable media approach" to new media, with responsibilities distributed between producers and consumers, "encourages creators to define a work in medium-independent terms so that it can be translated into a new medium once its original format is obsolete" (11). Over the past seventeen years, as new standards and possibilities have emerged, I have come to the conclusion that if the digitized content and material collections with which we have worked are "safe," then the structure that holds them together can be permitted to decay as new platforms take their place. In this, then, Digital Himalaya may be a simple object lesson in impermanence and nonattachment to form and structure, letting go of our now quite dated website so that the collections may live on through a generative process of rebirth and renewal.

■ AUDIENCE DEMOGRAPHICS: CHANGING EXPECTATIONS

When we established the project in 2000, we naively imagined that we were building a web portal primarily for academic users in the Global North who would have unfettered access to the internet through fast broadband networks and that communities in the Himalayas would be better served by us burning the digitized collections onto DVDs and depositing hard copies with institutes, colleges, and universities across Asia. How wrong we were!

Ever since we started tracking visits to and downloads from our website in 2005, a strikingly different pattern has emerged. Of the more than five hundred thousand unique "sessions" that Google Analytics has recorded, 19 percent have been from Nepal, 16 percent from the United States, 10 percent from India, and 8 percent from the United Kingdom. It is particularly satisfying that almost one hundred thousand web users in Nepal have accessed our content, offering a comprehensive challenge to our early assumption in 2000 that the "West" would have the web and the "Rest" would have hard discs and DVDs. Similarly striking are the data provided by Google about device category. While of the half million hits that the site has received since we started to track in 2005, only 9 percent have been on mobile devices and 2 percent have been on tablets, with the remainder from desktop or laptop computers; the use of handheld devices to access Digital Himalaya content has increased dramatically over time.

In the last year alone (July 2016–2017), mobile devices accounted for 20 percent of all visits and tablets for 4 percent, and given the increasing penetration of 3G mobile services across the Himalayan region, we can only expect this trend to increase in the coming years. At the same time, we receive as many requests from institutions in the Global North for offline copies of our collections on hard discs as we do from scholarly institutes in the Himalayan region. Some of our heaviest users download PDFs and films from our website using solar or hydropowered satellite broadband internet connections in Himalayan locations that would traditionally be described as "remote," as they have no vehicular access and/or are not on the national electricity grid.

■ CRITIQUES OF THE APPROACH

Over the years, Digital Himalaya has received its fair share of critical scholarly attention from archivists, librarians, museum curators, and fellow anthropologists who have explored both the potential and the limitations of our approach. Social sciences subject librarian at the Binghamton University Libraries Anne Larrivee (2013, 46) observes that while the "collections provide a unique array of culturally-enlightening digital resources on the Himalayan region," the "content is setup in an organizationally-limited way" and the "site feels like a pathfinder to available resources rather than a research tool to link to specific data." While we have worked closely with staff in libraries, archives, and museums, we acknowledge that none of our core project members are information management professionals, and this has led to limitations in our interface and organization. Other scholars have found more to praise in our applied approach, including archaeologist Sudeshna Guha (2012, 43), who suggests that Digital Himalaya "continues to remain theoretically useful for probing into relationships between digital replications and productions of cultural knowledge," and anthropologist Gina Drew (2012, 682), who suggests that Digital Himalaya's "efforts in resource sharing and collaborative publishing serve as a model for future endeavors to keep anthropological materials, from working papers to unedited video clips and field notes, in the public domain." All of these critiques and commendations are important and welcome and help us to refine, design, and look toward new opportunities for the project.

■ WHAT IS DIGITAL HIMALAYA? CHANGING EXPECTATIONS

As the project has aged and the internet has matured, I have been interested to observe a slowly changing perception of what Digital Himalaya is and how it works. Is it an archive? If so, by whom is it curated, and by what standards and selection process are materials included or excluded for dissemination? Or is Digital Himalaya more of an archive of an archive, a constantly mutating and transmigratory "collection of collections" that could never have been brought into conversation with one other than through a web interface. It has become clear to many of us working in this space that digital media impact both the subject and the tools of archival practice (Rinehart & Ippolito, 2014: 232).

By web standards, we are now an old project, designed and built before Google was a household name, when 4MB downloads were still large and all of our project team accessed our shared file folder through dial-up modems. While we have redesigned the website on a number of occasions, and have increased the size of our media collections as bandwidth has increased, I cannot escape the awkward feeling that our entire collection and approach are still rooted in an earlier, less interactive, and more traditional era of web technology. A large amount of the correspondence that we receive in the project e-mail inbox comes from scholars looking to publish in one of the many journals that we host online, even though we make it quite clear on our website that we are simply the online hosts, not editors or publishers. But as digital publishing has become the norm, and the front-end delivery of academic content becomes more widespread through open access initiatives, perhaps we are fulfilling part of the role of publisher, if only through dissemination, so this conflation of roles is to be expected.

As search tools have become more effective and more pervasive, we find that our collections are located, accessed, and downloaded without the user ever visiting or even knowing about our website. A simple search for a map, some census data, or a publication from the Himalayan region may send a prospective user to one of our file servers, bypassing the loose architecture of our website altogether. Whereas some technologists would perceive this as a problem, we view it as an asset: the visibility and discoverability of the collections hosted by Digital Himalaya have now reached the point that they no longer requires the fabric of our original website to facilitate access. It is striking how much you can achieve if you don't need or wish to take credit for it.

Similarly, we have opted for a redundancy approach to our multimedia collections, which are now housed on Cambridge University streaming servers, on the University of Virginia Tibetan and Himalayan Library, and also on YouTube. Not only is YouTube a very popular site for streaming video but it facilitates the very interaction, feedback, and commentary (in any number of languages) to which we originally aspired and which our own, much more basic website does not permit. Our thinking about the importance of our own interface has changed as standards have emerged over time and as some media-sharing sites have come to dominate the market. No longer are we allocating resources to developing sophisticated search and retrieval systems or pages that house images or audio and video collections, but we are rather focusing on pushing our content and the associated metadata to the places and platforms where they are most visible and best utilized. This is indicative of a wider reorientation among some digital projects that are moving away from developing customized and curated interfaces to collections of content to a "broadcasting" approach that makes use of free, albeit commercial, platforms to reach the widest possible audience.

■ THE DIGITAL FUTURE: BUILDING TOWARD SUSTAINABILITY

Sustainability for digital projects comes in various forms, with the two primary types being financial and technical. On the financial side, the project has turned away from relying on funding from research councils and foundations to a looser, flatter model of support from donations of time and money and some minimal advertising revenue generated through Amazon referrals and YouTube advertisements. I am sympathetic to colleagues who view such an approach as "selling out" but would remind them that open access is not free and that resources for servers, updates, and the digitization of new collections need to come from somewhere. While I don't believe that the micropayments from huge technology companies will float Digital Himalaya in the long term, I do think that it's worth experimenting with, if only because Digital Himalaya was always imagined to be a creative exploration of potential. While the project has done well in applying for and receiving operational grants, all of which are outlined and recognized online,[2] we have never had the comfort of core funding or institutional support on which to fall back.

The other primary vulnerability built into our system was institutional insecurity. Although Alan Macfarlane was an established professor at the University of Cambridge, the other three team members had relationships to the university that were more attenuated and less permanent. We often asked ourselves what the implications were of building a digital multimedia repository at a university to which only one of us had an enduring connection. Once again, time has proven to be an ally in our process. Our early commitment to DSpace, the University of Cambridge institutional repository, as the technical backbone for all of our collections provided deep security as two of our core team moved around the world on limited-term academic appointments. Now that Shneiderman and Turin have settled at the University of British Columbia (UBC), where both are tenured faculty, we have started to explore Digital Himalaya's next incarnation. Fortunately, UBC also uses the DSpace platform as its institutional repository, and I recently oversaw the bulk export of the entire Digital Himalaya collection from the Cambridge servers to a hard disc to enable its importation into UBC's Open Collections portal as a Featured Collection.[3] Following this data migration, which is planned for academic year 2017–2018, we believe that Digital Himalaya will finally be secure. While our current website may in time be retired, the collections that we have helped to digitize will have a new and permanent online home. As Rinehart and Ippolito (2014, 233) note, "new media works are going to need to be managed and migrated on a continual basis." Rather like the phoenix of ancient Greek mythology, I have now come to understand that Digital Himalaya will be cyclically regenerated and reborn, gaining new life by rising from the ashes of its earlier incarnation. And I have had to accept that the digital is just as transient, evanescent, and inconstant as other forms of analogue or corporeal existence.

Mark Turin (PhD, linguistics, Leiden University, 2006) is an anthropologist, linguist, and occasional radio presenter and an associate professor of anthropology at the University of British Columbia (UBC). From 2014 to 2018, Turin served as chair of the First Nations and Endangered Languages Program, and from 2016 to 2018, he was acting codirector of the university's new Institute for Critical Indigenous Studies. Before joining UBC, Turin was an associate research scientist with the South Asian Studies Council at Yale University and the founding program director of the Yale Himalaya Initiative. He continues to hold an appointment as visiting associate professor at the Yale School of Forestry and Environmental Studies. Turin directs both the World Oral Literature Project, an urgent global initiative to document and make accessible endangered oral literatures before they disappear without record, and the Digital Himalaya Project, which he cofounded in 2000 as a platform to make multimedia resources from the Himalayan region widely available online. Turin is the author or coauthor of four books and three travel guides and the editor of eight volumes, and from 2013 to 2017, he served as coeditor of the journal *HIMALAYA*. Turin also edits a series on oral literature with Open Book Publishers and is a regular BBC presenter on issues of linguistic diversity and language endangerment. He tweets @markturin.

■ NOTES

The author is grateful to Charlotte Eubanks, Pasang Yangjee Sherpa, and the external reviewers, who all provided welcome and substantive suggestions on ways to improve this short contribution. All remaining errors and infelicities are my own.

1. See the Digital Himalaya Project "Overview" page for more information: http://www.digitalhimalaya.com/overview.php.

2. See http://www.digitalhimalaya.com/support.php.

3. https://open.library.ubc.ca.

■ WORKS CITED

Drew, Georgina. 2012. "Digital Himalaya and the Collaborative Publishing Experience." *American Anthropologist* 114, no. 4: 680–81.

Guha, Sudeshna. 2012. "Curating Data, Disseminating Knowledge: Museums in the Digital Age." In *Proceedings ECLAP 2012: Conference on Information Technologies for Performing Arts, Media Access, and Entertainment,* edited by Paolo Nesi and Raffaella Santucci, 41–45. Florence: Firenze University Press.

Larrivee, Anne. 2013. "Digital Himalaya Project." *Reference Reviews* 27, no. 2: 45–46.

Rinehart, Richard, and Jon Ippolito. 2014. *Re-collection: Art, New Media, and Social Memory.* Cambridge, Mass.: MIT Press.

Shneiderman, Sara, and Mark Turin. 2002. "Digital Himalaya: An Ethnographic Archive in the Digital Age." In *Interarchive: Archival Practices and Sites in the Contemporary Art Field,* edited by Beatrice von Bismarck et al., 359–61. Köln: Buchhandlung Walter König.

Turin, Mark. 2011. "Born Archival: The Ebb and Flow of Digital Documents from the Field." *History and Anthropology* 22, no. 4: 445–60.

Turin, Mark. 2012. "Salvaging the Records of Salvage Ethnography: The Story of the Digital Himalaya Project." *Book 2.0* 1, no. 1: 39–46.

Turin, Mark. 2015. "The Unexpected Afterlives of Himalayan Collections: From Data Cemetery to Web Portal." In *The Anthropology of Expeditions: Travel, Visualities, Afterlives,* edited by Joshua A. Bell and Erin L. Hasinoff, 242–68. Chicago: University of Chicago Press.

Interface

**NAWANG GURUNG, ROSS PERLIN, DANIEL KAUFMAN,
MARK TURIN, AND SIENNA R. CRAIG**

Orality and Mobility: Documenting Himalayan Voices in New York City

OVER THE PAST TWO DECADES, the presence of people from the greater Himalayan region in New York City, particularly in the boroughs of Queens and Brooklyn, has expanded exponentially, from several hundred people in the 1980s to thousands of individuals from specific ethnic communities today (on Mustang, see Craig [2002] 2004, [2002] 2005, 2011; Craig and Gurung 2018; on Nepali women migrants, see Gurung 2015). As these new immigrants from Nepal, Bhutan, and North India, as well as diasporic Tibetans from India and culturally Tibetan regions in China, have settled into lives as New Yorkers, their senses of identity have begun to transform. Language plays a central role in these transformations. Himalayan voices can now be heard in the already hyperdiverse sociolinguistic landscape of a place like Jackson Heights.[1] Yet the processes of migration and assimilation have created new challenges for maintaining language diversity and cultivating a sense of social belonging through language. How are Himalayan New Yorkers finding a sense of community, navigating new transnational and intergenerational cultural dynamics, and responding to the relationship between "home" and being "over here" in New York? And what does language have to do with this?

These questions have guided a collaborative research project, Voices of the Himalaya: Language, Culture, and Belonging in Immigrant New York. Using the medium of video interviews, this project explores the lived experiences of migration and social change between the greater Himalayan region and New York City. The project has brought together a team of scholars and social activists, with expertise in linguistics, anthropology, and community-based participatory research (including the creation of digital archives), toward the production and curation of accessible narratives

64

told in an array of Tibetic Himalayan languages as well as several Tibeto-Burman languages close to the Tibetic area.[2] As a project, Voices of the Himalaya was designed to respond to the urgent challenges of language loss and rapid cultural change.

Beginning in 2016, the Voices of the Himalaya team has created and made publicly available twenty-five short videos with the dual goal of documenting Himalayan linguistic diversity in New York and encouraging language revitalization and cultural curiosity across generations, both within diasporic contexts and in "home" communities. These videos feature individuals of different generations and highlight a range of shared social issues: first impressions upon arrival in the United States; the challenges and possibilities of re-creating social networks in New York; balancing cultural continuity with American educational success; finding work and navigating the labor economy as nannies, construction workers, nail salon workers, and waiters or cooks; remembering and forgetting the cultural and natural landscapes of one's childhood. The videos also touch on unique personal experiences, from a Sherpa man who holds the speed record for climbing Everest to a Tibetan man who played a role in making it possible to Google in Tibetan and the Bhutanese equivalent of an *American Idol* superstar.

Voices of the Himalaya is not a traditional language documentation project. Unlike other such efforts, the project does not focus on one marginalized speech form but is rather transregional in scope. In addition, our goal is not the comprehensive documentation—through grammar, texts, and lexicon—of an endangered or minority language. As a collaborative team, we neither wish to exert scholarly authority over language use, nor in any way do we glamorize or valorize "endangerment" (see Pine and Turin 2017). Instead, the project seeks to showcase compelling stories that capture aspects of the happiness and suffering of everyday life and which are attuned and sensitive to a politics of (self)-representation. Since the first video was released in June 2016, the videos have been watched more than seventy thousand times and have been shared widely on social media.

In what follows, we sketch out our collaborative process, including the methodology we have used to generate and produce these videos. We then discuss how this work at once coheres with and departs from traditional "language documentation" efforts and explore several of the most compelling aspects of community responses to this work, including details on the analytics related to viewing, sharing, and responding to these stories.

■ OUR COLLABORATIVE COOPERATIVE

At the center of our core team of five anthropologists and linguists is Nawang Tsering Gurung, a young social entrepreneur and community mobilizer from the village of Ghiling, in Upper Mustang, Nepal. The eldest of ten children, only four of whom lived beyond childhood, Gurung's commitment to his cultural and linguistic heritage is both scholarly and deeply personal. He arrived in the United States on a student visa at the end of 2007 and lived variously in Dallas, then Boston, before finally making New York his home. Gurung observed that while both Texas and Massachusetts have strong diaspora communities of Himalayan origin, most hailed from more privileged backgrounds and urban social classes. Remote and ethnically Tibetan districts such as Mustang were almost entirely absent from the demographics of Nepalis in these locations.

Having completed an associate's degree from Quincy College in Boston while simultaneously holding down two full-time jobs and working more than seventy hours a week, Gurung moved to New York in 2011. He was immediately struck by how the entire urban landscape of New York City—and in particular the boroughs of Brooklyn and Queens—was saturated with more relatives and friends from his community than existed in the rest of the United States combined, and how these were more closely packed together than in his home district of Mustang. Relatives from villages a five-hour horse ride away in Mustang could now be reached through two stops on the subway. Rich social networks and complex economic relationships bound individuals from the higher reaches of Himalayan Nepal, India, and Bhutan together through religion, ritual, food, exchange, and language. Gurung heard not only Nepali on the street corners of Roosevelt Avenue and in the tea shops of Diversity Square but also the familiar rhythm of Mustangi Tibetan dialects along with Dzongkha, Thakali, Manange, and other Himalayan languages.

Gurung found employment at the New York Tibetan Service Center (NYTSC), a nonprofit organization dedicated to the social and economic mobility of Tibetan and Himalayan immigrants of New York City. Gurung served as development director at the NYTSC, a role that brought him into close contact with donors, scholars, and the city authorities of New York. Having worked previously as a research assistant with a number of ethnographically minded scholars, both at home in the Himalaya and in diaspora communities in the Global North, Gurung hatched the germ of an idea: would it be possible to document the languages, cultures, social histories, folklore, and community life of Himalayan New Yorkers through video and thereby explore the lived experiences of migration and social change in his own community?

In New York, Gurung observed that most of his fellow countrymen and -women were working such long hours and holding down so many jobs that their young, school-age children were growing up in a diaspora context without a clear sense of their cultural heritage. At the same time, as grandparents began migrating to the United States to join their families, these elders had a combination of considerable leisure time and great cultural knowledge from their home communities but often passed long days in solitude. Gurung wondered whether a collaborative multimedia project—provisionally titled Voices of the Himalaya—might be a way to collect, protect, and connect these untold stories of opportunity and challenge, a chance to showcase both the extraordinary sociolinguistic diversity and the cultural connectedness and unity of Himalayan communities in the diaspora.

Building on a strong preexisting relationship with Sienna Craig, a medical anthropologist at Dartmouth with whom he had previously worked and published, Gurung started to assemble his team. He reached out to Mark Turin, an anthropologist and linguist at Yale University who was then directing the Yale Himalaya Initiative, who put him in touch with linguist Daniel Kaufman, executive director of the Endangered Language Alliance (ELA), a nonprofit founded in 2010 with the goal of working with immigrant and refugee populations in New York and other cities, helping them document and maintain their languages. Kaufman in turn involved Ross Perlin, a writer and linguist specializing in endangered Tibeto-Burman languages spoken in southwest China who also serves as codirector at the ELA. Having composed the core team and procured seed funding from Dartmouth,[3] Voices of the Himalaya was ready to start work.

▤ METHODOLOGY

Our aim was to produce compelling, tightly edited web videos, usually no more than fifteen minutes each, that would appeal to a wide popular audience and compete with other online media. An implicit goal of this work was to establish a new public-facing domain for Himalayan languages, which are usually restricted to private settings such as the home. We believed that creating professional, subtitled videos in less common languages, perhaps especially when produced in the world-city of New York, could have a galvanizing effect on the language attitudes of speakers and nonspeakers alike.

Between May 2016 and March 2017, we conducted interviews with twenty-two men and women, young and old, from diverse Himalayan backgrounds, as shown in the following table.

Video title	Language	Gender	Hometown
Ama-la's Story	Ngari Tibetan	Female	Ngari, Tibet
Young and Tibetan in Queens	Tibetan	Female	Queens, New York, USA
From Mustang to Manhattan	Mustangi	Female	Marang, Upper Mustang, Nepal
Growing Up Between Words and Worlds	Tibetan (Ramaluk)	Female	Marang, Upper Mustang, Nepal
Mr. Speed, Fastest Up Everest	Sherpa	Male	Lhoding, Solukhumbu, Nepal
A Thangka Painter in New York	Tibetan/ Mustangi	Male	Chongur, Lower Mustang, Nepal
Cooking for the Community	Tibetan (Ramaluk)	Male	Tsum, Gorkha, Nepal
Trade and Travels from Manang to New York	Manange	Female	Manang, Nepal
Trade and Travels from Manang to New York	Manange	Male	Manang, Nepal
There Once Was a Storyteller . . .	Mustangi	Male	Tangye, Upper Mustang, Nepal
From the Farthest Valley	Tokpe Gola	Male	Papung, Taplejung, Nepal
After Us, No One Will Speak	Seke	Male	Tsuk, Kyangma, Mustang, Nepal
From Historic Capital to Diaspora Center	Lhasa Tibetan	Female	Lhasa, Tibet
A Restaurant of His Own	Tokpe Gola	Male	Papung, Taplejung, Nepal
A Kham Lady Renewing Tradition	Kham Tibetan (Dege)	Female	Dege, Kham, Tibet

Video title	Language	Gender	Hometown
A Superstar in Bhutan, a Newcomer to New York	Dzongkha	Male	Ula River, Wangdi Phodrang, Bhutan
Keeping up the Language, from Varanasi to Google	Tibetan	Male	Rongbu, Sog, Nagqu, Tibet
A Renaissance Man in Tibetan New York	Amdo Tibetan	Male	Arouxiang, Qilian, Qinghai, China
Nomad to New Yorker	Amdo Tibetan	Male	Changmuzhen, Guide, Qinghai, China
Bringing New York a Taste of the Himalayas	Thakali	Female	Jomsom, Lower Mustang, Nepal

After discussing the goals of the project using an English-language Institutional Review Board–approved information sheet as our guide, translated orally as needed into Tibetan and Nepali by Nawang Gurung, we elicited oral consent not only to the interviews but also to have edited videos made completely public and archived. Three female participants of the twenty-two people we interviewed later asked for their videos not to be made public for the time being, citing reasons of modesty and "face." Of the twenty-two interviews, five took place at the Manhattan office of the Endangered Language Alliance, while the others were held at people's homes and places of work (two restaurants and a store) in Queens and Brooklyn.

The participants came from a diverse set of linguistic and personal backgrounds, arguably representative of the new Himalayan community in New York. We also relied on a combination of convenience, chance, snowball, and targeted sampling techniques, facilitated and guided by Gurung's extended network and deep knowledge of the community and its most compelling stories. Indeed, in a few cases, interviews resulted from serendipity: a chance encounter at the Jackson Heights Dunkin Donuts; a friend brought along by another participant, and so on. In addition, a limited amount of "B-roll" footage and photography, shot by project members in neighborhoods or at events or supplied by the participants themselves, supplemented the interview footage.

Interviews typically lasted between half an hour and an hour, tracing a narrative arc from a personal introduction (often beginning with a "tashi delek" or "namaste," name, and place of origin) and life history to broader thoughts on language, culture, and community. No standard questionnaire was used, but Gurung (in all but a few cases the principal interviewer) used his knowledge of the participants and their communities, as well as general project themes, to guide the questioning. These questions were typically phrased in diasporic Standard Tibetan, in local Mustangi dialects, or occasionally in Nepali. Others present (Perlin in all but a few cases; Kaufman, Craig, and Turin in several; other videographers and advisors in some) added questions, usually in English. In keeping with project aims and our established conventions, all such questions and clarifications were edited out of the final videos. Footage breaks, text slides, and other devices may reveal the cuts to viewers with videography experience. Fuller, raw versions of the interviews are being archived.

As a project of and for the Himalayan New York community, Voices of the Himalaya took the self-representation and agency of participants seriously. Many participants chose to change out of New York street clothes just before beginning the interview and present themselves in their best traditional attire or cultural regalia. Likewise, participants were aware from the beginning that local languages were a focus of the project and were encouraged to speak their mother tongue despite fielding questions in Standard Tibetan or Nepali. While multiple speakers of the same variety interviewing each other might have been optimal in this respect (as was done in our Manange video), this was not usually possible for practical reasons and also not necessarily desirable in terms of larger project aims of widening access to historically marginalized voices. For most participants, it appeared to be quite natural for them to talk about themselves and their community in their mother tongue to an interlocutor (Gurung) who was assumed to understand most of what they said, although a few participants still opted for a more standardized language. For example, a chef from the Tsum region of northern Gorkha District, Nepal, chose to speak Standard Tibetan because of what he perceived to be the low status of his local dialect; a project manager at Google chose to do the same because he is professionally invested in Standard Tibetan rather than the eastern Tibetan (Kham) variety of his birthplace. Code-switching and mixed language use are present throughout the videos, representing a rich (if somewhat idealized) source of material for the study of multilingualism and language change in the Himalayan diaspora.

The relatively rapid "postproduction" process involved Gurung reviewing the entire recording and indicating cuts and reshufflings of material to streamline the narrative, avoid repetition, and, in some cases, steer clear of controversial material deemed potentially embarrassing to the participant or the community. In some cases, team members communicated with a participant who made requests for edits or answered questions, particularly in the translation process, which proceeded once a shortened "clean edit" had been made. Other small touches to provide narrative coherence and guide viewers—slides dividing topics, titles, occasional explanatory text—were added by Gurung and Perlin at this stage.

Gurung made first-pass translations of the varieties of languages he could understand—Mustangi (Loke), Seke, and Standard or Central Tibetan varieties—and enlisted several translators for those he could not (Manange, Sherpa, Kham, Amdo, Dzongkha), working with them through Nepali and Tibetan. Perlin, a native English speaker, then worked with Gurung to proofread and correct those English translations. One video, in a mixture of Mustangi and Tibetan, has a full phonetic transcription as well.[4]

Careful thought was given to release and dissemination, with social media considered to be the principal platform. In addition to being archived with full metadata at the ELA, videos have been uploaded to YouTube, where they are tied to the broader Voices of the Himalaya corpus by theme music, a unified YouTube playlist, and links back to the ELA site. New uploads were embedded and principally distributed by ELA and by Gurung personally via Facebook, with sharing and tagging helping to ensure a wide, community-based viewership. The preceding section outlines our process. But how does this relate to the discipline of linguistics and the field of "language documentation," particularly of rare or endangered languages?

■ VOICES OF THE HIMALAYA AS LANGUAGE DOCUMENTATION

In addition to being a de facto oral history project, Voices of the Himalaya was also conceived of as a language documentation project. The recent subfield of language documentation is mostly a reconfiguring of priorities and perspectives that have been present in some form for several centuries. Much of the traditional work of American linguists in the first half of the twentieth century involved describing the sound patterns, word structures, and syntactic configurations of Native American languages. The traditional outputs of such work were a descriptive grammar, a lexicon, and a text collection, occasionally referred to as the "Boasian trilogy" after the work of Franz Boas, one of the more prominent linguists and anthropologists of the later nineteenth and early twentieth centuries. What went on behind the scenes—the process and politics of fieldwork—

was often hidden to the public, including the primary data upon which those linguistic descriptions were based and the negotiations between the researchers and the communities whose languages and cultures they documented.

Several factors led to revisiting the values and priorities inherent in this work. A seminal publication by Michael Krauss (1992) highlighted the dire state of language endangerment today and, equally importantly, argued that linguists bear responsibility for remediating the situation. Rapid advances in digital technology also made it possible for linguists to create high-fidelity recordings that could be more easily preserved and shared across space and time. At the same time, there has been an increasing awareness of the ethical responsibilities of linguists toward the communities with which they work, especially Native and Indigenous communities, which has led to moving from a model of working *on* communities to working *with* and *for* communities.[5] Language documentation, as a subfield or simply a named movement, crystallized in the work of Himmelmann (2006, 1), with the oft-quoted goal of facilitating "a lasting, multipurpose record of a language."[6] This informal movement advocated for a new respect toward primary data and sought to answer questions of preservation and access and explore how an entire language could be properly represented in terms of its many genres, varieties, and speakers.

While the Voices of the Himalaya project is also meant to serve as language documentation, it clearly prioritizes certain principles of the field at the expense of others. The team focused on producing a sample of various Tibetic dialects and other Himalayan languages, many of them endangered and some undescribed, as they are spoken in a relatively new center of the Himalayan diaspora: New York City. The documentation is furthermore explicitly multipurpose: interviews were recorded in such a way that they could be used for linguistic analysis, for an oral history of the burgeoning Himalayan community, and for different types of pedagogical and learning contexts. These videos were also recorded, edited, and disseminated with the Himalayan community foremost in mind, with scholarly and research considerations a clear second.

However, given this orientation, coupled with concerns about the consequences of sharing sensitive information and opinions, the videos required rather heavy editing, which has not been a feature of many language documentation projects, the main concern of which has been to collect and disseminate primary data. The consequence of this approach is that Voices of the Himalaya is a unique collection of videos that are more watchable and popular than they would have otherwise been, although some of the original structure of the discourse has been lost through the editing process. The monologues were also structured into thematic chapters by the team in a post hoc fashion, not always reflecting the structure and sequence of the original conversation.

In terms of linguistic analysis, all the videos have been translated, and one has been transcribed using the International Phonetic Alphabet. While morphological and grammatical analysis is planned, it has not yet been undertaken. To what extent Voices of the Himalaya should be considered to be a language documentation project and to what extent it is more of an oral history project will largely depend on how users engage with the corpus and further extend its use. It is our hope that these annotated recordings can serve as a helpful baseline for the further study of these languages, but it must be kept in mind that the corpus, as of now, represents only how the interviewees speak in a controlled, one-on-one setting when asked to speak (on camera) in their native language and dialect.

■ COMMUNITY RESPONSES

As of mid-June 2017, the videos associated directly with the project had been viewed via YouTube more than seventy thousand times, with approximately 33 percent of views in the United States, 15 percent in Bhutan (principally the videos of our nationally celebrated Bhutanese participant), 14 percent in India, and then 6 percent each in Nepal, Switzerland, and Canada. In other words, the videos appeared to reach a representative cross section of the global Himalayan diaspora—even at the domestic level in the United States, where New York (half of all U.S. views), California, Massachusetts, and Minnesota were the states with the highest levels of engagement. Given that YouTube and Facebook are both blocked within China, we did not expect to reach viewers in that country, although there were a handful of such views. Thus far, efforts to upload videos to Youku and Tudou, with distribution via Weibo, were blocked.

Although such statistics must be treated with caution, according to YouTube analytics, most viewers are in the twenty-five to thirty-four age bracket (40 percent) and are male (69 percent), which may be a function of how videos were distributed, shared, and discovered. Approximately 60 percent of views occurred without subtitles, with that figure rising to 67 percent in New York. Although some may have had trouble finding the subtitles setting that sometimes needs to be toggled on or off within the YouTube interface, we take this figure to indicate that, for many viewers, subtitles were not necessary for comprehension—a compelling linguistic finding in its own right. The three most watched videos were *Young and Tibetan in Queens* (approximately fifteen thousand views), *A Superstar in Bhutan, a Newcomer to New York* (approximately twelve thousand views), and *Ama-la's Story* (ninety-four hundred views), after which there was a significant drop-off for smaller languages and for older speakers less connected to social media or less well known in the community.

Social media and YouTube commenters are certainly not a balanced cross section of the community. We realize that comment sections can be particularly contentious, and social media research was not a central focus of our methodology for this study (Sloan and Quan-Hasse 2017). However, we felt paying attention to the comments provided one lens onto how the Himalayan community was accessing and responding to this work, and the comments logged could be fruitfully compared with feedback elicited in different manners from segments of the community that are not well represented online. Social media "engagement" with the videos, through likes and comments, followed a broadly similar pattern and mostly came from the United States, India, Nepal, and Canada. All in all, the videos had 439 likes and 58 dislikes, as well as 48 comments, many focused on language choice and use (and principally in English; Tibetan, especially in *Young and Tibetan in Queens*; in Chinese; and in Manange for the Manange video). ELA, as manager of the YouTube account, attempted a light-touch approach to moderating these reactions, only directly posting once in a speaker's defense and in two cases removing inflammatory comments. In further work of this kind, we would hope to move from an ad hoc approach to a more considered policy on the ethics of community moderation around such a collection.

Comparing digital community reactions to *Young and Tibetan in Queens*, which features Tsejin Khando (a proud Tibetan American soon-to-be college student, born in New York, and a strong speaker of Tibetan), and *Growing Up between Words and Worlds* (approximately seventy-eight hundred views), with Chemi Chemi (a Mustangi college student in America who takes a more questioning stance toward certain aspects of community life), is instructive and illustrative. Most of commenters praised Tsejin as a model of cultural continuity, and three comments (in English) even directly address her as a friend or family member. Chemi's video, conversely, elicited several critical reactions to her code-switching, including two that themselves code-switch (one seems to be a transliteration of "um" into Tibetan characters, and the other apparently criticizes her patriotism), although other comments commended Chemi for her educational accomplishments and the way she speaks.

Public commentary on the corpus provides a new source of data that seems worthy of further analysis. As this data set grows, we can imagine taking a quantitative approach to studying the cause and effect between an interview and its responses. At what point, for instance, does an interviewee receive criticism for using too much English, Nepali, or Standard Tibetan? Does switching to these standard/national languages elicit the same types of reactions? In terms of ideas, what kinds of critical views elicit the most countercritiques, and which views find the most support? The social media and YouTube commenters are certainly not a balanced cross section of the community, but their comments can be fruitfully compared with feedback elicited in different manners from segments of the community that are not well represented online.

■ TRANSCRIPTION, TRANSLATION, AND LANGUAGE TRANSMISSION

Language documentation of the type exemplified in Voices of the Himalaya affords valuable learning opportunities by way of the transcription and translation process. For obvious reasons, it is typically the most fluent members of a linguistic community whose speech is prioritized for documentation. However, these fluent speakers, for lack of time and training, are often unable to transcribe and translate their own recordings on a computer. Traditionally, a linguist does this technical work with the help of native speakers by his or her side. Urban settings allow for a different dynamic, which may increasingly become the norm whether language documentation is carried out in situ or in centers of diaspora like New York City.

Specifically, younger community members can be trained to do time-aligned transcription and translation, which can in turn give them an opportunity to improve their own language skills. In the current project, two Tibetan undergraduate linguistics students at Queens College, Tenzin Namdol and Tsering Dolkar, were able to engage with the language of their parents in a systematic and rigorous way that was otherwise unavailable to them. Tenzin, in particular, who was raised in Dharamsala, Kashmir, and New York, had expressed remorse at never having learned the language of her mother, Mustangi (Loke), despite being very fluent in Tibetan, Hindi, and English. Nonetheless, Tenzin was familiar enough with Mustangi that she could create the outlines of an English translation, which could then be filled in with help from her mother and the interviewees themselves.

Through this process, Tenzin's own comprehension of Mustangi was appreciably improved, and the prospects of language transmission from her mother to her was given a second lease on life, albeit in a more limited context. While the finished corpus has great potential as a pedagogical tool, the process of creating the corpus should also be seen as a valuable opportunity for younger community members to improve their grasp of heritage languages. Most importantly, it offers diaspora youth a structured framework for engaging with their parents and elders on questions of language, culture, identity, and belonging.

■ CONCLUSION AND NEXT STEPS

Over the course of a twelve-month period, Voices of the Himalaya created a corpus of videos that are circulating within, and having a diverse impact on, Himalayan communities in both diasporic and Asian contexts. We have navigated our way through an evolving, collaborative methodology, documenting this research process with care and exploring complex questions of representation and voice. Based on community viewer feedback, we believe that such an endeavor has meaning and value to this community and that the project has scope for expansion.

One specific offshoot project that we are developing, based on this first year of research and video production, will focus on songs and singers in the Himalayan diaspora. During several of our interviews (and in a few of our completed videos), individuals offered examples of songs from their home communities. Song remains an incredibly rich source of cultural knowledge and linguistic diversity, including among those living in the New York Himalayan diaspora. Such a project would aim to document and showcase the diversity of Himalayan vocal traditions that are now uniquely concentrated—and in a critical moment of transformation and endangerment—in the diasporic center of New York City. This project recognizes that there is a shift under way to singing in the evolving Tibetan lingua franca, influenced either by popular music or by the conservatory approach of the Tibetan Institute of the Performing Arts. We aim instead to record the rural, vernacular genres as still practiced and sustained by small groups of enthusiasts in New York. Among the major themes and genres are male–female duets, drinking and wedding songs, songs particular to certain seasons, and songs about nature and specific sacred Himalayan geographies, honoring individuals such as *lamas* or commenting on religious themes.

In keeping with the goals of participatory action-oriented research, we also hope to use the next year to expand the corpus of Voices of the Himalaya videos and also to elicit more community-level feedback on the videos. We plan to do this in several ways: by conducting focus groups with elders and youth, in which we will play a few of the videos and elicit their responses, and by returning to some of the individuals represented in the initial videos and doing follow-up interviews or, if they are comfortable, capturing more of their unscripted daily-life interactions at home, with friends, and, as possible, at work. There is a tension concerning the aesthetics of presentation and the paramount goals of community access and use—custom-built platforms like Shanti, Voices of Tibet, and the Tibet Oral History Project might serve the former purpose, while existing commercial channels like YouTube and WeChat hold out the best hope for the latter. Digital Himalaya, discussed earlier in this *Interface,* raises questions about how much weight, with finite resources, to give long-term preservation and scholarly archiving. A related question concerns metadata structure and consistency: release onto larger platforms allows broader dissemination but simultaneously risks loss of control and decontextualization. No single platform can fully address all needs.

From a scholarly perspective, we hope to expand the phonetic transliterations of our completed videos and to write several other articles about this project for both public consumption and more specialist academic audiences. In addition, we are planning to develop additional pedagogical materials that can be shared with New York City schools and to engage in direct outreach in the form of guest lectures and/or teacher in-service presentations as a way of encouraging cross-cultural understanding and deepening productive discussions about new New Yorkers and their contributions to their own communities and to wider society.

Sienna R. Craig is associate professor of anthropology at Dartmouth College. She received her PhD from Cornell University (2006). She is the author of *Healing Elements: Efficacy and the Social Ecologies of Tibetan Medicine* (2012) and of *Horses Like Lightning: A Story of Passage through the Himalaya* (2008) and a coeditor of *Medicine between Science and Religion: Explorations on Tibetan Grounds* (2010), among other publications. In addition to her academic work, Craig writes creative nonfiction and fiction, children's literature, and poetry. From 2012 to 2017, she coedited, with Mark Turin, *HIMALAYA, Journal of the Association for Nepal and Himalayan Studies.* Craig is also a cofounder of DROKPA, a nonprofit organization that partners with Himalayan communities to support projects in education, community health, and social entrepreneurship.

Nawang Tsering Gurung is founder and director of Yulha Fund, a nonprofit dedicated to ensuring sustainable livelihoods and improving access to education and health care in the Himalayan communities of Nepal. He earned an associate's degree from Quincy College in 2011. He has served as a translator and assistant for National Geographic filmmaker Liesel Clark, on a documentary entitled *Cave People of the Himalayas.* Nawang has worked as a research assistant on several research projects in both New York and Nepal. Nawang is coauthor of several presentations and publications based on this work, including "The *Khora of Migration: Everyday Practices of (Well)-Being between Mustang, Nepal, and New York City.*" He is also coauthor of the book *Dogyab: Rituel Tibetain de Conjuration du Mal* (in French, 2017). Currently Nawang is coordinator of the Voices of the Himalayas project.

Daniel Kaufman is a founder and codirector of the Endangered Language Alliance and assistant professor of linguistics at Queens College, CUNY. He specializes in the Austronesian languages of Southeast Asia but has also focused for the last ten years on the documentation of endangered languages spoken by immigrant communities in New York City.

Ross Perlin is codirector of the Endangered Language Alliance, a non-profit based in New York City with a mission to document and support endangered languages and linguistic diversity. Ross received his PhD in linguistics from the University of Bern (2017) for his documentation and description of Trung, a Tibeto-Burman language of southwest China. He has also written on language, labor, and culture for the *New York Times, Time* magazine, the *Guardian,* and the *Washington Post,* among other outlets. His first book, *Intern Nation: How to Earn Nothing and Learn Little in the Brave New Economy,* was published in 2011.

■ NOTES

Thanks to all of the Himalayan community members who shared their stories and lived with us and to Tierney Brown for her assistance with YouTube analytics and comments.

1. The Endangered Language Alliance estimates that Jackson Heights, together with adjacent areas whose borders are not always strictly defined, is the most linguistically diverse part of New York City, the most linguistically diverse metro region in the United States, according to the Census Bureau. For ELA's map of the languages of Queens, first published in Solnit and Jelly-Shapiro (2016), see http://elalliance.org/programs/documentation/language-maps/.

2. Seke, Thakali, and Manange are among the Tibeto-Burman languages represented thus far in the project's corpus.

3. Dartmouth College, Office of the Provost, Global Exploratory/Development Grant 2016-17.

4. We hope to do more such phonetic transcription, pending additional funding.

5. Rice (2006) and Czaykowska-Higgins (2009) are two examples of these discussions among linguists, while Moskowitz (2015), Rylko-Bauer,

Singer, and Willigen (2006), and Stilltoe (1998) address the issue as anthropologists, and Smith (2012) is the work of an indigenous scholar working at the intersection of the two fields.

6. Other important sources theorizing language documentation include Lehmann (2001), Woodbury (2003), the handbooks by Gippert, Himmelmann, and Mosel (2006) and Austin and Sallabank (2011), and the journals *Language Documentation and Description* and *Language Documentation and Conservation.*

■ WORKS CITED

Austin, Peter, and Julia Sallabank. 2011. *The Cambridge Handbook of Endangered Languages.* Cambridge: Cambridge University Press.

Craig, Sienna. (2002) 2004. "Place, Work, and Identity between Mustang, Nepal, and New York City." *Studies in Nepali History and Society* 7, no. 2: 355–403.

Craig, Sienna. (2002) 2005. "A Tale of Two Temples: Culture, Capital, and Community in Mustang, Nepal." *European Bulletin of Himalayan Research* 27: 11–36.

Craig, Sienna. 2011. "Migration, Social Change, Health, and the Realm of the Possible: Women's Stories from Nepal to New York." *Anthropology and Humanism* 36, no. 2: 193–214.

Craig, Sienna R., and Nawang T. Gurung. 2018. "The Khora of Migration: Everyday Practices of (Well)-Being between Mustang, Nepal and New York City." In *Global Nepalis: Religion and Culture in a New Diaspora,* edited by D. Gellner and S. Hausner, 271–300. Delhi: Oxford University Press.

Czaykowska-Higgins, Ewa. 2009. "Research Models, Community Engagement, and Linguistic Fieldwork: Reflections on Working within Canadian Indigenous Communities." *Language Documentation and Conservation* 3, no. 1: 15–50.

Gippert, Jost, Nikolaus P. Himmelmann, and Ulrike Mosel. 2006. *Essentials of Language Documentation.* Berlin: Mouton de Gruyter.

Gurung, Shobha Hamal. 2015. *Nepali Migrant Women: Resistance and Survival in America.* Syracuse, N.Y.: Syracuse University Press.

Himmelmann, Nikolaus P. 2006. "Language Documentation: What Is It and What Is It Good For?" In *Essentials of Language Documentation,* edited by Jost Gippert, Nikolaus P. Himmelmann, and Ulrike Mosel, 1–30. Berlin: Mouton de Gruyter.

Krauss, Michael E. 1992. "The World's Languages in Crisis." *Language* 68, no. 1: 4–10.

Lehmann, Christian. 2001. "Language Documentation: A Program." In

Aspects of Typology and Universals, edited by Walter Bisang, 83–97. Berlin: Akademie.

Moskowitz, N. 2015. "Engagement, Alienation, and Anthropology's New Moral Dilemmas." *Anthropology and Humanism* 40: 35–57.

Pine, Aidan, and Mark Turin. 2017. *Language Revitalization.* Edited by Mark Aronoff. New York: Oxford University Press.

Rice, Keren. 2006. "Ethical Issues in Linguistic Fieldwork: An Overview." *Journal of Academic Ethics* 4: 123–55.

Rylko-Bauer, B., M. Singer, and J. V. Willigen. 2006. "Reclaiming Applied Anthropology: Its Past, Present, and Future." *American Anthropologist* 108: 178–90.

Sloan, Luke, and Anabel Quan-Haase, eds. 2017. *The Sage Handbook of Social Media Research Methods.* Thousand Oaks, Calif.: Sage.

Smith, Linda Tuhiwai. 2012. *Decolonizing Methodologies: Research and Indigenous Peoples.* London: Zed Books.

Solnit, Rebecca, and Joshua Jelly-Shapiro. 2016. *Nonstop Metropolis: A New York City Atlas.* Oakland: University of California Press.

Stilltoe, Paul. 1998. "The Development of Indigenous Knowledge: A New Applied Anthropology." *Current Anthropology* 39, no. 2: 223–52.

Woodbury, Anthony C. 2003. "Defining Documentary Linguistics." In *Language Documentation and Description,* vol. 1, edited by Peter K. Austin, 35–51. London: Hans Rausing Endangered Languages Project.

Codex

A Collaborative Review of *Trans-Indigenous: Methodologies for Global Native Literary Studies* by Chadwick Allen

In memorium of Teresia Teaiwa (August 12, 1968–March 21, 2017). We shall remember her strength, the power of her words, and her infinite wisdom, which have shaped our visions of a trans-Indigenous Oceania.

We sweat and cry salt water, so we know that the ocean is really in our blood.
　　—Epile Hau'ofa, "The Ocean in Us"

Toward the Trans-Indigenous Pacific: Islanding Perspectives

HSINYA HUANG

Chadwick Allen's 2012 monograph *Trans-Indigenous* proposes impressive tactics and practices for cross-cultural comparative studies of Indigenous cultural and literary (con)texts, specifically from Maori and Native North American peoples, a project he encapsulates in the idea of the "trans-Indigenous." As a response to contemporary debate on "transnationalism," "trans-Indigenous" questions the construct of the "transnational," "in its orthodox conceptions and in its typical attachments to dominant formations," such as the U.S.-based discipline of American studies, which "necessarily implies both a binary opposition and a vertical hierarchy of the Indigenous (always) tethered to (and positioned below) the settler-invader" ("A Transnational Native American Studies? Why Not Studies that are Trans-Indigenous?" 3). Replacing vertical Indigenous–settler (nation–state) relations with lateral Indigenous connections and challenging the borders of contemporary nation-states, Allen opens up the possibility of center-to-center conversations among Indigenous Nations and, ultimately, the possibility of a comparative critical methodology for global Indigenous literatures and arts.

This review evaluates the success of Allen's proposed methodologies and examines the ways to extend trans-Indigenous methodologies to new contexts, moving from Native American and Maori traditions to the broader context of debates surrounding global Indigeneity. In 2013, at the Native American and Indigenous Studies Association annual meeting in Saskatoon, Canada, Hsinya Huang, David Stirrup, and James Mackay, with Chadwick Allen as the commentator, presented a panel to acknowledge Allen's breakthrough in global Indigenous studies. Allen's rejection of transnational, (post)colonial, and multiethnic reading strategies in favor of Indigenous-specific methodologies is explicitly framed in activist terms, providing powerful counternarratives and critiques to oppose the ideology and practices of colonial and imperial fencing and mapping. In addition, Allen emphasizes the mobility, continuity, flow, interactions, and solidarity among Indigenous peoples in global contexts, arguing along a similar line to Epeli Hau'ofa's (2008) signature trope "our sea of islands" and Édouard Glissant's (1990) "poetics of relations." His logics also inform the revolutionary development for Native American and Indigenous studies advanced by Robert Warrior (2009) and others. In bringing Maori texts into his comparative framework, Allen furthermore challenges the spread of English-only ideology in relation to cultural imperialism and racial inequality. The cumulated effect of down-to-earth practice, close reading, and textual analysis is impressive, through which Allen recovers/interprets Indigenous genre, orature, linguistic mechanism, aesthetics, and technologies to subvert the writing culture of Euro-American colonialism.

Allen's critical focus, however, falls within Indigenous literary studies in English. The limitation in his selection of comparative cases exclusively devoted to Indigenous literature in English runs the risk of reaffirming settler state logics. The panelists in "Transindigeneity? Assessing the Possibility of a Comparative Critical Methodology for Global Indigenous Literatures" moved beyond the specific English-speaking settler colonial parameters of Allen's Fourth World model and set it in the broader context of debates in Scandinavia, northern Russia, central and southern Africa, and Asia Pacific to examine how definitions of Indigeneity transform and become unsettled. They suggested replacing the essentialist appeal inherent to trans- (as opposed to purely local) Indigenous discourse itself and bringing trans-Indigenous studies into conversation with the growing interest in transcolonial cultural movement. Can we prompt more radical deviation from orthodox shadows of literature in English, taking into account, for instance, Indigenous inheritance in Scandinavia, Asia Pacific, and so on, as aforementioned? Nevertheless, this moving away from the English-only ideology and practice can be a project of staggering proportions. How to implement the value of "trans-Indigenous" practically and manageably as we move beyond the English texts? We need to ensure that we ask important questions and seek answers within a framework of relevant issues. We need to gather relevant sets of issues crucial to diverse Indigenous groups and formulate positive notions of trans-Indigeneity, which in turn feed back into local native traditions. In Wai Chee Dimock's (2007) words, Homi K. Bhabha's "partial community" of the global/planetary life is "rendered partial by its off-center relation to the national government, and by its far-reaching and locally mediated kinship with other distant minority groups" (11).

In terms of "partial community," the juxtaposition of Allison Hedge Coke's *Blood Run* with Robert Sullivan's *Star Waka* in Allen's *Trans-Indigenous* may not be as productive as the comparative linkage between *Star Waka* and Indigenous texts of the Pacific islanders or Oceanians. Though both *Blood Run* and *Star Waka* represent Indigenous sophisticated technologies, and thus civilization, this comparative module nevertheless bypasses the significance of cultural traditions that inform the texts. *Blood Run* centers on earth work in Native America as land-based civilization, whereas *Star Waka* recovers seafaring tradition and orchestrates the common future of Oceania. In this sense, Sinophone writings by aboriginal poets of Taiwan, such as Syaman Rapongan of Pangso no Tau, appear akin to Sullivan's poetic trajectory across ocean as the pathway. Both Rapongan and Sullivan reinvent Indigenous grammar, words, and metaphors of the same Oceanian seafaring tradition. Allen speaks from his intellectual orientation in American studies and thus draws on English texts to illustrate the idea of the trans-Indigenous. And yet, Rapongan's work may be a more suitable candidate for comparison with Maori poet Robert Sullivan's eclectic waka poems in *Star Waka* than Native American poet Allison Hedge Coke's *Blood Run*. In terms of their common Oceanian heritage as well as linguistic/cultural implication to be reinvented in the transcolonial Oceanian context, Rapongan and Sullivan make a good pair of trans-Indigenous comparison mediated through Oceania. Can we shift the taken-for-granted life-forms of the land into to-be-generated, remapped forms of the sea, stars, and boat in the Pacific, which Rapongan and Sullivan brilliantly represent? While the "enchanted islands" in the Western literary canon set the paradigm of the "first contact" between the Pacific islanders and Euro-Americans, moving toward Oceania and using the island as a primary site of critical inquiry, postcolonial recuperation, sustainability, and dignity can be profitable (see Huang 2014). Can experiences, technologies, knowledge, and wisdom from a highlighted Oceanic/archipelagic world, as opposed continental ways of thinking, augment and expand a broader spectrum and enrich globally Indigenous and planetarily engaged fields of inquiry? The world of this Oceanic belonging named Austronesia (*austro* being "south" and *nesia* meaning "island"), in "the shape of a full sail" (Perez 2017), stretches from Madagascar to the Malay peninsula and Indonesia, north to the Philippines and Taiwan, and then traverses Micronesia and Polynesia. This Austronesian world includes a population of 400 million people, who speak more than one thousand different languages and have navigated "beyond the violent divisions of national and maritime borders, beyond the scarred latitudes and longitudes of empire, to discover the cartography of our most expansive legends and deepest routes" (Perez 2017).

In a graduate seminar titled Pacific Cultural Production that I taught in spring 2017, by reading and performing his poetry, Chamorro poet Craig Stanto Perez came to illuminate my students of diverse backgrounds, some from the U.S. continental interior and others born on Pacific islands with Taiwan as their genetic home. Upon return to his current home base in Hawai'i, Perez composed and publicized a poem, "The Fifth Map," dedicated to me to remember his journey and partnership in Taiwan as a widening circle of associations. From Guam as a center of his personal map to the Marianas Archipelago, Micronesia, and Oceania, and finally toward an expansive vision of a trans-Indigenous genetic/cultural family of Austronesia, Perez navigates "beyond the violent divisions of national and maritime borders, beyond / the scarred latitudes and longitudes / of empire, to discover the cartography / of our most expansive legends / and deepest routes." In this, the poet provides a trans-Indigenous worldview of interconnectedness through deep time, deep ecology, and deep mapping, which subverts the linear history and demarcated geography of empire.

In the same seminar, the spirit of Teresia Teaiwa as "Mother of Oceania" was commemorated a week after her passing through Kathy Jetñil-Kijiner's (2017) poetry "Three Poems of Mourning for Teresia Teaiwa." While Jetñil-Kijiner's poetry was on the reading agenda, Romina Lin, a local Taiwanese student, spontaneously brought to discussion Jetñil-Kijiner's mourning, which also brought tears to the eyes of each of the students in the seminar. I asked how an event that happened in Aetora, New Zealand, could have touched hearts that were geographically apart and remote. How did the students experience the loss and grief with Jetñil-Kijiner in her poetry mourning her "auntie" of Oceania? How did the students mourn in their unique ways as Jetñil-Kijiner did in her

"Marshallese" way? It is not historical contingency but rather genetic and cultural intimacy of a trans-Indigenous linkage that connects the world of Oceania and generates Pacific heartbeats as affect. It is the trans-Indigenous interactive ideo-affective experience, emerging with the flow of water, which overflows into tears. Each of the students feels a part of herself or himself was lost. And yet, in commemorating Teaiwa's strength, the power of her words, and her infinite wisdom, we remember ourselves. Together with Jetñil-Kijiner, we come up with our vision of a trans-Indigenous Oceania as commons, as a water pathway to (re-)shape our identity and the future of the islanders.

The endeavor to interpret texts repressed by Euro-American mapping/land-based ideology echoes Lisa Lowe (2015) in her *Four Continents of Intimacy*: the intimacy of the islanders resides in their shared history and common story of survival and trafficking of ethos and in their narratives of emotions and empathy. They are bound as a family not simply by (mixed) blood but by the contacts, trafficking, and communication and transmission of feelings among those living, working, and surviving together in the waters where Euro-American colonists demarcate. Can the trans-Indigenous create, in Allen's words, a "center-to-center-to-center" "Indigenous-to-Indigenous-to-Indigenous" space for intellectual activity as we use the island as a critical and central location for both the practice and the transformation of intellectual work in global Indigenous studies? Situated within the Pacific trans-Indigenous dynamics of cultural production and site-based work, poets and activists of Pacific Islands, such as Chantal T. Spitz (Tahiti), Hone Tuwhare, Albert Wendt (Samoa), Kathy Jetñil-Kijiner (Marshall Islands), Craig Santos Perez (Chamorro), and Teresia Teaiwa (Kiribati), among many others, push toward transnational and trans-Indigenous belonging, on one hand, and, on the other, toward a contemporary connection with Oceanic frameworks that would unsettle territorial ties to the Asian mainland and Euro-American continent and reframe the decentered island site as the niche for trans-Indigenous political and cultural commitment.

Hsinya Huang is director general of the Department of International Cooperation and Science Education, Ministry of Science and Technology, Taiwan, and professor of American and comparative literature, National Sun Yat-Sen University, Taiwan. She is the author or editor of books and articles on Native American and Indigenous literatures, ecocriticism, and postcolonial and ethnic studies, published in Taiwan and abroad, including *(De)Colonizing the Body: Disease, Empire, and (Alter)Native Medicine in Contemporary Native American Women's Writings* (2004); *Huikan beimei* *yuanzhumin wenxue: duoyuan wenhua de shengsi (Native North American Literatures: Reflections on Multiculturalism)* (2009), the first Chinese essay collection on Native North American literatures; *Aspects of Transnational and Indigenous Cultures* (2014); *Ocean and Ecology in the Trans-Pacific Context* (2016); and *Chinese Railroad Workers: Recover and Representation* (2017). She also edited the English translation of *Tai-wan yuan-zhu-min wen-xue-shi-gang (Literary History of Taiwanese Indigenous Literatures)*.

■ WORKS CITED

Allen, Chadwick. 2012. "A Transnational Native American Studies? Why Not Studies That Are Trans-Indigenous?" *Journal of Transnational American Studies* 4, no. 1: 1–22.

Dimock, Wai Chee. 2007. "Planet and America, Set and Subset." In *Shades of the Planet: American Literature as World Literature,* edited by Wai Chee Dimock and Lawrence Buell, 1–15. Princeton, N.J.: Princeton University Press.

Glissant, Édouard. 1990. *Poetics of Relation.* Translated by Betsy Wing. Ann Arbor: University of Michigan Press.

Hau'ofa, Epeli. 2008. *We Are the Ocean: Selected Works.* Honolulu: University of Hawai'i Press.

Huang, Hsinya. 2014. "Review of Trans-Indigenous: Methodologies for Global Native Literary Studies." *College Literature* 41, no. 1: 195–98.

Jetñil-Kijiner, Kathy. 2017. "Three Poems of Mourning for Teresia Teaiwa." https://www.kathyjetnilkijiner.com/three-poems-of-mourning-for -teresia/.

Lowe, Lisa. 2015. *The Intimacies of Four Continents.* Durham, N.C.: Duke University Press.

Perez, Craig Santos. 2017. "The Fifth Map: For Hsinya." *Dialogist: Quarterly Poetry and Art* 4, no. 3. https://dialogist.org/v4i2-craig-santos-perez/.

Warrior, Robert. 2009. "Native American Studies and the Transnational Turn." *Cultural Studies Review* 15, no. 2: 119–30.

Coming to Worlding Terms with "Trans": Methodologies in Chadwick Allen's *Trans-Indigenous*

ROB WILSON

Comparative literature as a disciplinary frame comes down from the proto-global modernizing times of Goethe, Matthew Arnold, Margaret Fuller, Emerson, and Marx with embedded center-and-periphery dynamics as well as Euro-American assumptions and predispositions that go on structuring "comparison" as such into an implicit hierarchy as to what counts (gets translated, published, circulated, read, compared) as "world literature" in shape, value, mores, audience, and impact. This consecrated inequity can still remain the case in these days of turbo- (often English-centered) globalization when interpreting and translating minor or (all the more so) Indigenous literatures as a core or reclaimed "center" for activating comparison across borders, cultures, sites, and areas. It is this dissatisfaction with structured hierarchy that might lead scholars to reach for a more fluid term of relationality that can cut across these older canonical divides, nation-centric patterns, and enduring post–Cold War areas of study. Such an affirmative turn to mobility, unsettling, and multiplicity is taking place in the emergent frameworks that now activate the transitive prefix *trans-*, as variously seen in the rise of "transpacific" to overcome Asia and Pacific segregations[1] or in "trans-Taiwan" in the *Inter-Asia Cultural Studies* journal; as in Chih-Ming Wang's (2013) *Transpacific Articulations: Student Migrations and the Remaking of Asian America*; in the framework of *Trans-Americanicity: Subaltern Modernities, Global Coloniaity, and the Culture of Greater Mexico* as used in the border-crossing Americas work of José David Saldivar (2012); in the "transatlantic" patterns reformulated in Paul Gilroy and Paul Giles et al.; and, all the more provocatively, as seen in the emergent and lesser-known reorientation around "trans-Indigenous" to be discussed here.

Amping the stakes and disrupting the normative terms of world literary comparability, Chadwick Allen's second comparative study of Indigenous literatures from within and across Pacific and Native American sites, *Trans-Indigenous: Methodologies for Global Native Literary Studies* (2012), emerges from within this global–local climate of theoretical restlessness and methodological dissatisfaction. It is a time of dismantling the humanities, when rethinking "world literature" has been reframed and is often set against the challenges of literary globalization as merely an Anglo-global or belatedly "Orientalist" form claiming to adjudicate the literary world republic of letters as such (see Mufti 2016).

Trans-Indigenous, to be sure, aims to shake up this canonical ex-Euro framework of adjudicated recognition and unexpected comparison as linked to world-transforming cultural–political ends. Allen's important new study raises issues and questions (of language, place, transdisciplinary reach, spatial and temporal frames, and global–local dialectics) that scholars like Gayatri Spivak, Rey Chow, Kuan-Hsing Chen, and Stuart Hall have long placed on the trans-area comparative agenda, from the transatlantic of postcolonial diasporas and the Black Atlantic to the decentering cosmopolitics of inter-Asia and the Asia Pacific Rim. But Allen's book is meant, at its most clearly articulated and theorized first level, to link up with, study, and affirm as well as compare Indigenous movements *across* (hence, "trans") their Indigenous sites and ongoing struggles not just for literary or cultural studies recognition but for the material and symbolic recovery of land, language, and sovereignty. So one crucial question (as I read it) becomes how to activate this world-transforming approach from within or across *(trans)* other disciplines, sites, and struggles as situated from within what we would call (after Epeli Hau'ofa) the *Pacific-becoming-Oceania* (see Wilson 2017). How does *trans-Indigenous* as such transform the identity-torn world of global and local strife not just in the Pacific but in broader domains of Indigenous struggle?

This larger question of comparison resonates at the outset of, if not throughout, Allen's study: "What if we question, instead, the efficacy of comparison as an analytic framework for studies of global Indigenous literatures written (primarily) in English?" (xii). This remains the case because anything in tactic or approach that is strongly "anticolonial" as such does not aspire to "sameness" of comparison with the colonial settler state literature or national culture frame, whereas "difference" (within the filtering domains of global culture) can be all too easily recuperated into some liberal add-on version of multicultural accommodation. Should not such literatures be studied as "together (yet) distinct"? (xiii), Allen asks, hence activating differences not so easily assimilated into "projects arranged by settler nation-state, by geographical or geopolitical area," and often aligned to the same interstate capitalist system (xiii). But even "Indigenous-to-Indigenous" comparison runs the risk of reduction to sameness, similitude, and an archived predictability of figure, tactic, form, and code, as is the danger here.

Chadwick Allen's (2002) first book, *Blood Narrative: Indigenous Identity in American Indian and Maori Literary and Activist Texts,* had elegantly convinced critical readers of these interpretive powers and cultural depths of literary and socially situated interpretation, and it is only fitting that it was named one of the ten most influential books in Native American and Indigenous studies by the scholarly association of that name. His new monograph, *Trans-Indigenous: Methodologies for Native Literary Studies,* will further secure and deepen the impact of this comparative, place-based, global, and native-aligned research upon "indigeneity" even as it raises some difficult questions in application, as suggested later. This second book presents an even more capaciously global–local framework around Indigenous narratives and forms that should impact the field-imaginary of these disciplines in ways that (1) not only sum up and refract prevailing hegemonies of cultural–political interpretation (as did his first book, with its focus on genealogy, narrative, and land) but also (2) bring them into more critically self-reflective and comparative transnational–local focus from New Zealand and the Native American homelands in Oklahoma and Ohio (to which Allen by birth and vocation is linked) to sites like Canada and Hawai'i, where related and translocally linked struggles over land, name, place, resource, language, community, voice, and sovereignty continue to come into recognition and adjudication.

With learned wit and broadly based transcultural learning, Allen here makes difficult postcolonial Maori texts like *Star Waka* and *Whale Rider* come alive as poem, story, and film in ways that are often not only formally insightful but also breathtaking in their detail, generic insight, and comparative linkages. Chapters 4 ("Indigenous Languaging: Empathy and Translation across Alphabetic, Aural, and Visual Texts") and 5 ("Siting Earthworks, Navigating Waka: Patterns of Indigenous Settlement in Allison Hedge Coke's *Blood Run* and Robert Sullivan's *Star Waka*") in *Trans-Indigenous* are rigorous and thorough in this regard as embodying this applied methodology of reading within and across demanding land-based and ocean-situated Indigenous texts. Allen activates a "trans" place-based command of local textual issues and performs the reach and range of comparative method for sites in and across the Pacific as it has come to be resignified as Oceania. He pushes toward a broader basis of comparison between Pacific-situated Indigenous struggles and those in North American Native communities, at the same time seemingly overcoming taken-for-granted oceanic/land or continental divides.

Allen's stress on "trans" thus aims to amplify and activate "the mobility and multiple interactions of Indigenous peoples, cultures, histories, and texts," recalling the unstable but productive actions of translation, transnational, and transform as "unequal encounters" (Allen 2012, xiv) across and through the many divides of a twofold dialectic he calls "recovery/interpretation" and "interpretation/recovery" that structures the two main sections of the book. The whole process of decolonizing "recovery" is haunted by an expanding liberal archive that merely seeks to activate what Allen calls "settler survey" and "settler celebration" (xvi), which can be added to the world national canon with a self-congratulatory multicultural smile. At times, while wary of recuperated difference serving the management strategies of the liberal state, Allen comes close to this canonical integration of methodological difference and formal distinction, as in his uncritical use of "aesthetic systems" and "technologies" (as well as "methodology" itself) as a quasi-systematic approach to form-focused, value-laden, and purposeful juxtaposition. Allen does this to ratify the power of the Indigenous at the basic level, while at the same time using such tactics still contaminated with the quasi-Kantian language and hermeneutic sublimity as systematic domination, even as he comes to terms with interpreting, recovering, and "prioritizing" the cultural and textual production of Native North American, New Zealand Maori, Hawaiian, and Indigenous Australian and Canadian works (xvi–xvii).

Allen's "methodological" approach to texts of high art and folkcraft is meticulous yet broad, shuttling between eras and across contexts and cultural terms—if at times wearying in its relentless historical detail and will to interpretive totality, never leaving gaps or linguistic aporias of untranslatability as Emily Apter (2013), in *Against World Literature: On the Politics of Untranslatability,* has urged can or should take place across discrepant frames of literary comparability to open up and preserve radical difference and otherness.[2] At other times, Allen's approach is dazzling in its tactic of juxtapositions across frames—probing, self-conscious, responsible both to literary discipline and to Indigenous peoples, as well as to form and place. Allen argues for "the idea of multiple and multiply informed Indigenous audiences [that] has not often occurred to literary scholars in the dominant academy" (142), hence a rethinking of how Indigenous literary criticism is formulated in most U.S. English or ethnic studies departments.

Allen's approach (claiming what I take to be the rigor, interpretive totality, and repeatability of a critical "method") would stay tied to the local site at the same time it is attuned to global forces and claims and would set up linkages of the literary to other cultural and artistic media, at the same time challenging the unmarked assumption (or model) of a "U.S.-based paradigm of Native American studies" (xxi). Oceanic and land-centric frames are elaborated in all the mobility, transition, linkage, and interconnection of the "trans" Pacific coming to be renamed Oceania: "Is the whale [sculpted between Maori and Pacific Northwest indigenous traditions and multimedia by Maori artist Fred Graham] not demonstrative of a mobile syntax for becoming tangata whenua, for becoming 'people of the land,' set outside a settler-Indigenous binary opposition?" (xxv). "Intertribal" connections across indigenous spaces and cultures here displace the priority of "international" as such, which is, after all, has been tied to the globalization of the nation-state system and its settler–state relations since the Treaty of Westphalia and the divisions of the New World. At the level of textual language, "bilingual punning" or "bilanguaging" is more and more stressed, thus helpfully engaging the politics and cultures in an asymmetrical contact zone of dictions, codes, and mores cutting across the taken-for-granted civilizational divides.

These *bilanguaging* tactics of reading become all-important as a way to enact the very coevalness of temporality and form central to applying Allen's reading method: "Across the chapters, as in *Blood Narrative*, I engage English and Indigenous languages on equal terms, outside the binaries familiar/exotic or domestic/foreign" (xxxi). The literary and cultural aim is to reveal complex and mobile patternings in texts, tactics, and forms so as to read these cultural productions that would help open the future to diversity and transformation adequate to the Global Indigenous reawakening. We could say that the blood–land complex central to *Blood Narrative* here gives way to a more mobile framing of language/movements or ocean/transitions as befits the methodology of "trans." But at the same time, this approach raises world-making or worlding expectations to deal with comparative Indigenous cultures beyond the two (Pacific/North American) that mainly occur here.

As Allen summarizes this textual and formal alliance of his method (echoing Gerald Vizenor and Édouard Glissant et al.) with ongoing acts of Indigenous recovery-through-interpretation, "Whether mourned as a loss or celebrated as survivance, the realities of contemporary Indigenous identities describe multiple kinds of diversity and complexity; often, they describe seeming paradoxes of simultaneity, contradiction, coexistence. These qualities are the contemporary Indigenous norm rather than its tragic exception" (xxxii). Allen employs a local–global dialectic of interrelations to reframe and relink these Indigenous forms and struggles, shuttling across *(trans)* specific and broader traditions and contexts: "The point is not to displace the necessary, invigorating study of specific traditions and [local] contexts but rather to complement these by augmenting and expanding broader, globally Indigenous fields of inquiry. The point is to invite specific studies into different kinds of conversations, and to acknowledge the mobility and multiple interactions of Indigenous peoples, cultures, histories, and texts" (xiv).

Does the book really help to open "the possibility for appreciation and interpretation of Indigenous literatures informed by multiple, distinct systems of Indigenous aesthetics across tribal, national, geographic and cultural borders" that are mainly just Indigenous centered and formally juxtaposed (106)? The claim is for a return to some kind of "*pan*-Indigenous" aesthetic based not in unity, archetype, and universality but in difference and locality, difficulty and distinction (106), as in Allen's reading of the same work (N. Scott Momaday's twelve-line poem *Carnegie, Oklahoma, 1919*) through Kiowa, Navajo, and Maori frameworks of cultural production in chapter 3. Allen shows as well that Momaday can "appropriate and innovate both Indigenous and settler (in some cases, colonial) artistic and rhetorical traditions to produce texts in all genres" (110). But the focus is on Momaday's transformation of Indigenous forms, mores, and modes via "productive connections" across the three frames: "The point is not to denigrate the dominant but to demonstrate the literary and political power of the Indigenous" (110), which becomes the main approach used throughout the study. If at times Allen's "Indigenous-centered" approach (138) to meaning making across discrepant systems comes close to an obsessive formalism driven toward reading/translating cosmic meaning (primordial or contemporary) into the slightest phoneme or syntactical turn, the overall result of the reading is mostly productive, shining light on what Kenneth Burke would call the text's "symbolic action" of *healing* through rhetoric and figurations of terminological unity: "Momaday's highly condensed poem both names and overcomes a contemporary anguish over Indigenous separation from ancestors, cultural traditions, and world views" (136).

We might also call this "trans-Indigenous" reading an innovative "worlding" or "world-making" temporal and spatial transaction of cultural recovery and change, as theorized by Eric Hayot (2012) and Pheng Cheah (2016) et al., or in *The Worlding Project* (Connery and Wilson 2007) activated as a challenge to dominant globalization tactics and patterns of capitalist time and space. Here, in such *worlding* modes, an ecopoetic worlding stance of belonging to Oceania becomes a matter of political and cultural commitment: becoming-Oceania means not only having a sense of history and cultivating a set of attitudes and beliefs; it means cultivating a sense of belonging to the planet and ocean as a bioregional horizon of care that calls for "trans-Indigenous" commitments in a crosshatched oceanic-land sense as well. Thinking with and beyond Epeli Hau'ofa's vision (2008), "Oceania" can thus activate (1) a worlding framework to help forge visions of ecological solidarity; (2) the site of alternative modes of belonging inside Asia and the Pacific, reflecting Pacific, Asia, and Americas linkages and knowledge formations; and (3) the oceanic imagination, which can prove helpful as a mode of transforming social and regional practices in the making of a trans-Indigenous worlding ecopoetics across (trans) the Pacific and Asia (see Wilson 2015). Allen's work is crucial as an approach to think with, through, and beyond the trans-Indigenous as such in this planetary era of climatological interconnection called the Anthropocene.

Still, it is hard to imagine that at such a STEM-driven time, when literary and humanities studies are being downsized and digitalized, that Allen's large-scale vision of reform (as in his repeated manifesto-like claims for reforming graduate study in the United States) would have much impact upon what Gayatri Spivak (2003) denominates the liberal-managed death of the comparative literary discipline at same time she urges literary scholars "to figure themselves—imagine themselves—as planetary rather than continental, global, or worldly" (72). As Allen admits of his disciplinary struggle to activate an Indigenous-based "trans" method, "the current system of graduate education in literature and culture studies, especially as these are enacted in most U.S. departments of English [like the one within which Allen was housed for years at Ohio State University], is not designed to enable the kind of engagements with Indigenous aesthetics I am proposing. Quite the contrary. In fact, our greatest challenge in formulating new models for Native American and Indigenous literary criticism may well be to overhaul graduate training so that it will be possible for future scholars to meaningfully engage Indigenous aesthetics and, thus, to engage Indigenous intellectual and artistic sovereignty. . . . We have barely begun to imagine what such [trans-Indigenous] collaborations might look like within the Indigenous literary and culture studies curriculum. Their potential impact on the future of the field may prove nothing short of revolutionary" (142).

In a climate of privatization, authoritarian reaction, phobic nationalism, and shrinking budgets, when comparative literature programs are being decimated language by language and site by site, as in the State University of New York system and even to some extent in the University of California system, area studies is being downsized, as are humanities programs being scaled back in contexts of STEM-centric consolidations. At a time when neoliberal privatization goes on tying universities to capitalist-driven vocations, it is hard to see this methodological revolution of "trans-Indigenous" study happening on any kind of large scale in literary or cultural studies departments, except perhaps in a few fortuitous sites or area formations (like Pacific studies at the University of Hawai'i at Mānoa, say) or for some multilingual scholarly individuals (like Allen himself, now teaching in the Pacific Northwest at the University of Washington, or for scholars in Maori/Pacific Islander New Zealand). In effect, Chadwick Allen's call to affirm and activate "trans-Indigenous" comparison, translatability, conversion, and recovery is a provocative exercise of methodology to help bring in the future, a manifesto elaborated for an audience, time, or space yet to come: *utopic* in that performative sense, learned, prodding, formal, experimental. Anglophonic literary studies and criticism do need to come to terms with this "trans-Indigenous" vision of translation, but it seems doubtful that, at this time of retrenchment in close or distant readings of global literature, precarious liquidity cum democratic dismantlement, and a recuperated formalism, it will do so in any kind of immediate way. This dialogue here in *Verge* is a multisited step in that transformative direction. The neoliberal turn of comparison against which Allen's *Trans-Indigenous* vision is posited can only aggravate the loss of alternative worldings and world-making frames direly needed within and against the planetary transformation of the Anthropocene.

Rob Wilson is professor of literature, creative writing, and cultural studies at the University of California at Santa Cruz. He is author of *Re-imagining the American Pacific: From South Pacific to Bamboo Ridge and Beyond* (2000) and of *Be Always Converting, Be Always Converted: An American Poetics* (2009) and is coeditor of *The Worlding Project: Doing Cultural Studies in the Era of Globalization* (2007), among other works.

■ NOTES

1. See Suzuki (2014, 352) on this large-scale discursive turn away from Pacific Rim and Asia-Pacific to "transpacific" as a framework "to describe the routes and infrastructures that enable the movement of goods and peoples across and around the Pacific."

2. One might recall here the trenchant and tactical defense of "opacity" made for Caribbean islander cultures and creolized poetics to resist translational claims to transparency made by hegemonic European cultures over the peripheries in Édouard Glissant's (2010, 11–120) "Transparency and Opacity." Not all Indigenous culture wants or needs to be world-translated.

■ WORKS CITED

Allen, Chadwick. 2002. *Blood Narrative: Indigenous Identity in American Indian and Maori Literary and Activist Texts.* Durham, N.C.: Duke University Press.

Allen, Chadwick. 2012. *Trans-Indigenous: Methodologies for Global Native Literary Studies.* Minneapolis: University of Minnesota Press.

Apter, Emily. 2013. *Against World Literature: On the Politics of Untranslatability.* London: Verso.

Cheah, Pheng. 2016. *What Is a World? Postcolonial Literature as World Literature*. Durham, N.C.: Duke University Press.

Connery, Christopher Leigh, and Rob Wilson, eds. 2007. *The Worlding Project: Doing Cultural Studies in the Era of Globalization*. Berkeley, Calif.: North Atlantic Books.

Glissant, Édouard. 2010. *Poetics of Relation*. Translated by Betsy Wing. Ann Arbor: University of Michigan Press.

Hau'ofa, Epeli. 2008. *We Are the Ocean: Selected Works*. Honolulu: University of Hawai'i Press.

Hayot, Eric. 2012. *On Literary Worlds*. Oxford: Oxford University Press.

Mufti, Aamir R. 2016. *Forget English! Orientalisms and World Literatures*. Cambridge, Mass.: Harvard University Press.

Saldivar, José David. 2012. *Trans-Americanicity: Subaltern Modernities, Global Coloniality, and the Cultures of Greater Mexico*. Durham, N.C.: Duke University Press.

Spivak, Gayatri. 2003. *Death of a Discipline*. New York: Columbia University Press.

Suzuki, Erin. 2014. "Transpacific." In *Routledge Companion to Asian American and Pacific Islander Literature, edited by* Rachel Lee, 352–64. London: Routledge.

Wang, Chih-Ming. 2013. *Transpacific Articulations: Student Migration and the Remaking of Asian America*. Honolulu: University of Hawai'i Press.

Wilson, Rob. 2015. "Toward an Ecopoetics of Oceania: Worlding the Asia-Pacific Region as a Space-Time Ecumene." In *American Studies as Transnational Practice: Turning toward the Transpacific, edited by* Yuan Shu and Donald E. Pease, 213–36. Hanover, N.H.: Dartmouth College Press.

Wilson, Rob. 2017. "Postcolonial Pacific Poetries: Becoming Oceania." In *The Cambridge Companion to Postcolonial Poetry,* edited by Jahan Ramazani, 58–71. Cambridge: Cambridge University Press.

Searching for the Trans-Indigenous

ALICE TE PUNGA SOMERVILLE

The title of this piece gestures toward Teresia Teaiwa's 1995 poetry collection *Searching for Nei Nim'anoa,* which in turn refers to a Banaban female navigator. The titular poem of the collection is about Teaiwa's own (scholarly, creative, cultural) search for Nei Nim'anoa. The poem opens "I need to learn how to navigate," a desire expressed in relation to the act of reading: "Read the stars, the wind, and the ocean swells / Like she did." Teaiwa the scholar, researcher, and writer "search[es]" for this ancestral and historical figure because of her "need" to "learn" how to "read," a move that—in the context of a collection that reflects over and over on her place in scholarly work and institutions—gently reframes and reclaims "read[ing]" within Indigenous Pacific knowledge traditions. Declaring that "drifting in a random sea" "has been too lonely," Teaiwa yearns to engage in deliberate and expert navigation. The purpose and outcome of navigation, then, is to counter loneliness: to find community. The idea of "searching" in the present piece does not suggest that the "trans-Indigenous" is out of sight, missing, or inadvertently mislaid. Instead, "searching" in Teaiwa's sense draws our attention to the deliberate, hopeful, careful, necessarily incomplete (and, for many, ancestral) work that underpins global Native literary studies. The present conversation between Huang, Wilson, and me—and Allen—is another instance or site of such hopeful, careful, and necessarily incomplete "searching": an attempt both to describe and to enact the transnational critical work suggested by the term *trans-Indigenous.*

Teaiwa's search is not only for location and direction but also for navigational expertise, for method. The idea of method—connective, collaborative, reciprocal method—is central to Allen's (2012) *Trans-Indigenous: Methodologies for Global Native Literary Studies* and his broader career-long work of which it is a significant part. The subtitle of Allen's book foregrounds its underpinning ambition: to variously propose, moderate, produce, and inspire a broad conversation about methodologies related to Indigenous literary studies. Questions of methodology have long energized Indigenous studies. Broadly, we can trace the language of methodology to the heavy influence of the social sciences in the development of the (inter)discipline, and more specifically, we might note the role of Linda Tuhiwai Smith's (1999) *Decolonizing Methodologies* as a text that has perhaps enjoyed singular mobility around the Indigenous scholarly world for almost two decades. (Allen acknowledges a debt to Smith's work in *Trans-Indigenous*.) There can be a temptation in the humanities (especially literary studies) to eschew concepts like "methodology" (or, indeed, method) in favor of theory; the book could plausibly have been subtitled "Theories of Global Native Literary Studies" or "Global Native Literary Theory." Instead, Allen's work—while certainly not antitheoretical—elaborates "methodologies" for global Native literary studies in (at least) two forms: analytical methodologies in relation to what one does with literary texts and institutional methodologies in terms of how we think about the structural contexts (discipline, scholarly association, reading list, graduate training) of literary studies and perhaps Indigenous studies more broadly. Lest this parsing of two kinds of "methodology" suggest these (method and context) are entirely extricable, Smith and others elaborate the ways in which the institutional context of scholarly work shapes, and is shaped by, the specific forms of analytical work undertaken in any one project or classroom.

At the level of analytical methodology, *Trans-Indigenous* practices what it preaches. Rather than gesturing toward possible or ideal engagements with literary and other cultural texts which one might undertake elsewhere, Allen's own method centers (and is explicitly derived from) his own careful engagements with specific texts. Much of the book involves long passages of detailed, productive, original, and often highly evocative working-through of specific texts (especially, but not only, poetry; more on this later). In their essays, both Huang and Wilson take time to elaborate Allen's methods of analysis, in which readings of specific texts (and especially pairings or clusters of texts) draw from and inform insights into cultural, aesthetic, and political contexts. Huang celebrates this approach, noting "the cumulative effect of down-to-earth practice, close reading, and textual analysis." Wilson acknowledges the value of various treatments of specific texts (e.g., "Allen here makes difficult postcolonial Maori texts like 'Star Waka' and 'Whale Rider' come alive as poem, story, and film in ways that are often not only formally insightful but also breathtaking in their detail, generic insight, and comparative linkages"), yet cautions later—belying perhaps a distinction between literary and cultural studies—that Allen's commitment to reading across specific texts "comes close to an obsessive formalism."

The kinds of things that count as texts for Allen's analysis are as broad as one would expect in twenty-first-century North American literary studies: poetry, novels, nonfiction, organizations, films. It does seem worth noting, however, that Allen engages a great deal of poetry. One wonders why this might be: Is the close reading of poetry sufficiently efficient to be most suitable for exploration in the context of a book (as opposed to, say, whole novels that might be profitably discussed in the context of the semester-long classroom rather than in a few pages)? Is there something about the focus of shorter poems that makes them easier to discuss alongside each other when so many other variables are at play in the global Indigenous comparative context (fewer moving parts, you might say)? Is poetry the preferred literary form for a greater range of Indigenous writers and therefore the most abundant source of texts for analysis for the would-be global Indigenous literary scholar (and/ or allied pragmatic questions about publication frequency, accessibility, rooms of one's own, and so on)?

It is unsurprising, given Allen's long-standing interest in thinking critically and productively about the context of analytical work, that he also turns his attention to the extent to which, and ways in which, the trans-Indigenous is produced and reproduced through institutional forms. We can think about this parallel strand related to contextual and institutional considerations as meta- or macro-methodologies for global Native literary studies. For example, Allen and Huang both specifically refer to the scholarly association Native American and Indigenous Studies Association (NAISA) as a form (in Allen's tracing of the genesis of the organization) and site (in Huang's recollection of a panel in which she and Allen participated) of the trans-Indigenous. Likewise, Allen, and in response Wilson, talk about graduate training. However, one can run into problems when attempting to generalize about structural forms, even when such generalization is at the service of positive visions for future or ideal arrangements, across the training of research/higher degree research/graduate/postgraduate students. Indeed, the range of terms just cited to refer to such students highlights the range of forms of (what we'll call for simplicity's sake) graduate education across different states. Although Allen is referring to PhD (and perhaps master's) students when he describes graduate education, attaining a PhD involves a wide range of requirements, lengths of expected time to completion, and supervision arrangements. For example, a PhD in Indigenous studies in my current institution (Waikato) is expected to take between three and three and a half years; commences when a student with a master's or honors degree applies with an initial thesis proposal, which is worked up into a full proposal within the first few months; and will involve a primary supervisor and two other supervisors who have less input into the process and usually function as additional resources or specialists in a niche area relevant to the topic of the student's research. The final thesis is assessed by external examiners in a process that is out of the hands of the supervisors. This is in stark contrast to the PhD I undertook at Cornell, which was expected to take between five and six years, commenced when students with undergraduate or master's degrees applied to a specific program and then took graduate-level classes (including classes to help satisfy a language requirement), and sat two sets of oral and written examinations (including the "comprehensives") before producing a dissertation proposal. The final dissertation was read by the supervisory committee, which also decided whether the student had passed the requirements for the degree. The differences in process are worth tracing in such detail, because when we are asking (important and timely) questions about graduate education and its possible forms in a future Indigenous studies, we need to imagine the kinds of interventions, structures, gatherings, and even advice that would be relevant for students in the "global" discipline. And specifically, as Allen cautions in his discussion of NAISA, for example, we need to manage the risk of U.S. hegemony if Indigenous studies is to be understood and practiced globally.

And here, of course, what might feel like mundane and instrumental considerations related to graduate training draw our attention to one of the quiet but insistent elements of the "global" in "global Native literary studies." Both Huang and Wilson foreground the idea of comparison, and respond to the questions Allen raises about the potential for comparative methods, which neither center the occupying/colonizing nation-state nor overstate what is shared between diverse Indigenous groups. A central question for Allen (2002), which in many ways extends the ideas raised in the final chapter of his prior book, *Blood Narrative*, is, how can we read globally without flattening out the objects of our analysis to the point of detached (and perversely colonial) abstraction? And if Indigenous literary studies is rooted in the local and the specific, how does a (global and comparative) literary studies that engages texts from more than one Indigenous context affirm these concepts rather than undermine them? How much should one know about a context in order to (productively, ethically) read a particular text, and how does this required knowledge expand when reading a number of particular texts? In *Trans-Indigenous*, Allen undertakes to provide an exploration as well as a demonstration of how a multiply grounded Indigenous literary studies might look.

Partway through the process of its preparation, this *Codex* paper conversation has been newly framed in relation to the untimely passing and unparalleled legacy of Banaban scholar and poet Teresia Teaiwa. This acknowledgment speaks to the impact of her writing and thinking around the Pacific and beyond. At the same time, it can be helpful— maybe even important—to gently nudge the relationship between the Pacific (Oceanic) and Indigenous worlds, and indeed between Pacific and

Indigenous studies. It would do Teaiwa, and her careful thinking about the relationship between the Pacific and Indigeneity, a disservice *not* to signal that her work has circulated widely in some critical contexts but has been less mobile around Indigenous studies; this in turn highlights the limited circulation of Pacific scholarship around the Indigenous studies world, and vice versa. In some ways, Allen's book naturalizes a connection between "the Indigenous" and "the Pacific" by engaging specific Pacific sites (especially New Zealand and Hawai'i) in the scope of a project clearly named "Indigenous." Although it can be tempting to thereby assume that Pacific studies and Indigenous studies are wholly and productively connected, in reality, they function as separate fields (with distinct genealogies and methods), and the overlap between the two fields, conceptually, academically, and pragmatically, is partial.

There are rabbit holes of definitions and categorizations—both of *Pacific* and *Indigenous*—down which we could disappear at this stage, and which are treated at length in other scholarship (and in classrooms around the world). For the purposes of this discussion, however, it is more helpful to reflect on how the fields actually function (and how they articulate their own origin stories) rather than to double down on abstract definitions and attempt to whip the disciplines into theoretical or ideal shape. I have argued elsewhere that these fields, like others, have been and continue to be produced by their respective scholarly bookshelves as much as they are by their objects of study (Te Punga Somerville 2015). These bookshelves might include shared texts (interestingly, in their essays, both Huang and Wilson draw on Glissant, whose Caribbean postcolonial work aids their engagement with the Pacific, despite his appearance on few Indigenous studies bibliographies) but also include rather different texts that make up the foundations (perhaps even the canons) of each field.

University of Hawai'i–based scholar Terence Wesley-Smith traced the genealogy and focus of Pacific studies in his 1995 essay "Rethinking Pacific Islands Studies," an essay he recently updated and published as "Rethinking Pacific Studies Twenty Years On," in which he notes that the most enduring legacy of the original essay was his identification of three distinct rationales for Pacific studies—pragmatic, laboratory, and empowerment (Indigenous centered)—that shape the way the field has operated in different sites. Teaiwa (2006, 2010, 2011, 2017) herself wrote extensively about the field both as a researcher and as a teacher and also published a cowritten piece with her longtime friend and colleague in the field April Henderson (Teaiwa and Henderson 2009–10). Pacific studies stands as a separate institutional entity in a small number of universities around the world, and in each place, the genealogy and focus of the field is different. Some of the more long-standing sites include University of Hawai'i at Mānoa, Brigham Young University–Hawai'i, Kapi'olani Community College, University of Papua New Guinea, University of Auckland, Victoria University of Wellington, University of Canterbury, and the Australian National University. More recently, the field has found feet at institutions like the University of Utah, University of the South Pacific, and City College of San Francisco, and at my own institution, the University of Waikato, which will offer an undergraduate major in Pacific and Indigenous studies from 2018. Still more institutions offer courses, classes, and emphases in the field; often these are determined by the presence of specific academic staff. There is not a single global or regional Pacific studies association, but the Australian Association for Pacific Studies runs an open-call conference every two years, and there are journals (especially *Pacific Studies* and *The Contemporary Pacific*) that function as key scholarly forums of the field.

Like Pacific studies, Indigenous studies spends considerable energy articulating the difference between objects of study and scholarly fields. Not all scholars of Indigenous people or cultures identify with Indigenous studies or make use of the wide variety of critical work the field has generated; conversely, there are Indigenous studies scholars (most notably Goenpul scholar Aileen Moreton-Robinson) who spend at least some of their time focusing on non-Indigenous rather than Indigenous subjects. Like Pacific studies, Indigenous studies is animated by critical reflection on the purpose, use, and limits of work in the academy, and many of its scholars are invested in critical, anticolonial, liberatory forms of community work and activism. Also like Pacific studies, Indigenous studies looks different in different sites and functions as a field through a loosely connected range of programs and institutional configurations, various conferences and journals. A number of recent published collections trace or attempt to represent the field, including *Native Studies Keywords* (Teves, Smith, and Raheja 2015), *Critical Indigenous Studies* (Moreton-Robinson 2016), and *Sources and Methods in Indigenous Studies* (Andersen and O'Brien 2017). And, of course, Allen himself traces some of this institutional and disciplinary genealogy in *Trans-Indigenous*. In universities, institutional forms of Indigenous studies have most often begun with a focus on the local Indigenous group and/or the Indigenous communities of the occupying nation-state. Few departments or programs recognized as "Indigenous studies" even have the term in their names. Although Indigenous people have been connecting with each other for as long as they have been connecting with Europeans, the "comparative" analytical (and institutional) work enacted and theorized by Allen emerged from these rather more locally focused fields and projects; Osage scholar Robert Warrior (2009) has described this as the "transnational turn" in Indigenous studies.

These two fields have seldom overlapped in the ways I have described them: they have distinct critical bookshelves, scholarly gatherings, institutional histories, and configurations. Those of us who work in Indigenous studies *and* Pacific studies are perhaps most keenly aware of their different emphases and of the reasons there is pushback on the part of both fields against being absorbed or delineated by the other. To point to the most obvious difference, Moreton-Robinson's edited collection *Critical Indigenous Studies* is subtitled *Engagements in First World Locations,* clearly foregrounding the First World (and Anglophone) emphasis of (Anglophone) Indigenous studies. The dominant focus of Pacific studies is independent or Indigenous-majority states, whereas the dominant focus of Indigenous studies is on nations that (by definition) are not nation-states but instead exist in parallel to various (usually settler) colonial states. Certainly there are specific non-Anglophone sites that receive (albeit marginal) critical attention, including Indigenous communities south of the U.S.–Mexican border, in Taiwan, and in Scandinavia. Some people working in Asia and Africa make use of the term *Indigenous,* but this is not necessarily connected to participation in or engagement with the critical body of scholarship that understands itself as Indigenous studies. (How this First World–Fourth World emphasis maps onto the range of communities represented in, for example, United Nations representative bodies is a complex question.)

It is important to note that there are specific sites that benefit from both a Pacific studies and an Indigenous studies analysis. For example, the Australia-based Fijian historian Tracey Banivanua-Mar (2007, 2016), who also tragically passed away in 2017, moved in both fields and made great use of Indigenous analysis in her work on Pacific histories, and she was committed to thinking about how these two connected in the context of Pacific communities living on (Australian) Aboriginal land. Most loudly, Hawaiian and Māori scholars have operated in both fields; as Polynesian places occupied by First World states, Hawai'i and Aotearoa both fit conventional definitions of *Pacific* and *Indigenous.* Other sites in which there is articulation of and with Pacificness and indigeneity include Guam, Taiwan, Rapanui, and much of the French-occupied Pacific.[1] Indeed, I would suggest that an overlap between the Pacific and Indigenous studies is implied or naturalized in sites such as the present cluster of essays because of the specific contexts out of which we write: Huang is based in Taiwan; Wilson in California, but with an emphasis on Hawai'i in terms of his thinking about the Pacific; and I am based in New Zealand.[2]

Teaiwa's poem "Searching for Nei Nim'anoa" ends with the speaker of the poem identifying the resources she will use to "chart [her] course": "my broken Gilbertese" and "my broken heart," a pairing that explicitly foregrounds "broken[ness]" wrought by region-sized historical events and individual experiences. In the context of searching for the trans-Indigenous, we might consider that global Native literary studies is about the richness as well as the loss of language (as represented by "my broken Gilbertese") but is also accompanied by the "broken heart" that simultaneously evokes desire and destruction. As Wilson points out when he identifies the Anglophone focus of Allen's work, searching for the trans-Indigenous cannot help but rely on the "breaking" of Indigenous languages. Reading texts from a vast range of Indigenous sites, after all, rests on the existence of texts in a common language, and that common language is colonial.[3] Despite this, Allen fruitfully draws on his own partial knowledge of various Indigenous languages as he engages texts in relation to their respective cultural contexts and thereby demonstrates the kind of analytical navigation that can be undertaken even with "broken" languages. Likewise, the "broken heart" draws attention to the emotional, affective, traumatic, historically grounded, relational, and hopeful element of this work. Global Native literary studies is neither apolitical nor trite but responds to violence and disappointment as much as it also recognizes the significance of personal and collective histories to analytical work.

Ultimately, Teaiwa admits the very real possibility that her best attempts to "search[] for Nei Nim'anoa" still might not be enough: "If I don't find her." The poem does not end there, however; nor does it end with Teaiwa "drifting in a random sea." Instead, it ends with a confident and hopeful acknowledgment of reciprocity: "Tao / She'll find me." In these final two lines, we find a balance between Gilbertese and English as well as a balance between Teaiwa and Nei Nim'anoa. Trusting that the ancestor (and her "read[ing]") is able to find her relieves Teaiwa of the burden of fixing either the loneliness or the brokenness mentioned earlier in the poem. If Nei Nim'anoa has the capacity to "find" the speaker of the poem, logically, she too is "searching"—because one cannot find what one has not been looking for. Allen, and we, find ourselves searching for the trans-Indigenous because "drifting in a random sea" when reading comparatively is analytically unsatisfying and potentially dangerous. We seek to counter the loneliness of Indigenous literary studies that is bound by the same borders as the nation-state and national literatures. The sheer range and richness of Indigenous texts draw attention to brokenness but also to language and the heart. Does Allen find the trans-Indigenous? Do we? Teaiwa's poem disagrees with itself: she is searching for Nei Nim'anoa to learn how to navigate, and to conduct her search, she charts a course. In the end, the trans-Indigenous may be produced by Allen's arguments, but perhaps reciprocally—and deliberately, hopefully, necessarily incompletely (and, for many, ancestrally)—it finds us in the kinds of transnational conversations we have held here.

Alice Te Punga Somerville (Te Ātiawa, Taranaki) is associate professor in the Faculty of Māori and Indigenous Studies at the University of Waikato. She is the author of *Once Were Pacific: Māori Connections to Oceania* (2012).

■ NOTES

1. One key location for further consideration is Fiji, where recent political and cultural shifts hauntingly echo forms of Indigenous repression in settler colonial states. The politics of race and indigeneity function there in such a way that some suggest that an Indigenous analysis problematically challenges attempts to address perceived racial privileges and disadvantages; of course, an Indigenous analysis of these claims would itself suggest that the blurring of race and Indigeneity is problematic.

2. Given the publication of the present scholarly conversation in a journal titled *Verge: Studies in Global Asias,* it seems worthwhile also to mention that the relationship between Asia and the Pacific is variable and complex and has been treated by a number of scholars.

3. Texts here include critical scholarship, such as the present cluster of *Codex* essays.

■ WORKS CITED

Allen, Chadwick. 2002. *Blood Narrative: Indigenous Identity in American Indian and Māori Literary and Activist Texts.* Durham, N.C.: Duke University Press.

Allen, Chadwick. 2012. *Trans-Indigenous: Methodologies for Global Native Literary Studies.* Minneapolis: University of Minnesota Press.

Andersen, Chris, and Jean M. O'Brien. 2017. *Sources and Methods in Indigenous Studies.* New York: Routledge.

Banivanua-Mar, Tracey. 2007. *Violence and Colonial Dialogue: The Australian-Pacific Indentured Labor Trade.* Honolulu: University of Hawai'i Press.

Banivanua-Mar, Tracey. 2016. *Decolonisation and the Pacific: Indigenous Globalization and the Ends of Empire.* Cambridge: Cambridge University Press.

Moreton-Robinson, Aileen. 2016. *Critical Indigenous Studies: Engagements in First World Locations.* Tucson: University of Arizona Press.

Smith, Linda. 1999. *Decolonizing Methodologies: Research and Indigenous Peoples.* London: Zed Books.

Teaiwa, Teresia K. 1995. *Searching for Nei Nim'anoa.* Suva, Fiji: Mana.

Teaiwa, Teresia K. 2005. "The Classroom as a Metaphorical Canoe: Cooperative Learning in Pacific Studies." World Indigenous Nations Higher Education Consortium. http://citeseerx.ist.psu.edu/viewdoc /download?doi=10.1.1.486.843&rep=rep1&type=pdf

Teaiwa, Teresia K. 2006. "On Analogies: Rethinking the Pacific in a Global Context." *The Contemporary Pacific* 18, no. 1: 71–88.

Teaiwa, Teresia K. 2010. "Specifying Pacific Studies: For or Before an Asia-Pacific Studies Agenda." In *Remaking Area Studies: Teaching and Learning across Asia and the Pacific,* edited by Terence Wesley-Smith and Jon Goss, 110–24. Honolulu: University of Hawai'i Press.

Teaiwa, Teresia K. 2011. "Preparation for Deep Learning: A Reflection on 'Teaching' Pacific Studies in the Pacific." *Journal of Pacific History* 46, no. 2: 214–20.

Teaiwa, Teresia K. 2017. "Charting Pacific (Studies) Waters: Evidence of Teaching and Learning." *The Contemporary Pacific* 29, no. 2: 265–82.

Teaiwa, Teresia K., and April K. Henderson. 2009–10. "Humanities and Communities: A Dialogue in Pacific Studies." *Pacific Studies* 32, no. 4: 421–38.

Te Punga Somerville, Alice. 2015. "Unpacking Our Libraries: Landlocked, Waterlogged, and Expansive Bookshelves." *American Quarterly* 67, no. 3: 645–52.

Teves, Stephanie Nohelani, Andrea Smith, and Michelle Raheja. 2015. *Native Studies Keywords.* Tucson: University of Arizona Press.

Warrior, Robert. 2009. "Native American Studies and the Transnational Turn." *Cultural Studies Review* 15, no. 2: 119–30.

Essays

YU LUO

Alternative Indigeneity in China?
The Paradox of the Buyi in the Age
of Ethnic Branding

THE MUSIC BEGAN. A dozen female villagers stepped out onto the newly built performance stage and started dancing slowly to the sweet and gentle melody they had prerecorded. Broadcast through basic audio equipment, it was a song these middle-aged women created in Buyi, a northern Tai language.[1] Under an overcast sky, their Buyi costumes appeared all the more vibrant. Ruby- and emerald-colored patches of embroidery decorated the indigo-dyed batik clothes with drip and whirlpool patterns. And as the dancers turned, their long, ruffled skirts fluttered just like the butterflies in the lyrics of the song.

Watching from across the plaza, I noticed an elderly female villager in her sixties standing right next to me. She was deeply engrossed in the performance onstage. Intrigued, I turned to her and asked in Buyi, "Is this [performance] good to watch?"

She answered in Buyi, with specific words borrowed from Han Chinese. "Yes, very good. Wearing the Buyi costume to dance looks pretty. The Bouxnongz and the Miao are called minority nationalities [*shaoshu minzu*, 少数民族] too; but only here live the genuinely qualified [*zhenzige de*, 真资格的] minority nationalities."

This was the Spring Festival celebration of 2013, when the county government initiated a three-day event in Wuyang Village. Participants from nearby villages and the county seat enrolled to perform songs and dances for the competition. Situated in a small basin amid karst limestone hills in China's southwestern province of Guizhou, the village—composed of almost three hundred Buyi households—was branded the "Thousand-Year-Old Buyi Village" in 2010. In the hope of promoting this out-of-the-way village and bringing it to the forefront of cultural tourism destinations, this celebration also exemplified a quotidian mode of cultural governance in which the local state and the villagers themselves joined forces.

In a landlocked province like Guizhou, which has suffered from chronic underdevelopment, cultural industries appear as a promising pathway to alleviate poverty. Cultural traditions have in turn been showcased by locals to gain a share of state support and market benefits, which largely depend on the promotion and reputation of these local cultures. Nevertheless, rural villagers and ethnic minorities in China "have yet to assert local traditions for claims of intellectual property and land rights" (Wu 2015, 5). Their limited recourse is potentially further constrained because they cannot claim the status of "indigenous peoples," a transnationally celebrated notion that has not been officially endorsed in China (Elliott 2015; Hathaway 2010; Sturgeon 2007; Yeh 2007) and in other Asian contexts where national governments deny the concept's relevance (Baird 2016).[2]

The display and celebration of ethnic cultures in present-day China, instead, follow parameters set out by the *minzu* (民族) scheme in the early 1950s. Drawing on intensive sociolinguistic surveys, the nascent People's Republic of China categorized non-Han populations into "minority nationalities" *(shaoshu minzu)* per the Stalinist model borrowed from the Soviet Union (Mullaney 2010). The Buyi, or Buyizu (布依族), was one of the minority nationality groups designated by the state in 1953. New dispensations, preferential benefits, and substantial advantages were granted to ethnic minorities under the *minzu* policy to offer them cultural freedom, rights, and economic aid and to advance the political objective of consolidating national unity (Kaup 2000).[3] In essence, all of the designated fifty-six nationality groups—the Han and fifty-five minority nationalities—have been regarded by the Chinese state as native to Chinese territory. With all citizens deemed to be "heritage residents" *(shiju minzu,* 世居民族), as I shall elaborate later, there are no "indigenous peoples" in China's official discourse.

Nonetheless, as indigenous populations have experienced worldwide, local ethnic peoples like the Buyi are still inevitably enlisted in the cultural production of the "periphery," a process that is persistently influenced by the "dominant center" (Mathur 2007, 8). In contemporary China, minority groups are at once subjected to histories of the socialist present and to market logics, the latter having encouraged the productive development of the individual through the pursuit of economic self-interest (Litzinger 2008, 234). This is a moment of late socialism, when the burgeoning cultural economy remains largely supervised by the party state, which attempts to prosper from the market forces it has unleashed in its post-

Mao reforms (Kipnis 2008; Siu 2007; Zhang 2001).[4] In turn, revivals of folk traditions in China's "late socialist modernity" have become increasingly integrated with party-state rhetoric and have also mingled with tourist spectacles, consumption practices, and heritage debates (Wu 2015, 5).

The female spectator's remark left me puzzled. With no intention of challenging the Chinese state's classification of non-Han populations as minority nationalities, her comment nevertheless hinted at decade-old debates over the authenticity of local ethnic cultures. The calculus of cultural purity and authenticity at work is seen in many other contemporary indigenous experiences (cf. de la Cadena and Starn 2007a). Through art performances and heritage-tourism regimes, not only outside spectators but minority villagers themselves have grown keen on comparing culturally "genuine" ethnic minorities against the "fake" ones (Kendall 2017; Tenzin 2017). In other words, to be "genuinely qualified" is to demonstrate certain marked differences—such as the distinctive set of Buyi costume—that are made visible through contemporary China's cultural production.

Therefore, as cultural symbols are mobilized through a proliferation of territorial brands—oftentimes promoted by state entrepreneurship—for the sake of commercial development (Oakes 2009), we see the social imperative to perform and, more precisely, to instrumentalize culture. These brands create the archetype of a "thingified culture" (Lash and Lury 2007) and "make visible aspects of global production, distribution, and consumption perhaps more powerfully than any other cultural forms" (Yang 2015, 15). As John and Jean Comaroff (2009) have exemplified, worldwide emphasis on "branding," or making visible a particular identity or image through distinctive design and cultural promotion, opens up new regimes of cultural production and commodification. As for China, it entered the age of "culture as capital" in the 1990s, when culture started to be reconstructed as a site to accumulate revenue (Wang 2001). Since then, branding visual identities and national images that are attention catchers (Wang 2010, ix–x) has allowed Chinese cultures and arts to compete in a globalizing economy, not only as producers or imitators but also with a certain extent of creativity (Wong 2013; Yang 2015).

Drawing from my long-term fieldwork among local Buyi communities in Guizhou province as well as my own experience as a Buyi hailing from the same province, this article probes the convergence of cultural branding and identity politics among variegated ethnic populations in southwest China as they jockey for regional, national, and global visibility. I argue that, alternative to engaging directly and explicitly with the notion of "indigenous peoples," ethnic branding in contemporary China could potentially enhance a parallel kind of "indigenous space" (Hathaway 2010, 303–4; Hathaway 2016, 3) by articulating a positive presence of minority peoples in public discourse, media, and other realms. This tactic of (self-)branding proves especially useful as a safe, legitimate, state-recognized means in a context in which indigenous minority groups have limited recourse to lodge critiques that might well seem dangerous to or critical of the state (such as highly contentious protests, court cases, or demonstrations). In addition to being a savvy, entrepreneurial move, I suggest that cultural branding can serve important agential roles in the self-articulation of local identity.

In what follows, I first introduce the contemporary Chinese context in which the concept of *yuanshengtai* (原生态, which translates literally as "original ecology") both parallels and diverges from the transnational ideal of "indigeneity," intersecting with environmental concerns, heritage preservation, traditional knowledge, and folkloric art performances. In earlier work, I have argued that the romanticized expression and appropriation of *yuanshengtai*—similar to deployments of indigeneity—valorize cultural distinctiveness and environmental stewardship, while deflecting attention from politically contentious issues and transnational claims for rights (Luo 2018). In this article, I discuss how the branding of *yuanshengtai*, which emphasizes cultural diversity and historical authenticity, may not be in the best interest of ethnic groups such as the Buyi, who may be deemed "not exotic enough" due to historical attachment to civilizational centers and lack of transnational linkages. I argue that, while there are discourses and practices that can serve as alternative ways to articulate indigeneity in China, certain groups may well be facing a dilemma in such identity politics. This inquiry into the Buyi in an age of ethnic branding thus allows us to ponder the trajectories and limits of indigeneity in contemporary China and to reckon with powerful socioeconomic forces that are giving shape to emerging state spaces and collective identities.

■ FROM AUTHENTICITY TO *YUANSHENGTAI*: THE EMERGENCE OF AN ALTERNATIVE "INDIGENOUS SPACE"

The social and intellectual processes around the notion of *yuanshengtai*—as one way of branding the cultural distinctiveness of ethnic, rural peoples—demonstrate that a concept commensurate with "indigeneity" has emerged domestically in China. This parallel current may entail the forming of an alternative "indigenous space" (Hathaway 2010, 303–4)—one that does not directly engage with the highly politicized notion of "indigenous peoples," which are not officially recognized. With a focus on cultural economy, *yuanshengtai* allows the emergence of a particular kind of indigenous identity with shifting valences and social relationships.

The neologism *yuanshengtai* first gained currency at the beginning of the twenty-first century, when artistic experiments were designed to integrate ethnic, rural elements of southwest China. Chinese film-makers and performance artists drew from cultural practices of ethnic minorities that were deemed unpolished, authentic, grassroots, and, very importantly, nurtured by nature. Valorizing the symbiosis of untarnished landscapes and culturally distinct inhabitants, the concept has since been synergistically taken up as a desirable brand by multiple interest groups in arts, academia, government, business, and mass media (*Baidu baike* 2015). For instance, Guizhou province, with its modest level of development compared with the rest of the nation, has capitalized on the opportunity to claim an alternate distinction as the flagship in *yuanshengtai*—that is, Guizhou has gained a reputation based on its spectacular ethnic diversity and life-nourishing environment (Luo 2018).

What the *yuanshengtai* phenomenon has revealed, in particular, is national-level concerns about the perceived loss of cultural traditions and values as well as anxieties about urban lifestyles and environmental pollution in a rapidly changing China. These trends have driven a desire to look back into the "past," to search for natural and cultural purity, and to recapture Chineseness. The perpetual pursuit of "authenticity" draws from certain Chinese philosophical roots that worship the "eternal yesterday" as an object to be preserved (Levenson 1968). This reverence for the "past" is given new life in the contemporary hope to keep up with the worldwide heritage fad, which swept across China in the early 2000s (Blumenfield and Silverman 2013; Breidenbach and Nyíri 2007; Harrell 2013).

Contemporaneous to the global trend in preserving intangible cultural heritage, China also witnessed a new environmental movement that has arisen in the context of massive social transformations (Hathaway 2013; Rees 2016). The emphasis on nature in present-day China draws attention to the role of local knowledge systems in maintaining biodiversity and sustainability (McLaren et al. 2013; Yeh 2014). This focus on biodiversity, in particular, has facilitated the entry of the global concept of "indigenous knowledge" into the field of nature conservation in China's southwest (Hathaway 2010; Sturgeon 2007). Therefore, as Helen Rees (2012, 2016) has argued, the idea of "ecology" latent in the term *yuanshengtai* has acquired an almost magical aura, stressing the causal relation between cultures and their geographic setting as well as conjuring up a sense of pure, unspoiled, and natural origins. The conceptual foundation of *yuanshengtai*, to some extent, reconfigures the long-standing symbolic relationship between "nature" and minority populations in China that were historically seen as "closer to nature" in state and popular perceptions.[5] Moving away from classifying ethnic groups as more primitive and less evolved, the *yuanshengtai* discourse seems to signify a shift to valorizing traditional knowledge and environmentally sustainable practices.

Notably, the expression and appropriation of such romanticized rhetoric, seen as antidote to distasteful urban pollution and cultural loss, primarily transpired in an intermediate realm. Local intellectual elites and policy makers in Guizhou, for instance, established cultural industries and sustainable growth initiatives partly in conversation with Taiwanese academics, as well as transnational nongovernmental organizations, both of which acknowledge aboriginal peoples and indigenous cultures (Luo 2018). However, as people from different locales deploy this discourse to engage valences of ethnic and cultural authenticity on their own terms (Kendall 2017), the disjuncture between grassroots struggles and middle-class imaginaries becomes manifest. Underpinned by specific imagery that focuses on the integration of local cultures and natural habitats as quintessentially pure and exotic, *yuanshengtai* performances and ensuing cultural industries tend to spotlight certain ethnic groups and cultural features while dismissing others. Similar to what Michael Hathaway (2016, 14) suggests about the political identity and political strategy associated with "indigenous groups," it is not a question of whether there *are yuanshengtai* peoples in China but *which* groups are *yuanshengtai* (or not), and to what extent.

If compared to "indigeneity," defining features of which include historic continuity, cultural purity, and environmental sensibility (Dove 2006), *yuanshengtai* puts a similar emphasis on local knowledge and grassroots wisdom. The articulations of *yuanshengtai* resemble contemporary trans-cultural ideals, discussed by Beth Conklin and Laura Graham (1995), which highlight ethnic, rural peoples as potentially paradigmatic exemplars of core values, instead of treating them as peripheral members of society whose traditions are insignificant (if not backward or detrimental). Thus the characteristics of *yuanshengtai* resonate with those of "indigeneity," the rise and global spread of which has served as a counterpoint to the delocalizing impact of modernity and to the dominant development discourses (Dove 2006, 192, 195). However, where *yuanshengtai* diverges from the discourses and practices of indigeneity is, significantly, the ways in which it deflects attention from historically and politically contentious issues and transnational claims for rights and justice that would call for official recognition of "indigenous peoples" by the Chinese state (Luo 2018). The idea of *yuanshengtai* portrays local minority peoples as culturally "unique" and naturally "pure," yet it does so with no mention of any historical precedence that could potentially trigger unsettling issues, including land and labor rights as well as self-determination. As its usage expands and diffuses, sometimes *yuanshengtai* is meant to include anything quintessentially Chinese, while no longer making a clear distinction between the Han and the non-Han, who are fused in the official discourse as "heritage residents" *(shiju minzu).*[6]

The rhetoric of "heritage residents," instead of "indigenous peoples," has to do with the alleged common inheritance of both local Han and non-Han groups, who have mixed and mingled for centuries, even millennia, through migration, intermarriage, and conflict. The Chinese state maintains that all of the fifty-six state-defined ethnic groups (the Han and fifty-five minority nationalities) are native to its territory as "heritage residents"—or, more precisely, heritage *minzu* groups—and therefore there are no "indigenous peoples" in China. The rationale for the central state's position, which avoids admitting the existence of "indigenous peoples," is, perhaps, to skirt the need to engage with the United Nations protocols on "first nations" that address the rights of land and resource allocation for minority communities (Elliott 2015, 207–12). Thus *heritage residents* has become an expedient term to refer to local populations in multiethnic regions (used, for example, in the title of a research center at Guizhou Minzu University).

Therefore, while the articulation and appropriation of *yuanshengtai* undergirds a positive valence of minority cultures in the public domain, it does not call for the recognition of any "indigenous peoples" in China. Nor does it touch on marginalization and power asymmetry, as experienced by ethnic, rural residents over time, which have shaped not only domestic ethnic policies but also transnational indigenous-rights movements (Elliott 2015, 206–7). This approach, with its limitations on making political claims for indigenous peoples and justices, hinges on the contemporary state-market mechanism and espouses the legitimacy and sovereignty of the polyethnic Chinese nation (Luo 2018, 90). The rhetoric of *yuanshengtai* takes for granted the existing *minzu* categories under China's territorial and citizenship status, simply valorizing natural endowments and cultural traditions in an atemporal way.

However, a question persists for the various groups of "heritage residents" who hope to articulate their distinctiveness through the discursive and material productions of *yuanshengtai*, namely, what are the cultural and identity politics involved? Indeed, ethnic minority cultures over the past three decades or so have come to be represented in more diverse, complex, and nuanced ways, rather than simply standing as a foil to Han civilization or being portrayed as components of Chinese national unity, as was the case in earlier decades. The rankings of certain cultural traditions on the heritage lists are intimately connected to local governments' tourism revenue, scholars' research funding, and the market share of folk commodities (Wu 2015, 53–55). Because ethnic pride and economic profit become intricately entwined (Harrell 2013), multiple social groups in China, from regional elites to local villagers, are now struggling to brand something readily recognizable and ultimately marketable. In a country where the "expression and exploitation of local or group culture" has broadened in the twenty-first century (Pieke 2014, 130), spotlighting and celebrating uniqueness based on selective difference comes to be an increasingly important tactic in the attempt to outperform other groups and localities in China.

■ CAUGHT IN A DOUBLE BIND: THE "WATERLIKE" BUYI

One late evening in summer 2015, when I returned to Wuyang Village two years after my initial eighteen months of fieldwork, I received a phone call from Kun, an artist friend of mine then teaching at a university in Guiyang, the capital city of Guizhou province. Kun needed my suggestions because she was confounded by a design project on which she was collaborating with other Han artists. The project endeavored to manifest the essence of the Buyi ethnic group through sculpture.

"The sculpture, to be erected at the public square in the county seat, is part of an effort to attract more attention and to promote the local tourism economy, because this county in southwestern Guizhou with a predominant Buyi population has been so chronically impoverished," she bemoaned. "Earlier on, we tried to incorporate ethnic elements such as the bronze drum and the ox head into the sculpture. But local government officials were rather dissatisfied. They were concerned about such symbols being indistinguishable from other ethnic groups, for instance, from those of the Miao in southeastern Guizhou, which is famous for its ethnic tourism." She therefore asked if I, a native of Guizhou registered as Buyi on my national ID, as well as an academic who has been studying the Buyi, could pinpoint something distinct about the Buyi.

I first met Kun in mid-June 2013, when she followed a team of professors from her alma mater, the Sichuan Academy of Arts, to visit Wuyang Village and to seek inspiration for the team's artistic creations. Like many domestic tourists who have grown to appreciate Guizhou as an ideal summer getaway to avoid urban China's intense heat, Kun and the other artists embraced the *yuanshengtai* feel of the village, from breathing fresh air to drinking its well water, from enjoying the tranquility and lush greenness to collecting and ingesting wild vegetables and fish. During their noon breaks from composing all types of paintings, woodblocks, and collages, I sat down and had long chats with these visitors about their aesthetic perceptions of the local natural and cultural landscapes. The leading artist mentioned the salience of ethnic trademarks that could make a locality stand out as "the one and only" in an increasingly competitive cultural market. Such cultural trademarks, demonstrated through the old Buyi stone residences, are historically accumulated and arise within the context of a given environment and should thus be highlighted and preserved from the "encroachment of homogenizing modern transformations"—or so the artists contended.

Two hundred kilometers away from Wuyang Village, the county where Kun was helping to erect a Buyi sculpture doubtlessly faced a similar kind of endeavor in branding a readily recognizable ethnicity, whether such branding was conveyed in the form of an art project or through rural community development. On my end of the phone, I remained baffled and silent. Once again, I ruminated on my enduring doubts that I could glean any features of the Buyi that differed from similar Tai-speaking peoples, or from other populous and influential groups—such as those identified as the Han and the Miao—in highly multiethnic regions where people have mixed and mingled over time. And even if I could think of something unique about the Buyi inhabiting a particular locality, would that be adequate to capture the entirety of an internally heterogeneous ethnic group with an alleged population of nearly 3 million today, scattered across Guizhou and other parts of the Sino-Southeast Asian borderlands?

What I noticed, at the same time, was also the disjuncture between the expediency of branding an ethnic village like Wuyang as "an exemplar of the Buyi culture" at the local level and the challenge of branding the Buyi ethnic group on a more general level. Within China, the Buyi—in contrast to other ethnicities, such as the Miao (Hmong) or the Dong (Kam)—have a lower profile today and are less closely identified with the exoticized, multiethnic Guizhou. Moreover, little is known about the Buyi, China's tenth largest minority group, in Western scholarship. As I shall illustrate, the juggling act in the effort to highlight distinctiveness captures a contemporary challenge faced by the Buyi, in particular, with their seemingly unremarkable ethnic character.

Two months after our phone conversation, Kun showed me a blueprint of the sculpture they had designed. The blueprint, having received approval from the local government, had been implemented and undertaken as a major construction project for the county seat. It was completed in late 2015. Apart from incorporating the shape of a set of musical instruments typically used by local Buyi in that region, the designers added a number of wavy patterns to cover the entire sculpture piece. These curves, as Kun told me, were meant to symbolize whirlpools, something ostensibly signifying the Buyi ethnicity.

Indeed, the Buyi, along with other Tai-speaking groups, have mostly lived along highly irrigated river valleys. A Guizhou proverb alludes to this stereotype: "The Han live in townships, the Buyi live by waters, and the Miao live on mountaintops." While oversimplifying ethnic groups as occupying distinct ecological niches, this telling phrase nevertheless implies the in-between identities and places that the Buyi have stereotypically maintained. As explicated in the following pages, the Buyi's association with "water" in a multiethnic region that is densely mountainous, on one hand, suggests the historical advantage of versatility that thrived on agrarian livelihoods, but on the other hand, it may also generate a contemporary disadvantage related to a lack of distinguishable ethnic trademarks.

■ A BRIEF HISTORY OF THE FORMATION OF THE BUYI

By no means suggesting a teleological process of organic evolution, I nevertheless use major scholarly discourse for reference about the forbears of present-day Buyi. Far from being a monolithic group, they belonged to the proto-Tai peoples and originated from the ancient Hundred Yue (*Baiyue,* 百越) tribes as the indigenes of southern China as early as 2000 BCE (Holm 2003; Weinstein 2014).[7] While the imperial Chinese state treated local indigenes as objects of civilizing discourse and policy, state enterprises at the time were culturally vigorous and yet institutionally weak (Crossley, Siu, and Sutton 2006). China's southwestern borderlands, heavily crisscrossed by mountains and rivers, hence undergirded the emergence of what James Scott (2009, 241, 281) called "ethnic amphibians," capable of "social shape-shifting" within a broad range of identities.

Water, in this sense, contributed to the flourishing of rice paddy agriculture. At the same time, it enabled central authorities to gradually take control of sedentary populations and garner taxes. In particular, those who occupied fertile land and controlled sufficient water sources (which were easier to find in flat valleys and in small basins in the interior of hilly regions) may have come into closer contact with new Han settlements established to (re)claim land and "civilize" frontier populations. Intensive cultural borrowing between various groups and strategic interactions with the imperial regimes produced a range of "in-between" or intermediary non-Han groups along the progressively civilized spectrum from "raw" to "cooked" (Blum 2001; Hostetler 2001). Similar to other Tai-speaking groups (Holm 2003; Kaup 2000), the Buyi's forbears are believed to have maintained patriarchal structures and to have developed a sense of cultural superiority, some inventing a mythical Han origin for themselves in the hope of gaining higher social status. They have hence maintained a Janus-faced identity depicted in historical archives as "both Sinicized (*hanhua*, 汉化) and intractable" (Weinstein 2014, 26–27) or at once pliable and stubborn.[8]

Despite being depicted as a riverside ethnicity, the Buyi ascendants classified themselves according to the quality and elevation of the land they farmed (Weinstein 2014, 22), similar to the ecological and ethnic stratifications described in Edmund Leach's (1960) classic study of mainland Southeast Asia. Lowland dwellers were often called "people of the rice paddies" (*bouxnaz*), a name that differentiated them from "people beyond the rice paddies" (*bouxnongz*) and "people of the hills" (*bouxloeh*) (Holm 2003, 9; Zhou 1996). These autonyms, which have lasted to present day as relational terms, might provide "badges of self-identity" (Holm 2003, 9), but they may not imply any real sense of primordial or monolithic ethnic solidarity.

After the turbulent years of the Republican era in the early twentieth century, the formation of *minzu* under the socialist regime was marked by an unprecedented institutionalization of state power. Drawing on precedent Republican-era surveys and borrowing from the Stalinist model of nationalities, the identities of the enormously diverse populations were made concrete through the classifying label of *minzu* (Harrell 2001; Joniak-Lüthi 2015; Mullaney 2010). Rather than a top-down imposition, *minzu* identification involved interactive processes in which visiting missions were sent out by the state authority to conduct ethnolinguistic and social surveys as well as negotiations with local peoples.[9] Officials and scholars consulted with minority elites and held symposiums to greet locals. They also organized exhibitions, film screenings, and art performances, inviting minority peoples to sing and dance together as a way of harmonizing multiethnic relations. A special meeting of the Minzu Affairs Commission was subsequently convened in Guizhou and made a decision to use the autonym "Buyi/Bouyei" for the group's name, after considering at least twenty other names (Mullaney 2010, 111–12).[10] In 1953, Buyizu became one of the first thirty-eight minority nationality groups identified by the socialist state.

Since then, group consciousness has grown apace with nation building and state integration among local Buyi—both administratively and ideologically defined by a socialist government—who also incorporated a considerable amount of Han vocabulary and internalized the language of the state in support of national unity and socioeconomic progress. As Erik Mueggler (2001, 5) put it, the state is "not external to the fundamental concerns of daily life, nor does it penetrate this intimate sphere only from the outside"; it is "a constitutive force at the heart of the social world." An increasing number of minority cadres were trained in government-organized sessions, and public education in minority areas was promoted (Chen, Yan, and Ma 2008, 327). At the same time, ethnic literature and arts from respective minority groups were collected, cataloged, and studied. Such efforts also helped sustain the imagery of a Chinese culturalism, which, in fact, was wrapped around a solid Han core through the processes of Sinicization (Leibold 2007) and contributed to the construction of a myth of national belonging. Therefore, as fluid ethnolinguistic distinctions have become hardened and various layers of local societies have been penetrated by the party state, the Buyi identity—"primordially framed" and yet "de facto constructed" (Joniak-Lüthi 2015, 23)—has been but one marker locals reproduce for themselves to adapt to changing life-worlds.

■ INTERETHNIC REFERENCING: THE BUYI VERSUS THE MIAO

Within China's multiethnic borderlands, newly classified identities were thus carved out of a formerly shifting set of cultural practices through which people had cultivated multiple axes of relatedness. As the Buyi have actively marched "forward" with the socialist nation, they have continued to "other" the adjacent Miao ethnic group. The Miaozu (苗族), also forged from a diverse assemblage of local populations, have been historically regarded by the state as "harder to control" and thus ranked beneath the Buyi in an ethnically based hierarchy. The Buyi have distanced themselves from the Miao, who were being indirectly pushed or even forcefully chased into mountains and higher-altitude areas. Many legends attached to the limestone hills and caves around Wuyang Village involved conflicts and disputes with the Miao as well as ancient treasures hidden in haste by fleeing Miao. On the mountains, some of the Miao practiced swidden (slash-and-burn) agriculture, often regarded as more "primitive"—an evolutionary predecessor of wet-rice cultivation. An old saying Wuyang Villagers told me was "the Miao move their villages around." Rather than sedentarizing, the "mountaintop Miao" allegedly changed residence immediately upon using up the fertility of their land. Furthermore, and perhaps perceived as a consequence, some Miao do not worship their ancestors and have no ancestral places to which they return.

With features such as these deemed typical of "raw and untamed barbarians" in Chinese state and popular imaginations, the Miao were stigmatized to the extent that Buyi, if mistakenly referred to as "Miao," would react as if insulted. A nonreciprocal linguistic pattern has also existed, as most Buyi know how to speak Han Chinese but not the Miao language, which they regard as utterly unintelligible and perplexing, given the considerable number of subdialects. Buyi villagers often refer to any language they do not understand as that of the Miao and believe that the Miao language is the hardest to learn and Han Chinese the easiest (especially with more recent help of mass media, state education, and labor migration).

In the eyes of many Buyi, the Miao used to be those who could "barely catch up with the times [*ganbushang shidai,* 赶不上时代]." This interethnic dynamic persists in the contemporary postreform era, but now with an ironic twist. Mr. Yang, a retired elementary school teacher in Wuyang Village (pers. comm., November 7, 2013), articulated the puzzle as follows:

> We barely intermarried with the Miao; don't know if we were foes with them or what. Miao daughters-in-law were unwanted, and the meals they cooked for New Years and ritualistic events would not be touched or consumed by our ancestors. We used to smear them for not being clean. But now they are advanced [*xianjin,* 先进]; the Miao are broadcast on the TV so much more. It's as if we Buyi are not as good as they are?

The conundrum here is that the Buyi, having endeavored over time to become more socioeconomically "advanced," are now less "exotic." Historically seen as almost but not quite Han (Unger 1997), the Buyi consequently face a contemporary predicament in response to the market imperative to highlight cultural qualities as historically authentic and ethnically unique. Even though the Buyi have long been sedentarized and able to claim ancestral places (previously favored, "cooked" qualities), these same traits are now undesirable in the *yuanshengtai* paradigm. In a reversal of the old hierarchy, those deemed "raw" have come to be preferred as "closer to nature."

Distinct from (and stigmatized by) the mainstream Han, yet not as distinct as other ethnic minority groups, the Buyi are caught in a double bind. Now that the context has shifted, neighboring groups, such as the Miao, are far ahead in this new game. For instance, the traditional Buyi women's costume for life-cycle rituals (such as marriage and burial) and public performances may represent a visual element that distinguishes the Buyi from other groups and evokes local pride. And yet, displaying these costumes and ornaments in the village museum of Wuyang reminded some Buyi elites and villagers that they have not inherited—and are thus not able to display—as many silver ornaments as the Miao people. In addition, at various county-level cultural events, Buyi villagers from

Wuyang have noticed that the Miao groups were able to stage a unique form of dance using *lusheng* (the bamboo reed pipe that is the emblematic musical instrument of the Miao), whereas the Buyi choreography relied on simple movements recently created.

The ambivalence of Buyi-ness, very importantly, epitomizes a fundamental paradox in China's national history—that is, the tension between the impulse to preserve roots of cultural purity and the drive for civilizational progress (Duara 1995; Oakes 2012). This paradox, in the late socialist context, is manifested in the fact that local ethnic groups are still deemed to be "backward" minorities who ought to be transformed into "modern" citizens, even while they are simultaneously required to highlight a distinctive cultural identity to effectively gain a share of a state-controlled market. Thus Chinese ethnic minorities inhabit spaces of underdevelopment that are in need of improvement, and yet at the same time, these are sites of "tradition" threatened by development. This impossible conundrum may, in fact, lead to multivectored possibilities. Are the Buyi left to step on others' toes, or can the Buyi embrace greater freedom in labeling their own cultural difference?

■ "A CULTURE OF WATER"

Intriguingly, the aforementioned imagery of water was prominent in my interlocutions with Buyi villagers, who have relied on fresh water for rice growing and everyday survival, as well as with local elites, who described water as the metaphorical psyche of the Buyi. Uncle Wu, who continued to study Buyi rituals and cultural histories after moving out of his natal village Wuyang to receive higher education and work for a state-owned enterprise, reiterated this idea during my interviews with him in June 2013:

> Because our ancestors have historically occupied fertile soils with sufficient irrigation in a region with limited availability of farmable land, we have inhabited advantageous terrains in southern China. There was no need to compete with others like the Miao or those in the north. We have been rather content with the status quo and go with the flow. Just like the water, we Buyi are too "soft," not tough, very friendly and adaptable to others. We don't fight for ourselves at the forefront, and thus, we are less visible and less united.

As elaborated by some Buyi educated elites hinting at the lack of distinctiveness and offering an explanation for the invisibility of the Buyi in local cultural politics, the "waterlike" character may not necessarily be desirable at present, because it is too fluid and adaptable, without unique qualities of its own. The flip side, as suggested, was intragroup competition within the Buyi, as compared to that within the Miao. Despite huge variance among those identified as Miao, some Buyi elites still regard the Miao as more united. They believed that the Miao's core identity and solidarity, derived from having withstood a long history of warfare and constant attack from powerful opponents (especially the central authorities), is what caused Miao representatives and political elites to engage in mutual aid and collegial support on the regional level. In contrast, according to many Buyi, "It is always about 'me' and 'you,' even within the same ethnic group. It is fine to maintain deeply rooted ethnocentric awareness [minzu yishi, 民族意识], but why compete against each other in the spirit of localism? Each of the Buyi areas is eager to be the 'first' or the 'best,' now that they are constructing cultural attractions. It is just a means of branding anyway."

According to these reckonings, the Buyi—a "waterlike" ethnicity that has always adapted its mode of being to thrive—has been reduced to a collection of self-interested fragments, united only by the minzu label they share. The Buyi's flexibility and malleability throughout history have become liabilities, undermining the Buyi's ability to be "distinctive" in the contemporary context. This rhetoric of Buyi's lack of distinguishable features also echoed the urgent sense of loss among my Buyi informants, as well as my relatives, who fear the fading away of Buyi traditions because of the so-called assimilation to Han Chinese culture. The case of the Buyi hence speaks to the plight of many interstitial ethnicities, who are neither integrated into the power center nor oppositional against or obviously distinguishable from the mainstream. They are somehow turned into the "weaponless weak," because they are lacking in "weapons of the weak" (cf. Scott 1985)—in this case, the resistant, "exoticized" attributes possessed by more marginalized ethnicities.

In a geopolitical context as well, Buyi elites perceived themselves to be at a relative disadvantage. As a group, the Miao—internationally known as the Hmong—have many subvariations across the Sino-Southeast Asian borderlands and are thus transregional and even transnational. The Buyi, on the other hand, with nearly 90 percent of the population resident in Guizhou, are largely constrained to one province.[11] Guizhou, furthermore, is a hinterland province without any international borders and has been described as a chronically "disadvantaged interior region" (Oakes 2000, 669) and as socioeconomically "remote" (Schein 2014, 371). This leaves the Buyi in an undesirable situation and results in Buyi intellectuals feeling unable to "reach out" to translocal arenas.

Therefore the Buyi face a dilemma as to whether and how such a group can develop capacity for the kinds of scale crossing needed to allow discursive resources to travel and translate (Fortun et al. 2010, 231). The Buyi resemble the indigenous populations described by Elizabeth Povinelli (2002, 253) as "trapped between too much and not enough cultural difference." Indigenous peoples consistently fail at difference and indigeneity "because the inspection regime of recognition requires them to be radically different, and yet, at the same time, cannot actually recognize radical alterity" (Cattelino 2010, 237). As "heritage residents" of the Chinese nation, the Buyi are indeed *not* Han, and yet *are* comparatively "Sinicized."

According to a Han township cadre in charge of Wuyang Village, most people have only heard of Miao culture, whereas there is no well-known Buyi place. "You see, the Buyi inheritance is gradually disappearing. And compared to that of other groups in Guizhou, the promotion and development of the Buyi culture is already lagging behind [*luohou, 落后*]." As he put it, without a well-created brand to bring publicity, tourism development and cultural promotion cannot be converted into materialized benefits for local populations. In other words, called upon by the state to mobilize individual capacities for self-governance and self-improvement (Litzinger 2008, 233), the cultural economy in late socialist China that stresses "uniqueness" thus tends to create uneven spaces and variegated subjects, with some caught in a double bind. Whether making historically and socially marginalized people into a political category such as "indigenous" (Hathaway 2016) or simply generating an alternative indigenous space such as *yuanshengtai* through a commercialized route, persistent efforts and massive mobilizations are required. A critical challenge therefore arises when none of the resources required to do so are available to the Buyi's advantage.

■ INDIGENEITY AND INVISIBILITY IN THE AGE OF CULTURAL BRANDING

The economic dimension of such double binds experienced by the Buyi reveals a paradox that ensues not only from the failure to be different enough but also from the simultaneous unrecognizability of difference (Cattelino 2010, 237). Given how much ethnic boundaries defining Han and minority groups have actually shifted over time (Wu 1994), the obsession with authenticity we witness today has resulted from multiple groups—especially those with "between and betwixt" status—having long negotiated the terms of coexistence with each other (Tenzin 2017, 563). Similar to other populations seeking to define themselves within and against indigeneity's dense web of symbols, fantasies, and meanings (de la Cadena and Starn 2007b, 2), China's minority peoples, as its "internal others," have also been managing the complex dynamics of categorization.

The processes of symbol making and identity branding for cultural promotion in turn reveal tremendous borrowings from and mimicking of others (Tenzin 2017, 559), which somehow resemble the ways in which ethnic groups have negotiated and interacted with each other throughout history. The construction of cultural difference entails, on one hand, efforts to distinguish oneself from others using multifaceted reference points for comparison and, on the other hand, cross-reference and even imitation. In other words, ethnic branding is not necessarily about essence but often about relative difference, often by gradation—something bigger in terms of size or scale, older in terms of the historical origin claimed, or more appealing for the public gaze. At the same time, however, the processes of nation building that help to bridge local differences and to distinguish China from the rest of the world have resulted in an increased degree of commonality in lived experience and communicative practice across China (Kipnis 2012). While new productive and consuming selves are not merely copycats, as is often implied in global representation of China (Wong 2013; Yang 2015), efforts at difference indeed tend to follow one of very few available paths. Success in making indigenous subjects visible, then, means crafting "originality" or "authenticity" as exemplified by *yuanshengtai* through actively assuming certain kinds of arbitrarily distinctive characteristics and power.

Throughout my eighteen months of fieldwork, I observed how Wuyang Village tried to spruce up visible aspects of Buyi culture, ranging from rituals and performances to architectural sites and material objects, to showcase Buyi uniqueness. A key strategy for ethnic branding, I would like to pinpoint here, is the common practice of learning from "models" that already have much publicity. With years of state-financed propaganda and entrepreneurial promotion, Xijiang Thousand-Household Miao Village in southeastern Guizhou has become an exemplar of ethnic rural tourism, even despite having become so commercialized. Local governments, in turn, often organized fieldtrips for selected village cadres to visit, who then regularly referenced such model sites in developing their own. It seems particularly ironic that the Buyi were encouraged to emulate the Miao example, which is more "advanced" in branding *yuanshengtai*, though historically the Miao ranked beneath the Buyi on the ethnic hierarchy.

For those in Wuyang Village who visited Xijiang, the experience was unhelpful at best. While a female representative from Wuyang Village recalled that "good-looking houses" in Xijiang offered the most direct visual experience and served as a primary attraction for tourists from afar, she and other villagers felt that Xijiang was not as scenic as Wuyang Village.

However, they understood that Xijiang received much state funding and large-scale planning, with the tourist income generated being shared by each household—a practice they suspected may not happen in their own village. While certain "cultural heritage" attached to the Buyi has been produced and often valorized over the past decade, the number of such state-recognized items and sites is far from comparable to that of the Miao.[12] The profiles of these cultural object-forms factor into determining how much attention and state support an ethnic group or area might gain, especially in terms of poverty alleviation and general social welfare.

Rival claims of authenticity—or who is more *yuanshengtai*—exist not only between the Buyi and the Miao but also among the various subgroups that have been assigned a common ethnic label, all defined under the umbrella of "Buyi." Just as the female villager indicated in the opening vignette, some subgroups who have also been categorized as Buyi (such as the Bouxnongz) are still deemed different and not "genuinely qualified."[13] Localist desires to promote *yuanshengtai* through cultural industries may resonate with the fact that villagers tend to view themselves as members of several distinct populations, depending on when and under what circumstances their ancestors started to inhabit the area.[14] Therefore, while it may be relatively convenient to brand a Buyi locale as *yuanshengtai*, a coherent and distinct branding of the Buyi in general may nonetheless remain challenging.

Meanwhile, another question demands critical attention: to what extent can villagers take control of the promulgation of *yuanshsengtai*? Similar to the entry of "indigenous knowledge" discourse (Hathaway 2010; Sturgeon 2007), *yuanshengtai* discourse remains stuck in an intermediate realm. Even at present, it is primarily disseminated by artists, officials, intellectuals, and media professionals, many of whom view the situation with an urbanite and elitist gaze. Borrowing from Tracey Heatherington (2010), I suggest that the global dreamtimes of indigeneity—that is, the tension between the cultural realities and living landscapes of local populations and the social-ecological imaginaries envisioned through policy discourse and new media—deserve critical attention. While officials often regard culture as both a rich vein of untapped economic ore and a salve for the social instability wrought by decades of uneven growth, cultural development has tended to increase incomes only for a very small minority of rural elites, provoking new forms of economic alienation and social discontent rather than ameliorating problems (Oakes 2006, 2009).

On the other hand, villagers have also come to understand the expediency of culture in terms of its potential to bring new sources of income, prosperity, and pride. While gaining recognition of indigenous status by the Chinese state is not the ultimate goal, *yuanshengtai* makes a case that there may be possibilities for strengthening indigenous identities that are not antithetical to state sovereignty and citizenry but that are articulated more on their own terms in local and even translocal settings. The state-market mechanism upon which *yuanshengtai* hinges exemplifies the convenience of culture both as a new model of local governance and as a resource for new forms of capital accumulation and market expansion (Yúdice 2003). This, in fact, gives rise to the utopian conception that treats culture as a "rooted pure space" needing protection from the impurities of the wider world and that, in turn, becomes highly marketable itself (Oakes 2009, 1076). As long as "these new expressions and claims of cultural difference" are made within the bounds of national unity (Yeh 2007, 86), the market-oriented economy in contemporary China will continue to allow a valorization of minority cultures through ethnic branding.

■ CONCLUSION

In Asia and Africa, many national governments recognize the existence of indigenous peoples in other parts of the world. In their own countries, however, either all or none of the citizens are recognized as indigenous to the country (Baird 2016, 501). In China, specifically, there is little grassroots support for and long-standing official opposition to the category. This exemplifies Hathaway's (2016) argument that the emergence of indigenous identities is often difficult and always political. Therefore "becoming indigenous is always only a *possibility* negotiated within political fields of culture and history" (de la Cadena and Starn 2007b, 13), which, in the Chinese case, must be negotiated within the nation-state framework. Indigenous populations have to use cultural and political frames that are comprehensible within the nation-state, which continues to be the locus of most negotiations (Tsing 2007, 39). The challenge for China's ethnic minorities is thus to address the possibilities of indigeneity by engaging with the party state rather than withdrawing from it, even though this creates a very limited space in which to maneuver.

Addressing the question of whether indigenous subjectivity can be practiced in the context of China, this article has attended to cultural commodification as one of the only viable avenues for local minority populations. Currently the only available frame and relevant category for talking about cultural difference (Yeh 2007), *minzu* has been the identity label locals have embraced and reproduced in quotidian cultural production. Ethnic branding in line with *minzu* categories—exemplified by the *yuanshengtai* phenomenon—could potentially enhance an alternative indigenous space by propagating positive valences of minorities, in contrast to older representations of them as primitive and backward. This could only have emerged alongside the rise of the market economy and the environmental movements in contemporary China, making *yuanshengtai* at once a protean concept and a lived reality, much like indigeneity. At the same time, for minority populations, a multilayered sense of belonging is embedded in such processes as we see the convergence of cultural revitalization, ethnic pride, and economic profit.

While *yuanshengtai* differs from the category of indigenous that embodies intrinsically political qualities and international orientations (Hathaway 2016), identifying whether and to what extent a group is *yuanshengtai* is a politicoeconomic strategy as much as it is an identity label. *Yuanshengtai,* having taken root in highly multiethnic provinces like Guizhou, where the party state allows minorities to enjoy a relatively high level of cultural and religious freedom (Sautman 2012, 16), enables minorities to perform creatively as long as they remain within the permissible limits of public ethnic identity (Davis 2005, 37). Therefore mainstream China's growing interest in pristine nature and in exotic cultures may foster the existence of alternative indigeneity, yet with limited capacity. Unlike the spatially framed notion of indigeneity, which ties a particular group to a specific locale, the rhetoric of "heritage residents" embedded in *yuanshengtai* naturalizes the notion of coinhabitance by Han and non-Han in multiethnic regions of China (Yeh 2007, 84). In this formulation, all residents should ideally contribute to the safeguarding of social harmony through economic advancements and cultural expressions. This works to the state's best interest, obscuring the historical marginalization of non-Han groups and the transnational linkages with other minoritized peoples, increased awareness of which may lead to rights-related issues.

Insofar as a notion like *yuanshengtai* reminds us of the need to acknowledge the efficacy of particular categories and generalizations despite the dangers of relying on them (Fortun et al. 2010, 232), it could also entail the obscuration of economic and cultural struggles of certain groups like the Buyi. As I have demonstrated, the Buyi find themselves caught in a double bind by virtue of their close relationship to Han Chinese and relatively high degree of Sinicization. Moreover, with limited transnational connections and with a history of allying with the Chinese state, the Buyi have become relatively invisible in contemporary cultural politics. The Miao, in contrast, have historically crossed the borders of multiple nation-states and resisted state rules due to oppression from various authorities.[15] The culturalization of indigenous life thus may not end up resolving inequalities but redistributing them (Bessire 2014). Indeed, while "representations of and claims to cultural difference are expedient insofar as they multiply commodities and empower community" (Yúdice 2003, 25), the shift from cultural survival to survival via culture entails a simultaneous process of empowerment and yet alienation.

The focus of this article on cultural economy primarily derives from my observation of local aspirations among the Buyi I have encountered, who have no intention to defy or even to challenge the state. While my analysis of ethnic branding barely touches upon legal rights—typical in other indigenous experiences in relation to autonomy and sovereignty—this does not mean that struggles over rural land rights or tensions resulting from uneven distribution do not exist. Owing to land dispossession and excessive commercialization, many ethnic rural communities in China's southwest are beginning to lose control over their economies, cultures, and lifestyles. This will continue to pose a challenge for scholars, especially indigenous scholars such as I, who are constantly engaged in a balancing act between of whom and for whom we speak.

Yu Luo is an assistant professor in the Department of Chinese and History at the City University of Hong Kong. Her recent publications have appeared in *Modern China* and the *Handbook on Ethnic Minorities in China*.

◾ NOTES

1. While the characters for the modern ethnonym are rendered "Buyi" in pinyin Romanization, "Bouyei" is the transcription adopted for foreign publication since 1991 (Weinstein 2014, 136n2).

2. As Ian Baird (2016) pointed out, many government leaders in Asian countries accept the validity of the concept of indigeneity, but consider it inapplicable to their own countries, which did not experience high levels of European settler colonization. A significant exception applies to Taiwan (Baird 2016; Elliott 2015), where aboriginal peoples are officially identified as "Taiwan's indigenous peoples" and where political issues related to land restoration and indigenous rights have risen to importance (Teng 2004, 105).

3. Katherine Kaup (2000) has examined some of the new *minzu* policies under Mao, including new political and administrative posts, preferential access to technical schools and higher education, and exemption from the "one-child" policy.

4. Distinct from the metanarrative of postsocialism that implies a teleological transition from socialism to liberal capitalism (Zhang 2001), "late socialism" entails the state exerting itself to regulate nascent national

industries, avoid potential chaos in the market, and structure new modes of private and public life (despite pressure to retreat from the market and everyday social spheres to substantiate its claim in promoting the market economy) (Yang 2015, 20–21).

5. Textual and visual illustrations recorded by the late imperial authorities from the sixteenth to twentieth centuries had placed "barbarians" along a continuum from wild to tamed, from "raw" to "cultured" (Hostetler 2001), which saw new incarnations right up to modern-day perceptions of ethnic minorities (Blum 2001).

6. The translation of *minzu* here embodies the ambiguity inherent in the notion itself (Mullaney 2010): when modified by *Zhonghua, minzu* is used for people of the Chinese nation in aggregate (the *Zhonghua minzu*); when modified by *shaoshu,* it refers to "minority nationalities" *(shaoshu minzu)*; and additionally, it is used without modification to denote "ethnic groups," usually non-Han.

7. Groups that have been considered ascendants of the Buyi included what was called "Zhongjia," "Bunayi," "Bunongyi," "Shuijia," "Zhuang," etc., some of which appear to have lived in proximity to one another (Chen [1942] 2004, 79–80).

8. See also Zhongguo difangzhi jicheng bianji gongzuo weiyuanhui ([1948] 2006), juan 170, 13502.

9. In winter 1950, the renowned scholar Fei Xiaotong led the third branch of the Central Nationality Delegation's Southwestern China Visiting Mission to some minority regions of Guizhou (Zhenning Buyizu Miaozu zizhixian gaikuang bianxiezu 1985).

10. Whilst "Bu" in the autonym "Buyi/Bouyei" is a prefix used for most human-denominating vocabularies in the Buyi language, the second syllable "yi") has more linguistic variations among those inhabiting different Buyi areas of Guizhou.

11. Granted, there are Buyi communities in Yunnan province and a few in northwestern Vietnam. Various trans-Tai connections (e.g., based on similar languages and rituals), including Buyi and Zhuang linkages, are also developing, by both local state and grassroots initiatives. The precedent for this alliance is that from 1956 to 1981, a set of uniformed scripts for both groups was created using Latin alphabets. Nevertheless, the Miao ethnicity is undoubtedly more populous on a national level and more influential worldwide.

12. For instance, among the 202 villages from Guizhou cataloged by the central government as the second batch of "Ancient/Traditional Chinese Villages" in 2013, there are only three Buyi villages listed, the rest being predominantly Miao and Dong.

13. While "Buyi" is the only ethnonym that is state recognized and is most commonly used, the reality is much more complicated because of variance in language and geographic location. Those in Wuyang Village, for instance, refer to those who hail from a different Buyi subdialect area that is situated farther from the county center as Bouxnongz, while calling themselves Bouxnaz.

14. A similar case has been examined by Tim Oakes (2009, 1086) on how *tunpu* culture in Guizhou imposes a unity that villagers themselves do not experience and obscures the significant variation from village to village in terms of actual histories, meanings, and practices.

15. Some scholars have proposed that indigenous peoples in Asia should be considered "colonized peoples," or peoples who have been oppressed by other ethnic groups throughout history, rather than simply "first peoples," because many are not actually the first to inhabit the places where they currently live (Gray 1995). For instance, significant numbers of ethnic Hmong people were forced to migrate to Southeast Asia over a century ago due to oppression in China and were subsequently further oppressed by new authorities and colonial powers in Southeast Asia. At least according to some, the Hmong should qualify as indigenous peoples in Southeast Asia (Baird 2016).

■ **WORKS CITED**

Baidu baike [Baidu online encyclopedia]. 2015. "'Yuan sheng tai' citiao" [A glossary of "yuanshengtai"]. http://baike.baidu.com/view/105755.htm.

Baird, Ian. 2016. "Indigeneity in Asia: An Emerging but Contested Concept." *Asian Ethnicity* 17, no. 4: 501–5.

Bessire, Lucas. 2014. "The Rise of Indigenous Hypermarginality: Native Culture as a Neoliberal Politics of Life." *Current Anthropology* 55, no. 3: 276–95.

Blum, Susan. 2001. *Portraits of "Primitives": Ordering Human Kinds in the Chinese Nation.* Lanham, Md.: Rowman and Littlefield.

Blumenfield, Tami, and Helaine Silverman, eds. 2013. *Cultural Heritage Politics in China.* New York: Springer.

Breidenbach, Joanne, and Pál Nyíri. 2007. "'Our Common Heritage': New Tourist Nations, Post-'Socialist' Pedagogy, and the Globalization of Nature." *Current Anthropology* 48, no. 2: 322–30.

Cattelino, Jessica. 2010. "The Double Bind of American Indian Need-Based Sovereignty." *Cultural Anthropology* 25, no. 2: 235–63.

Chen Guo'an, Yan Yong, and Ma Qizhong. 2008. *Zhongguo shaoshuminzu xianzhuang yu fazhan diaocha yanjiu congshu: Zhenningxian Buyizu juan* [Research on the contemporary conditions and development of

Chinese ethnic minorities: The Buyi in Zhenning county]. Edited by Hao Shiyuan and Ren Yifei. Beijing: Minzu chubanshe.

Chen Guojun. (1942) 2004. "Beipanjiang Miao Yi de fenbu." In *Guizhou Miao Yi shehui yanjiu* [A study on the society of Miao and Yi people in Guizhou province], edited by Wu Zelin and Chen Guojun et al., 79–80. Beijing: Minzu chubanshe.

Comaroff, John, and Jean Comaroff. 2009. *Ethnicity Inc.* Chicago: University of Chicago Press.

Conklin, Beth A., and Laura R. Graham. 1995. "The Shifting Middle Ground: Amazonian Indians and Eco-Politics." *American Anthropologist* 97, no. 4: 695–710.

Crossley, Pamela K., Helen F. Siu, and Donald S. Sutton, eds. 2006. *Empire at the Margins: Culture, Ethnicity, and Frontier in Early Modern China.* Berkeley: University of California Press.

Davis, Sara. 2005. *Song and Silence: Ethnic Revival on China's Southwest Borders.* New York: Columbia University Press.

de la Cadena, Marisol, and Orin Starn, eds. 2007a. *Indigenous Experience Today.* Oxford: Berg.

de la Cadena, Marisol, and Orin Starn, eds. 2007b. Introduction to *Indigenous Experience Today,* edited by Marisol de la Cadena and Orin Starn, 1–30. Oxford: Berg.

Dove, Michael R. 2006. "Indigenous People and Environmental Politics." *Annual Review of Anthropology* 35: 191–208.

Duara, Prasenjit. 1995. *Rescuing History from the Nation: Questioning Narratives of Modern China.* Chicago: University of Chicago Press.

Elliott, Mark. 2015. "The Case of the Missing Indigene: Debate over a 'Second-Generation' Ethnic Policy." *The China Journal* 73: 186–213.

Fortun, Kim, Mike Fortun, and Steven Rubenstein. 2010. "Editors' Introdution to 'Emergent Indigeneities.'" *Cultural Anthropology* 25, no. 2: 222–34.

Gray, Andrew. 1995. "The Indigenous Movement in Asia." In *Indigenous Peoples in Asia,* edited by Robert H. Barnes, Andrew Gray, and Benedict Kingsbury, 35–58. Ann Arbor, Mich.: Association of Asian Studies.

Harrell, Stevan. 2001. *Ways of Being Ethnic in Southwest China.* Seattle: University of Washington Press.

Harrell, Stevan. 2013. "China's Tangled Web of Heritage." In *Cultural Heritage Politics in China,* edited by Tami Blumenfield and Helaine Silverman, 285–94. New York: Springer.

Hathaway, Michael. 2010. "The Emergence of Indigeneity: Public Intellectuals and an Indigenous Space in Southwest China." *Cultural Anthropology* 25, no. 2: 301–33.

Hathaway, Michael. 2013. *Environmental Winds: Making the Global in Southwest China.* Berkeley: University of California Press.

Hathaway, Michael. 2016. "China's Indigenous Peoples? How Global Environmentalism Unintentionally Smuggled the Notion of Indigeneity into China." *Humanities* 5, no. 54: 1–17.

Heatherington, Tracey. 2010. *Wild Sardinia: Indigeneity and Global Dreamtimes of Environmentalism.* Seattle: University of Washington Press.

Holm, David. 2003. *Killing a Buffalo for the Ancestors: A Zhuang Cosmological Text from Southwest China.* DeKalb: Southeast Asia Publications Center, Northern Illinois University.

Hostetler, Laura. 2001. *Qing Colonial Enterprise: Ethnography and Cartography in Early Modern China.* Chicago: University of Chicago Press.

Joniak-Lüthi, Agnieszka. 2015. *The Han: China's Diverse Majority.* Seattle: University of Washington Press.

Kaup, Katherine. 2000. *Creating the Zhuang: Ethnic Politics in China.* Boulder, Colo.: Lynne Rienner.

Kendall, Paul. 2017. "The Location of Cultural Authenticity: Identifying the Real and the Fake in Urban Guizhou." *The China Journal* 77: 93–109.

Kipnis, Andrew. 2008. "Audit Cultures: Neoliberal Governmentality, Socialist Legacy, or Technologies of Governing?" *American Ethnologist* 35, no. 2: 275–89.

Kipnis, Andrew. 2012. "Constructing Commonality: Standardization and Modernization in Chinese Nation-Building." *The Journal of Asian Studies* 71, no. 3: 731–55.

Lash, Scott, and Celia Lury. 2007. *Global Culture Industry: The Mediation of Things.* Cambridge: Polity.

Leach, Edmund. 1960. "The Frontier of 'Burma.'" *Comparative Studies in Society and History* 3, no. 1: 49–68.

Leibold, James. 2007. *Reconfiguring Chinese Nationalism: How the Qing Frontier and Its Indigenes Became Chinese.* New York: Palgrave Macmillan.

Levenson, Joseph R. 1968. *Confucian China and Its Modern Fate: A Trilogy.* Berkeley: University of California Press.

Litzinger, Ralph. 2008. "Afterword: Beyond the Corporate Leninist Box." In *Privatizing China: Socialism from Afar,* edited by Li Zhang and Aihwa Ong, 230–36. Ithaca, N.Y.: Cornell University Press.

Luo, Yu. 2018. "An Alternative to the Realm of the 'Indigenous' in Early 21st-Century China: Guizhou's Branding of *Yuanshengtai*." *Modern China* 44, no. 1: 68–102.

Mathur, Saloni. 2007. *India by Design: Colonial History and Cultural Display.* Berkeley: University of California Press.

McLaren, Anne, Alex English, Xinyuan He, and Catherine Ingram. 2013. *Environmental Preservation and Cultural Heritage in China.* Champaign, Ill.: Common Ground.

Mueggler, Erik. 2001. *The Age of Wild Ghosts: Memory, Violence, and Place in Southwest China.* Berkeley: University of California Press.

Mullaney, Thomas. 2010. *Coming to Terms with the Nation: Ethnic Classification in Modern China.* Berkeley: University of California Press.

Oakes, Timothy. 2000. "China's Provincial Identities: Reviving Regionalism and Reinventing 'Chineseness.'" *Journal of Asian Studies* 59, no. 3: 667–92.

Oakes, Timothy. 2006. "Cultural Strategies of Development: Implications for Village Governance in China." *Pacific Review* 19, no. 1: 13–37.

Oakes, Timothy. 2009. "Resourcing Culture: Is a Prosaic 'Third Space' Possible in Rural China?" *Environment and Planning D: Society and Space* 27: 1074–90.

Oakes, Timothy. 2012. "Looking Out to Look In: The Use of Periphery in China's Geopolitical Narratives." *Eurasian Geography and Economics* 53, no. 3: 315–26.

Pieke, Frank N. 2014. "Anthropology, China, and the Chinese Century." *Annual Review of Anthropology* 43: 123–38.

Povinelli, Elizabeth. 2002. *The Cunning of Recognition: Indigenous Alterity and the Making of Australian Multiculturalism.* Durham, N.C.: Duke University Press.

Rees, Helen. 2012. "Intangible Cultural Heritage in China Today: Policy and Practice in the Early Twenty-First Century." In *Music as Intangible Cultural Heritage: Policy, Ideology, and Practice in the Preservation of East Asian Traditions,* edited by Keith Howard, 23–54. Burlington, Vt.: Ashgate.

Rees, Helen. 2016. "Environmental Crisis, Culture Loss, and a New Musical Aesthetic: China's 'Original Ecology Folksongs' in Theory and Practice." *Ethnomusicology* 60, no. 1: 53–88.

Sautman, Barry. 2012. "Paved with Good Intentions: Proposals to Curb Minority Rights and Their Consequences for China." *Modern China* 38, no. 1: 10–39.

Schein, Louisa. 2014. "The Edges of Alterity." *HAU: Journal of Ethnographic Theory* 4, no. 1: 361–81.

Scott, James C. 1985. *Weapons of the Weak: Everyday Forms of Peasant Resistance.* New Haven, Conn.: Yale University Press.

Scott, James C. 2009. *The Art of Not Being Governed: An Anarchist History of Upland Southeast Asia.* New Haven, Conn.: Yale University Press.

Siu, Helen. 2007. "Grounding Displacement: Uncivil Urban Spaces in

Postreform South China." *American Ethnologist* 34, no. 2: 329–50.

Sturgeon, Janet C. 2007. "Pathways of 'Indigenous Knowledge' in Yunnan, China." *Alternatives: Global, Local, Political* 2, no. 1: 129–53.

Teng, Emma. 2004. *Taiwan's Imagined Geography: Chinese Colonial Travel Writing and Pictures, 1683–1895.* Cambridge, Mass.: Harvard University Press.

Tenzin, Jinba. 2017. "Seeing Like Borders: Convergence Zone as a Post-Zomian Model." *Current Anthropology* 58, no. 5: 551–75.

Tsing, Anna. 2007. "Indigenous Voices." In *Indigenous Experience Today,* edited by Marisol de la Cadena and Orin Starn, 33–67. Oxford: Berg.

Unger, Jonathan. 1997. "Not Quite Han: The Ethnic Minorities of China's Southwest." *Bulletin of Concerned Asian Scholars* 29, no. 3: 67–78.

Wang, Jing. 2001. "'Culture' as Leisure and 'Culture' as Capital." *Positions: East Asia Cultures Critique* 9, no. 1: 69–104.

Wang, Jing. 2010. *Brand New China: Advertising, Media, and Commercial Culture.* Cambridge, Mass.: Harvard University Press.

Weinstein, Jodi. 2014. *Empire and Identity in Guizhou: Local Resistance to Qing Expansion.* Seattle: University of Washington Press.

Wong, Winnie Won Yin. 2013. *Van Gogh on Demand: China and the Readymade.* Chicago: University of Chicago Press.

Wu, David Yen-ho. 1994. "The Construction of Chinese and Non-Chinese Identities." In *The Living Tree: The Changing Meaning of Being Chinese Today,* edited by Tu Wei-ming, 148–67. Stanford, Calif.: Stanford University Press.

Wu, Ka-Ming. 2015. *Reinventing Chinese Tradition: The Cultural Politics of Late Socialism.* Champaign: University of Illinois Press.

Yang, Fan. 2015. *Faked in China: Nation Branding, Counterfeit Culture, and Globalization.* Bloomington: Indiana University Press.

Yeh, Emily. 2007. "Tibetan Indigeneity: Translation, Resemblances, and Uptake." In *Indigenous Experience Today,* edited by Marisol de la Cadena and Orin Starn, 69–97. Oxford: Berg.

Yeh, Emily. 2014. "The Rise and Fall of the Green Tibetan: Contingent Collaboration and the Vicissitudes of Harmony." In *Mapping Shangrila: Contested Landscapes in the Sino-Tibetan Borderlands,* edited by Emily T. Yeh and Chris Coggins, 255–78. Seattle: University of Washington Press.

Yúdice, George. 2003. *The Expediency of Culture: Uses of Culture in the Global Era.* Durham, N.C.: Duke University Press.

Zhang, Li. 2001. "Migration and Privatization of Space and Power in Late Socialist China." *American Ethnologist* 28, no. 1: 179–205.

Zhenning Buyizu Miaozu zizhixian gaikuang bianxiezu. 1985. *Zhenning Buyizu Miaozu zizhixian gaikuang* [A general survey of Zhenning Buyi-Miao Autonomous County]. Guiyang: Guizhou renmin chubanshe.

Zhongguo difangzhi jicheng bianji gongzuo weiyuanhui, ed. (1948) 2006. *Minguo Guizhou tongzhi* [Republican-era Guizhou gazetteer]. Chengdu, China: Bashu shushe.

Zhou, Guoyan. 1996. "An Introduction to the Kam-Tai (Zhuang-Dong) Group of Languages in China." In *Languages and Cultures of the Kam-Tai (Zhuang Dong) Group: A Word List,* English–Thai ed., edited by Zhou Guoyan and Somsonge Burusphat, 1–65. Bangkok: Sahadhammika.

MEGUMI CHIBANA

An Artful Way of Making Indigenous Space

IN 1995, the Okinawan community of Yomitan, which had been dispossessed of their lands during the Pacific War to allow for the building of a Japanese airfield, revealed their plans for the future of their village (Yomitan-son 1995). Village leaders placed an image and a poem at the center of this new vision, an artful way of imagining indigenous space:

> *Yutasa aru funshii*
> *Masaru chimugukuru*
> *Sachifukuru hana ya*
> *Mura nu miati*

> The richness of nature
> Good hearted people
> The culture, shining with all its glory
> is the guideline of the village[1]

According to this vision, known as the Phoenix Plan (J: *ōtori keikaku*),[2] the cape of Yomitan is a phoenix about to take off toward the East China Sea. The Yomitan Hills and Takō Mountain become wings with flying capability. Holding a lei of corals in its beak, the phoenix welcomes *kariyushi* (O: prosperity) arriving from *nirai kanai,* the faraway land across the sea whence, according to traditional Okinawan belief, happiness comes. The energy of *hito* (J: people), *mono* (J: goods), and *bunka* (J: culture) flows into the center, swirls like a windmill, and generates its energy (Yomitan-son 2013a). Drawing from a philosophy of feng shui, which represents the interconnectedness of communities with nature, Yomitan envisions the resurgence of the village, rising again like a phoenix. Reinforcing the visual imagination, the accompanying poem, written in the 8–8–8–6 style

135

Figure 1. The Phoenix Plan of Yomitan Village. Courtesy of Yomitan village.

common to Ryukyuan poetry (O/J: *ryūka*), suggests that following the "guidelines of the village" (O: *mura nu miati*), this artfully constructed space of nature–people–culture will result in "a healthy community" (O: *ganjuu nu shima*).[3]

In 1995, the village government of Yomitan adopted this Phoenix Plan based on indigenous community orientations and has continued to use it as the groundwork for local government planning (Yomitan-son 1995). The municipality incorporated the principle into its master plan, and the phoenix became a new icon to symbolize the village and its vision of the landscape. Continuing to guide current community-building efforts in Yomitan, the phoenix with its autochthonous wings of mountains works to slowly repossess bits of farmland, reclaiming them from their designation as Japanese (and, later, U.S.) military airstrips.

This article explores the emergence of indigenous space in Yomitan village of Okinawa. Indigenous space, Michael Hathaway (2010, 304) argues, pertains to "the ways that the concept of indigenous people is engaged with and used in specific locales at specific times." Examination of indigenous space requires posing questions of "how and why indigeneity becomes relevant or even possible, and how it changes over time"

(Hathaway 2010, 304). Following these inquiries, this article examines the land disputes of the Yomitan Airfield in Okinawa, how indigenous space has emerged, and the resultant new accounts and boundary politics of belonging and exclusion created through artful envisionings of indigenous space. Debates and disputes over the use of the Yomitan Airfield had long revolved in a circuit of Okinawan struggles for land rights, political autonomy, and culturally (and ethically) appropriate forms of governance. Through an examination of micro-level politics and indigenous notions of community ties in Okinawa, I argue that indigeneity has been used as a translocal tool of political organizing and resistance, in which local organizers and leaders can ground globally circulating discourse on indigenous rights to exert pressure on the state for the purposes of gaining community recognition, acknowledgment of cultural distinctiveness, and (at least limited) land use rights.

■ SHIFTING THE APPROACH FROM IDENTITY TO AGENCY

Published before the resolution, in 2007, of the United Nations Declarations on the Rights of Indigenous Peoples, Benedict Kingsbury's (1998, 422) article on the so-called Asian controversy argued that the language to describe the social and political concepts and "political consciousness of the modern territorial state" has made it difficult for people in Asia to apply international legal terms like "indigenous peoples" to their own populations. As Kingsbury noted, the transnational circulation of "indigeneity" has consistently gained traction on the ground when endorsing the recognition and the rights of indigenous peoples as a distinct group of people (see Baird 2015, 2016; Erni 2008; Gray 1995; Niezen 2003). In the case of Okinawa, a discourse of indigeneity puts pressure on the Japanese state's refusal to recognize Okinawans as such and any Okinawan claim over land based on indigenous rights of self-determination and sovereignty (Yokota 2015). As elsewhere in Asia, the various difficulties inherent in conceptualizing indigeneity continue to cause local controversies in its application (Keating 2013). The questions of who is indigenous and how we can determine who is are still under discussion by states and international organizations (Baird 2015, 55; Corntassel 2003), and not everyone acknowledges the term as an appropriate political tool for Okinawan self-determination.

As Hathaway (2010, 303) argues, it is important to see "indigenous people not as a natural category, but as a social and political category." My perspective also refuses to understand indigeneity as something natural or essential. Therefore I aim to move away from exploring indigeneity through identity politics of Okinawa/ns (which questions whether they are indigenous or not, for instance), focusing instead on questions of local agency to examine how, at which point, and to what extent, Okinawans have translated, adapted, and embraced various aspects of "indigeneity" for the purpose of practicing self-determination.

While the global circulation of indigenous rights discourse sounds appealing and promising, as Jeff Corntassel (2008, 2012) has shown, an overly tight focus on the language of rights often belies local agency as expressed through acts of land care "responsibility." Arguing that the fundamental point of indigenous struggles lies in "one's relational, place-based existence," Corntassel (2012, 89) suggests reframing indigenous self-determination by adding the concept of resurgence and everyday acts of renewal that focus more on relationships and responsibilities to the land and people. In this article, I follow Corntassel's lead and explore more of the complex nature of indigeneity and people's everyday relationship to the land in Okinawa. Adopting and adapting this approach opens crucial new pathways for exploring Okinawan politics, scholarship on which has heretofore been mainly dominated by narratives of oppression and suffering. Viewing contemporary Okinawan micropolitics instead through the lens of indigenous organizing around land responsibility opens a new vantage, recognizing the everyday agency of Okinawan villagers in sculpting their own self-determination.

My essay thus brings the fields of Okinawan studies, indigenous studies, and political science into a conversation. This article highlights how Okinawans have cautiously engaged with, taken up, adopted, and translated a discourse of indigeneity not only to resist military occupation but also to commit to and reactivate autochthonous understandings of belonging and communities' connections to lands, cultures, and spiritualities. This article fills in the gap that emerges when researchers study indigenous populations from the field of political science where the self-determination of indigenous people tends to be examined through rights-based political and legal frameworks (Corntassel 2008). This essay adds understandings of indigenous cultural values and ways of being that come along with, and are inseparable from, political self-determination. To the field of indigenous studies, which is still heavily situated in the Western settler societies, such as Australia, Canada, New Zealand, and the United States, my work contributes to expanding the theoretical concepts of indigeneity, settler colonialism, and militarism by extending these to the Okinawan case of challenging U.S. and Japanese empires. Finally, this essay intervenes in the field of Okinawan studies by moving beyond state-centered or settler-centered discourses of Okinawan indigeneity. I consider the extent to which Okinawan villagers' resistance and resurgence efforts align with global indigenous discourse, and I propose reconsidering the significance of local agency, political and economic aspirations, and cultural and spiritual understandings of the land, drawing connections between these indigenous narratives and local political movements.

■ CONTEXT: LAND GRABBING IN OKINAWA

Okinawa, the southernmost and most recently added administrative region of Japan, has gradually gained more international scholarly attention due to increasing media coverage of, and transnational protests by activists against, the ongoing issue of U.S. military base construction in northern Okinawa. Since 1996, activists and activist scholars from Okinawa have started articulating their indigeneity at the United Nations, going so far as to assert their right to self-determination over the land while contesting a disproportionate military occupation (Association of the Indigenous Peoples of the Ryukyus [AIPR] 2004). Okinawa prefecture, only 0.6 percent of Japanese national territory, has been burdened with approximately 74 percent of the U.S. military forces stationed in Japan (Okinawa Prefectural Government [OPG] 2016). These forces occupy 18 percent of the Okinawa Island, where much of the Okinawan population lives (OPG 2016). This article focuses on Yomitan village, located on the western coast of the central part of Okinawa Island.

In the history of Okinawa, major land grabbing occurred in three forms: state-building projects, war, and military occupation. First, the military invasion and the early formation of settler colonial space in the Ryukyuan Islands by the Japanese feudal domain of Satsuma was the major turning point in control over the land (Matsumura 2015, 28–33; Okinawa-ken [1972] 1977, 24–30). After the disposition of the Ryukyu Kingdom and the annexation of the newly designated territory of "Okinawa" within the context of modern Japanese nation-state building, Japan's Meiji government used two strategies to transform Okinawa's land use and economic structure significantly. One is the Preservation of Old Customs Policy (J: *Kyūkan onzon seisaku*) enacted by prefectural government officials, who were directly appointed by the Meiji state (Okinawa-ken [1972] 1977, 60–66). This policy aimed to preserve the old land divisions, administrative structures, and taxation while not allowing farmers to own land (61). With this policy, the Meiji government secured a monopoly to buy up and to make a significant profit from sugar production in Okinawa, which served as an intermediary until 1903 (Okinawa-ken [1972] 1977, 200; Ryūkyū Seifu [1972] 1989, 147, 343).

The other strategy of land grabbing was the Land Reorganization Project (J: *Tochi seiri jigyō*) begun in 1899, which converted much of the communal land to private ownership (Okinawa-ken [1972] 1977, 409; Ryūkyū

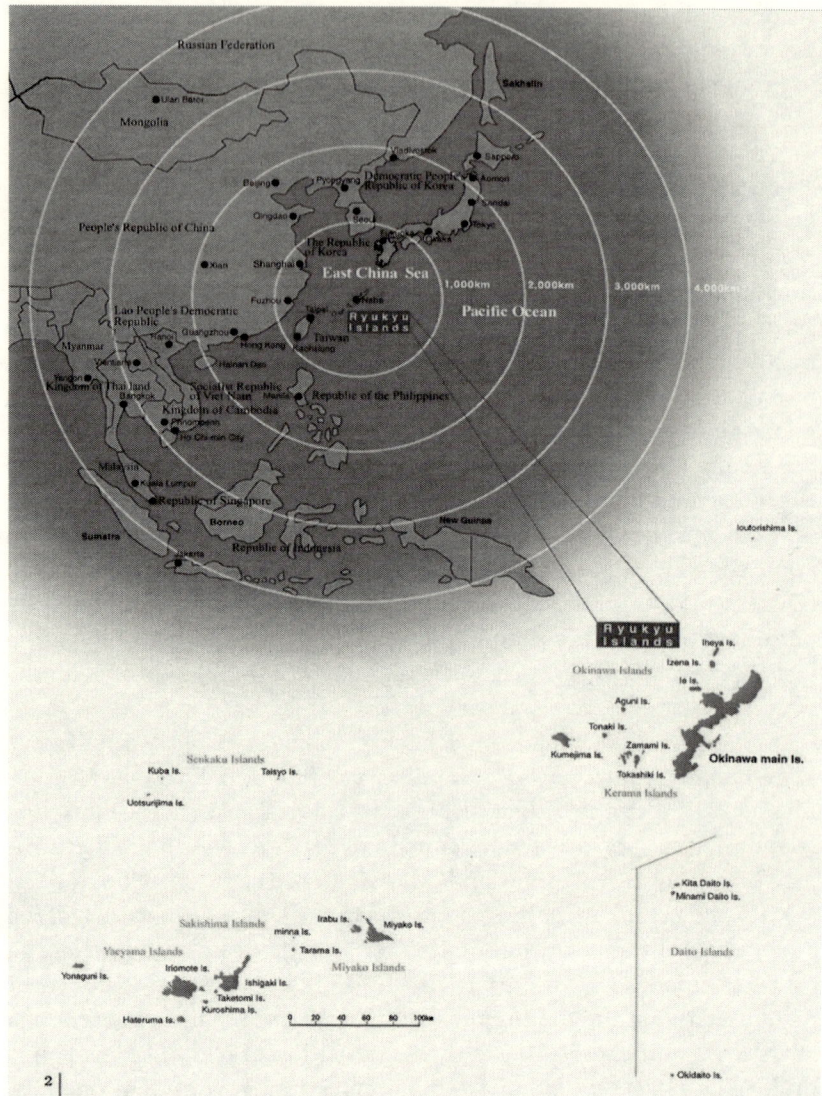

Figure 2. The location of Okinawa prefecture. Courtesy of Okinawa Prefectural Government.

Seifu [1972] 1989, 305–10). This project consolidated landownership into few parties (Okinawa-ken [1972] 1977, 429–36). This project also laid the foundation of unification of the administrative system under Imperial Japan (Okinawa-ken [1972] 1977, 434). Okinawa historians have pointed out that these two state strategies were significant factors that delayed the economic development of Okinawa (Okinawa-ken [1972] 1977, 429–36;

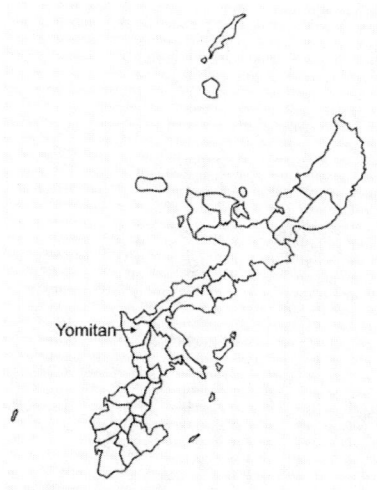

Figure 3. The location of Yomitan village in Okinawa Island.

Ryūkyū Seifu [1972] 1989). Meanwhile, the exploitation of the Okinawan economy in connection to the sugar industry served to support the Japanese capitalist development (Okinawa-ken [1972] 1977, 429–36).

Second, land grabbing through war involvement was carried out both by the Japanese and the U.S. armed forces. Before the American invasion of the island of Okinawa, the Japanese Army declared martial law and began constructing its army bases on various Okinawan islands (Okinawa-ken [1972] 1977, 464–79; Shimabukuro 2010; Yomitan-son Yakusho 1969, 220–21). The Japanese Empire, before World War II, emphasized developing a territorially unified national identity, positioning the Imperial family as a symbol of the Japanese nation (Okinawa-ken [1972] 1977, 464–79). Okinawan civilians gave up their farmland and homesteads for the sake of the Japanese emperor. Furthermore, the actual ground battle, which lasted from April to June 1945, physically and brutally damaged and displaced the indigenous peoples of Okinawa from their homeland.

Third, postwar land grabbing was carried out by U.S. military forces in two waves. Soon after the U.S. military landed on Okinawa Island, the U.S. Navy issued the Nimitz Proclamation and established the U.S. military government (Asato et al. 2004, 302). The U.S. military government of the Ryukyu Islands (1945–50) occupied the islands located south of 29 degrees north latitude and suspended the administrative and judicial powers of the Japanese government in these areas (Asato et al. 2004, 302). The U.S. military secured military bases by enclosing the necessary land as much as possible while they detained Japanese soldiers in prisoner of war camps and Okinawan residents in displaced person (DP) camps set up throughout the island. In 1951, the San Francisco Peace Treaty and the Security Treaty (ANPO) between Japan and the United States officially separated Okinawa from the rest of Japan to utilize the island for U.S. military reinforcement in the Far East. In 1953, the U.S. civil administration of Ryukyuan Islands (1950–72) in Okinawa issued the Land Acquisition Procedure, during the implementation of which its military, with bayonets and bulldozers, forced farmers and landowners to relinquish their lands (Asato et al. 2004, 304).

The legal backing of land seizure by the U.S. military galvanized a sense of crisis among Okinawans and triggered a majority of them to stand up and join in a demilitarization movement, which is locally known as "the island-wide struggles" (Asato et al. 2004; Tanji 2006). The island-wide land struggles eventually led Okinawans to demand immediate and unconditional restitution of military land and Okinawa's reversion to Japanese administration (Asato et al. 2004). Today, the U.S. military occupation continues in Okinawa, even though, officially speaking, forty-six years have passed since Okinawa was "returned" to Japanese administration.

In the following pages, I examine both external and internal forces that have encouraged and obstructed efforts to mobilize native people with respect to their use of land. Conflicts over land in Okinawa are not homogenous. Okinawan struggles for the land are multilayered in ways that challenge and empower people to reinvigorate indigenous space. On many occasions, indigenous land claims focus too much on who owns the land, who is entitled to it, and who can be defined as the indigenous people. The result is that other forms of being in the place are left out of the picture, although different modes of engagement with the land have also contributed to our understanding of indigeneity and have been carried out in social movements and through rural livelihoods.

In Okinawa, autochthonous understandings of communities' connection to lands, cultures, and spiritualities, although still present and active, have been overtaken by a rights-based conception of being "indigenous" and have been replaced by a nation-state projection of land, power, and belonging. First, I describe the historical organizations and orientations of communities in Yomitan. I discuss what has changed and what has remained stable in terms of social belonging throughout the processes of postwar displacement and relocation. I show that genealogical and cultural connections have played tremendous roles in shaping spatial and political claims to the land in Yomitan. Next, I delve into the trajectory of land use disputes over the past forty-six years since Okinawa's reversion to Japanese administration in 1972. The restoration of the former military airfield that I examine in this article highlights internal political tensions under the Japanese state. I illustrate several phases of indigenous land claims and examine various strategies that Okinawans have adopted to mark, zone, claim, occupy, and access the militarized land. Finally, I close by revisiting Okinawan indigeneity and what it reveals about processes of making indigenous space. Throughout, I argue that the understanding and use of "indigeneity" by Okinawans has changed and reemerged as a new component within international political identification and regarding issues of landownership, entitlement, and access.

MICROCOMMUNITY: *AZA* POLITICS, PEOPLE, LAND, BELONGING, AND POWER

A community is a form of abstract social organizing that develops, evolves, includes, and excludes members. Formations of communities similarly engage a variety of elements, including people, history, climate, geography, social and political conditions, and legal structures. Therefore characteristics of a community are diverse in their orientation, definitions, conditions, and activities. In Japan since 1940, micro-level community organizations called *jichi-kai* 自治会 or *chōnai-kai* 町内会 (J: neighborhood associations) have become institutionalized and unified by the central government through the enactment of community association maintenance policies (Nakachi 1989, 203; Nakata 2017). These policies were implemented by the state for the top-down management of its population and to urge the modernization of the nation (Nakachi 1989; Nakata 2017). In mainland Japan, *jichi-kai* (J: neighborhood associations) cover their own territory and population. Its membership is based on households rather than individuals. A *jichi-kai* is responsible for a wide variety of activities, ranging from organizing cultural events to providing disaster management assistance (Nakata 2017).

The Okinawan communities discussed in this article are slightly different from Japanese *jichi-kai* and administrative districts in terms of how communities have historically evolved and survived "diasporically."[4] Okinawan microcommunities are integrally interrelated with the lands of specific villages and locales. Cultural and spiritual connections and attachment to the land are notably strong at a village level. Furthermore, the Okinawan understanding of "community" (O: *shima*)[5] does not correspond with racialized or affiliation-based organizing like those often found in Western, settler colonial societies. Thus though Okinawan indigeneity has been shaped by multiple waves of displacement (whether Japanese annexation or the U.S.-led militarization of land), the conceptual structure of indigeneity in Okinawa cannot be understood solely in terms of nativity versus settler colonialism. Nor is Okinawan indigeneity commensurate with "*minority minzu* (nationality)" (Yeh 2007, 82; Elliott 2015, 186) or "heritage-residents" (Elliott 2015, 211; Luo 2018, 95) ideas of indigenous peoples, as articulated by other Asian states. Rather, Okinawan indigeneity hybridizes both models on an intensively local scale that might be termed *micro-indigeneity*.

In rural Okinawa, microcommunities under the municipal level have been called *aza,* and *aza* is used as a unit system with a community name. For example, in Yomitan, there are twenty-three microcommunities, such as *aza* Sobe, *aza* Kina, and *aza* Zakimi. These *aza* are self-governing entities slightly different from the administrative-based neighborhoods. Some communities own a community hall called *aza kōminkan,* which serves as a place for the members to gather and hold events and meetings. Predominant members of a community are the residents, who historically live around the area, their descendants, and newcomers, who have moved into the area by marriage.

Aza serve four main functions.[6] First, an *aza* generates a cultural sense of belonging to the community. In general, the governing body of each *aza* takes responsibility for performing the traditional ceremonies and rituals of a community. Sacred sites in the area are usually preserved and maintained by representatives and volunteers of the *aza.* Each *aza* also encourages preserving and teaching youth and children folk cultures, such as dance, music, and theater, that are associated with and unique to a particular place and people. Second, each *aza* functions as a self-governing body. Each community holds events and activities, such as a sports day and a clean-up day. Third, the *aza* plays a role as a subsidiary organization of the municipality. Yomitan village, for instance, delegates administrative tasks to each *aza* community. Fourth, the *aza* serves as an intermediary between community members and the municipality.

Geographical and demographical boundaries between communities are often ambiguous. Some people are members of the community where they grow up. Others join the community organization to which their parents belong, regardless of their own place of current residence. Based on these characteristics, Nakachi Hiroshi[7] (1989) argues that communities in Yomitan are genealogy based, while those in other towns of Okinawa are mostly place-based organizations. Each community has slightly different characteristics. Theses "genealogy-based" communities in Yomitan have been disrupted and reconstructed by two historical processes of land grabbing—the Preservation of Old Customs Policy in the early Meiji period and the ongoing presence of the U.S. military (Nakachi 1989).

The annexation of the Ryukyu Kingdom in 1879 made Okinawa into an

Figure 4. Twenty-three *aza* communities of Yomitan. Names in a circle indicate communities that relocated after villagers' displacement and dispossession of the land.

internal colony of Japan and placed Okinawans in a "second-class citizen" status. The Preservation of Old Customs Policy was the Meiji government's strategy to delay land reform in Okinawa. Under this policy, the premodern system of collective landholding (J: *jiwari seido*), taxation, and the Ryukyuan *magiri*[8] governance was maintained. While the Japanese state had carried out land reform in 1873 in the other parts of Japan, the old land tenure system remained in Okinawa until 1903 (see Asato et al. 2004; Nakachi 1989; Ryūkyū Seifu [1972] 1989). In *The Limits of Okinawa: Japanese Capitalism, Living Labor, and Theorizations of Community*, Wendy Matsumura (2015, 49) describes how the Preservation of Old Customs Policy turned Okinawa into a "domestic site of sugar extraction" to serve the rapid economic development of Japan as a nation-state. While Okinawan farmers were exploited in the system of capitalist accumulation, labor and heavy taxation implanted a sense of "common" responsibility among agrarian villagers (Nakachi 1989).

Comparing various colonial situations in Asia, Tania Li (2010) argues that indigeneity is a socially constructed concept and coemerged with capitalism through the process of colonialism. Borrowing Li's perspective on a critical role of capitalist dispossession in making indigenous subjects, I claim that indigeneity in Okinawa was constructed by and coemerged with the Preservation of Old Customs Policy, in which a colonial and capitalist project by the Japanese state pressured the Okinawan populations to restrict their mobility in a particular geographical area while maintaining the customary tenure system. This intermeshing of Okinawan indigeneity and Japanese colonialism is not surprising when one considers how the Japanese government simultaneously implemented assimilationist policies and encouraged simplification of indigenous languages and customs (Asato et al. 2004, 292; Okinawa-ken [1972] 1977, 816–19). Therefore the "indigeneity" constructed and used to refer to Okinawans at that time was a product of Japan's colonial projects that fixed people in time, representing them as a static and stagnant culture.

Moreover, repeated dispossessions and forced dislocations of communities have helped to foster a collective spirit and subjectivity for self-governance among villagers. After Japan's surrender in World War II, the administrative rule of Okinawa transferred from Japan to the United States via the Peace Treaty of San Francisco. Establishing the U.S. Civilian Administration of the Ryukyus (USCAR), the U.S. military took control of and priority over all administrative, legislative, and judicial powers in Okinawa. As mentioned earlier, the 1953 Land Acquisition Procedure issued by USCAR forced farmers and landowners to hand over their lands. With the military fortification of the island, indigenous communities in Okinawa underwent repeated processes of dispossession and repossession of their lands.

In postwar Yomitan, the areas released for residents to return from DP camps were limited. Therefore many of dispossessed villagers ended up moving to a neighboring area different from their original homeland. For example, the postwar military occupation made the people of *aza* Uza move to *aza* Takashiho and Nagahama (Figure 4). While losing physical access to the ancestral land, Uza people built the Uza Community Hall for gathering and maintained a cohesive sense of belonging with a hope of returning to their land in the future (Yomitan-son Kyōikuiinkai Bunkasōgōka 2014). The Uza community continued to function as an autonomous body with the authority of this invented space as known as "Uza Community Hall." Just like other *aza*, the Uza community organizes traditional ceremonies and community events in their community hall in Nagahama. Ceremonies and rituals held by Uza still cherish the genealogical connection to the "original" Uza area rather than Nagahama. As a result, in Nagahama, there are two genealogy-based communities, Nagahama and Uza. In this manner, in Yomitan, names of *aza* communities indicate not only places but also groups of people, who identify themselves and trace their ancestral roots to particular places. *Aza* community halls then are considered important as meeting places and spaces in which to exercise governance of the community.

Development of contemporary *aza* communities in Yomitan is complicated locally. This genealogy-based organizing of micro-unit communities certainly exists as an extension of collective landholdings and major land dispossessions imposed from the outside. This matrix of overlapping community spaces further increases in complexity when other forms of occupying and claiming the space are brought into consideration.

▪ MAKING INDIGENOUS SPACE ON MILITARIZED LAND

What I refer to as Yomitan Airfield in this article is an area located at the center of the village. In the airfield, there was a 1.2-mile-long runway and a 1-mile-long taxiway (Yomitan-son 1983; see Figures 5 and 6). While remnants of the airfield are still there, the area is now open to a vast sky with sugarcane fields, a few blocks of greenhouses, new roads that run by a government office, a public school, and a farmer's market. In 2006, village organizers, including those involved in envisioning the Phoenix Plan, reaped the rewards of long years of community organizing when 191 hectares of the airfield were transferred officially from U.S. military control and usage returned to the Okinawan community (Okinawa-ken Yomitan-son 2005, 7). This achievement of the land restoration reflects more than sixty years of native struggles. With the phoenix vision of Yomitan, the former airfield is seen in the midst of a significant trans-formation, a repossession of—and artful re-creation of—indigenous space. Here I reconstruct the main steps that Yomitan leaders took over the last half-century, steps that ultimately resulted in partial reposses-sion of the airfield.

"Is Yomitan Airfield state land?" As soon as the political regime of Okinawa changed, elders of the *aza* Zakimi community raised the ques-tion (Shimabukuro 2010, 6). Upon Okinawa's return to the Japanese administration in 1972, villagers learned that the Yomitan Airfield was registered as a state property, which the U.S. Army was using for para-chute training. Under the falling parachutes, villagers were working in the field growing sugarcane and sweet potatoes. Villagers were bothered by helicopters circling overhead and by the risk of falling objects that had caused fatal accidents in the past (Shimabukuro 2010). Okinawans at that time anchored their hopes on the reversion to the Japanese ad-ministration to stop the military occupation and control of the island. However, the reversion did not change the situation in a way that many Okinawans wished, at least not for the people from Zakimi, the former landowners and residents of the Yomitan Airfield. A series of colonial projects on Okinawan land had historically and systematically pushed native people out of their ancestral land for the sake of a Japanese nation-state. Okinawa after the reversion faced a mountain full of unprecedent-ed issues that raised questions about who was responsible for the dis-

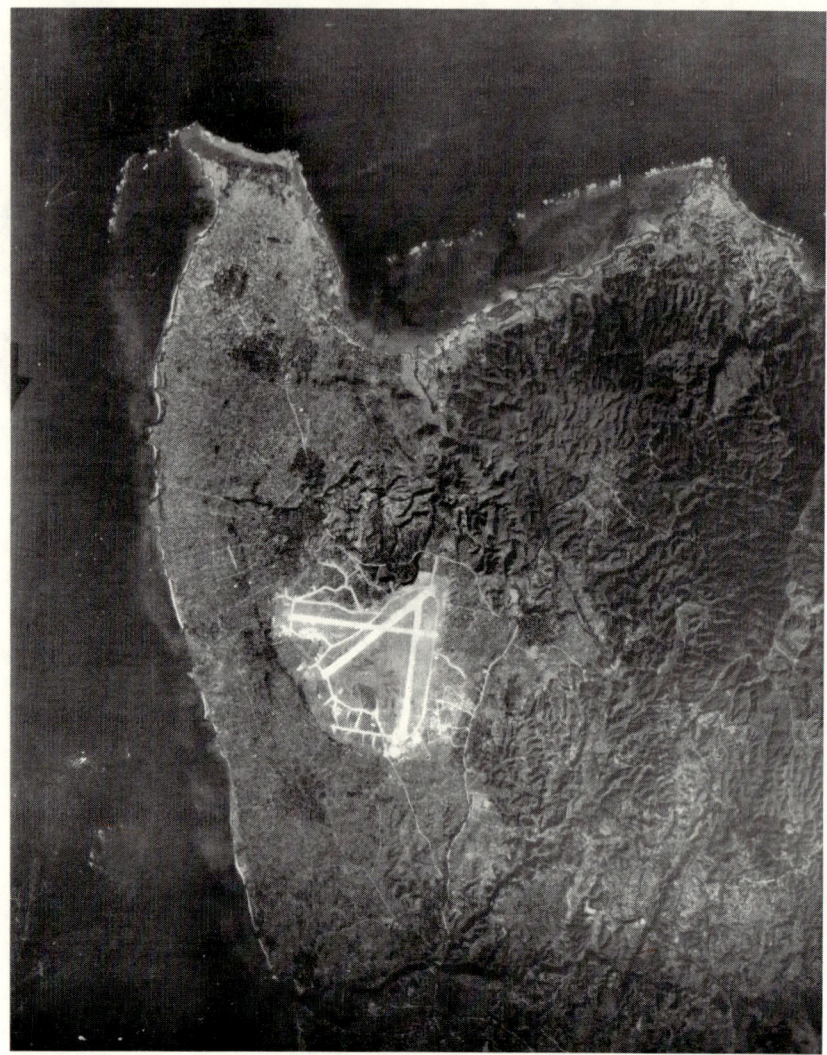

Figure 5. An aerial photograph of Yomitan village taken by the U.S. military on January 3, 1945. The Yomitan Airfield, which the Japanese Imperial Army had prepared to engage the enemy, was located at the center of the village. Courtesy of Yomitan village.

placement and dispossession that happened over the course of the war.

As the title of Yomitan Airfield became a hot topic of conversation among senior residents in the Zakimi community, four men from the community soon volunteered to conduct fact-finding research on whether the Yomitan Airfield was state land and how it had become so (Shimabukuro 2010, 4). These men collected information, interviewed people concerned,

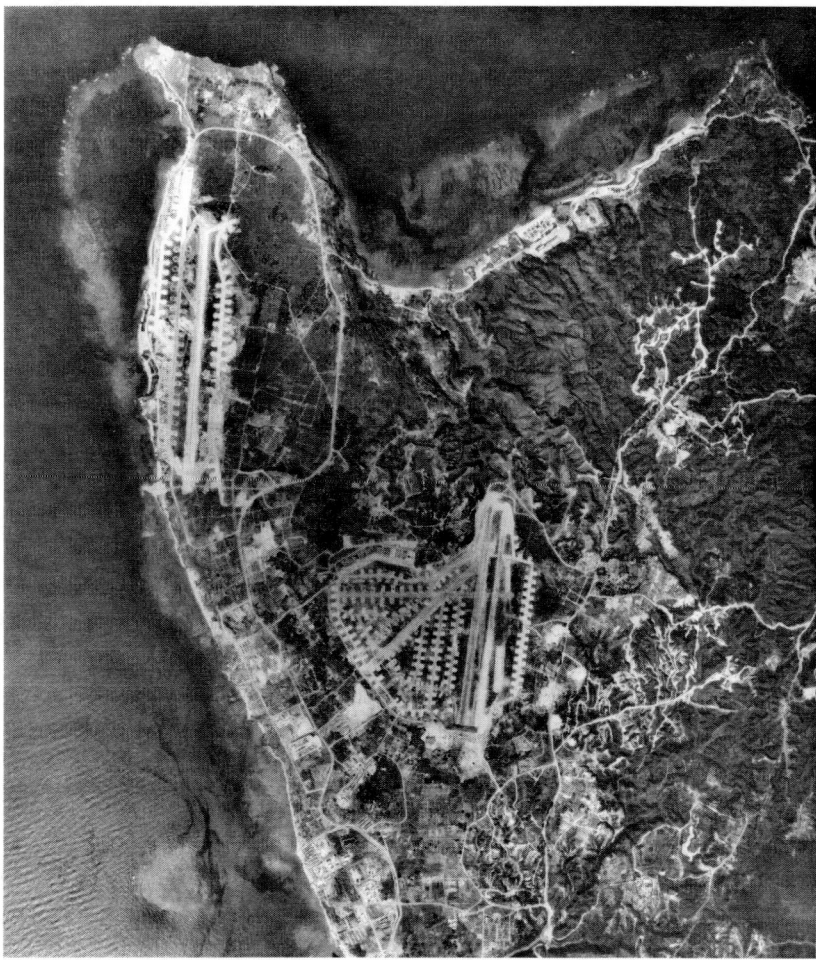

Figure 6. An aerial photograph of Yomitan village taken by the U.S. military on December 10, 1945. Eight months after the U.S. military landing on the island, the U.S. military expanded the Yomitan Airfield and constructed the Bolo Airfield on the coastline. Courtesy of Yomitan village.

and submitted a report to the *aza* Zakimi Community Board. Receiving the report, the board soon set up a meeting with nineteen representatives from the village assembly, the senior group, the youth group, the women's group, and so on (Shimabukuro 2010, 4). Residents of Zakimi remembered that five *aza* communities, Zakimi being the largest, had previously occupied the area where the Yomitan Airfield was constructed. On June 12, 1973, the *aza* Zakimi Community Board formally inaugurated a coalition to restore ownership of the Yomitan Airfield with more than 150 "former landowners" (J: *kyū jinushi*) and concerned people (Shimabukuro 2010, 4). With the participation of "former landowners" from other *aza* communities, an endless battle over the acquisition of Yomitan Airfield landownership began.

■ PHASE 1: THE QUESTION OF OWNERSHIP

"The Yomitan Airfield is not state land. Per Article 15 of the National Mobilization Act, the airfield should be returned to landowners. Its usage can be discussed later" (Shimabukuro 2010, 6). The four Zakimi men, who submitted the written report, made this clear statement based on their three-year-long voluntary research. The request report included a description of the traditional land tenure system in Okinawa, the agricultural situation in Yomitan, and the National Mobilization Act, which had drastically changed the political situation of Okinawa/ns.

The construction of Yomitan Airfield for the Japanese Imperial Army began in 1943 as an operation to protect Japan from its enemies (Shimabukuro 2010). Upon conducting a preliminary survey for the airfield construction in Yomitan, Lieutenant Colonel Jin Naomichi made a verbal promise to landowners for the return of the land when the Japanese Army no longer required the airfield (Shimabukuro 2010, 11; Yomitan-son 1983, 24). Because of their urgent need for the land, the Japanese Imperial Army decided on the tactic of land seizure and offered compensation for cultivated products and house evictions. The compensation and eviction fees were paid through the purchase of government bonds instead of cash payments (Shimabukuro 2010, 11). Unfortunately for villagers, in the confusion of wartime, such forms of money turned out to be inaccessible and useless. The postwar government has never bought back these bonds, leaving the villagers without any compensation to this day (Shimabukuro 2010, 11; Yomitan-son 1983, 22).

The Zakimi people stated, "It was not too much to say that was compulsory relocation" (Shimabukuro 2010, 11). Under the pressure of the wartime regime and the National Mobilization Act, airfield construction was executed without providing an option for landowners to reject it. No matter how Zakimi landowners recalled or regretted the past, the then-Japanese citizens had been forced to follow the national policy. People who resisted were treated as unpatriotic and suffered sanction (Shimabukuro 2010, 11; Yomitan-son Yakusho 1969). Many citizens believed cooperation with the military was the duty of the Japanese Imperial subjects (Shimabukuro 2010, 11). It was also common for villagers to offer their land and donate the eviction fee to the state (Shimabukuro 2010,

11). Meanwhile, there were also landowners who became involuntarily engulfed in giving up their land. For example, Tōyama Seitoku testified that his land was condemned for the airfield while he was absent, in Tinian Island (Shimabukuro 2010, 187).[9] In the end, prewar Japanese Imperialism created a situation in which approximately 256.1 hectares of the property in Yomitan were occupied and used by the military free of cost (Okinawa-ken Yomitan-son 2005, 7).[10] The airfield was constructed on the private properties of more than six hundred different landowners (Shimabukuro 2010, 26).

The main request by the Zakimi men was to regain ownership of the land from the state, as provided for under Japanese law (Shimabukuro 2010, 6). The first step for the landowners' coalition, therefore, was to testify to the indigenous presence of "former landowners," the chaotic process of land seizure, and the need for war reparations. Meanwhile, villagers requested that the state clarify how Yomitan Airfield had become state property. The response by the National Property Division was unsatisfactory to the villagers. While the state claimed that there were land sales contracts, under war conditions, there was no record found of either purchasing or renting the land from indigenous landowners (Yomitan Hikōjō Yōchi Shuken Kaifuku Jinushikai 1980, 6).

In response, indigenous landowners' counteractions and resistance took various forms and emphasized their ancestral relationship to the land. They soon started gathering testimony explaining the absence of land sales contracts. They also created a detailed map of the area based on aerial photographs and their memories of the prewar communities (Yomitan Hikōjō Yōchi Shuken Kaifuku Jinushikai 1980). It is worth noting that indigenous landowners added in their request statement, "For farmers, the land is the source of life. It is the place to converse with ancestors' spirits, and it is the spirits of ancestors themselves" (Shimabukuro 2010, 6). Thus not only did these previous landowners claim the economic importance of the land for farmers but they also stressed their cultural and spiritual attachment to the land. They believed that their elders or youths would repeatedly raise the airfield issue before the government could succeed in whitewashing history (Shimabukuro 2010, 6).

The core of the problem was that the Yomitan Airfield was managed by the state as a state property without fact-checking of its title. Under the postwar constitution, the state had merely claimed the Yomitan Airfield and offered it to the U.S. Army. Without enough material proof of the title, communication between the indigenous landowners and the state came to a deadlock (Yomitan-son 1983).

■ PHASE 2: CLAIMING "COLLECTIVE" LANDOWNERSHIP

In 1979, the deadlock situation slowly changed to a path to reconcilia-tion. After repeated Diet proceedings over landownership, the Okinawa Development Agency,[11] which was established to promote infrastruc-ture after Okinawa's reversion to Japan, suggested employing the Act on Special Measures concerning Promotion and Development of Okinawa of 1971 (Yomitan-son 1983, 26). With an effort to negotiate a solution in a step-by-step manner, the state suggested Yomitan village come up with planning for the effective use of the state land (Yomitan-son 1983, 21–39). With local government planning, the state intended to grant the airfield to Yomitan village eventually. While the dispute over the landownership between the state and indigenous landowners was not settled, Yomitan village invested a large budget in developing the Yo-mitan Airfield Conversion Plan, involving a series of consultations and discussions with the committee members, including assemblymen, village officials, scholars, former landowners, farmers, senior groups, women's groups, local economic organizations, and *aza* community board leaders (Yomitan-son 1983). While the consultation gave priority to the will of former landowners, the planning as a village, with expected land restora-tion as a village property, underpinned villagers' intentions of collective landownership.

In contrast to the steady progress in local government planning, how-ever, the process of land restoration from the U.S. military was proceeding at a slow pace. According to an official at the National Property Division, who was unwilling to go forward with Yomitan's Conversion Plan, then mayor Yamauchi Tokushin specifically pledged to make space for Yomitan villagers by adding a plausible feng shui theory of "indigenous" land use (Yamauchi 2014; Figure 1). Yamauchi explained how feng shui of the land would assure the importance of public space in the middle of Yomitan Airfield, although he later wrote in his autobiography that he was un-certain about the feng shui of the place at the time he spoke to the state officials (Yamauchi 2014, 95). Later, Yamauchi sent village officials to a feng shui specialist in Korea and confirmed that the prewar indigenous community was located and oriented well according to the principle of feng shui (Yamauchi 2014, 96). Fortunately, Yamauchi's feng shui theory worked to provide the reason for the village to build public facilities in the middle of the military airfield.

On June 29, 1995, the Japanese–U.S. Special Action Committee on Okinawa (SACO) agreed on joint use of the Yomitan Airfield by the Yo-mitan village (Yamauchi 2014, 106).[12] In this way, making "indigenous space" on the military land was successful. The construction of the village office at the center of the airfield was completed in 1997, and the villagers celebrated its inauguration as an "edifice of self-governance, decentralization, participation, democracy, and peace" (Yamauchi 2014, 111). Although the permission provided only for "interim use," the repossession and use of the airfield by the village opened a new space for the community. Through self-organization and the reconfiguration of space, the village successfully refuted the military use of indigenous space and regenerated the landscape as a democratic hub for deliberating alternative futures. It is not clear how convincing Yamauchi's theorization of the landscape's feng shui was for the state officials. However, for the villagers, creating a community space with a land-based vision on the militarized area was a redefining moment, a reclaiming of colonized space by indigenous hands, minds, and spirits and the beginning of exercising autonomy over the space where public meetings could be hosted and cultural events could be held. It was meaningful for villagers that local governance could be exercised on the land that everyone worked together to regain through protests and planning.

In December 1996, SACO approved the final report that promised the total return of the entire airfield by 2000 (Yomitan-son 2013b). Although the return proceeded behind schedule, the ownership of the airfield was transferred from the state to the village through the land-space exchange. Yomitan sold a smaller piece of village property currently occupied by the U.S. military for the exchange with a total of 222.8 hectares of state property, which was known as the Yomitan Airfield (Yomitan-son 2013b; *Ryukyu Shimpō* 2006). Yamauchi reflects on this land restoration process:

> The power of the U.S. military and the state is big. When the weak stand against the strong, we cannot resist by force. That is why we thought carefully and rendered "artful ways." Meanwhile, we continued asking for "compassion" from the U.S. military and police officers. Even if they had a duty to stop our protests, I believed there was something that connected us as human beings. (Yamauchi 2014, 74, my translation)

Interestingly, Yamauchi often shares the story of when he met a U.S. Army garrison representative in Yomitan to request the land return to Yomitan people. Yamauchi (2001, 232–35) well remembers that the representative replied to Yamauchi saying that he was a Native American descendant and understood Yamauchi's feeling about land struggle. This meeting with a Native American military commander seems to have made a strong impression on Yamauchi, causing him to realize the complexity within U.S. militarism and to reflect on indigenous commonalities within legacies of colonialism.

While standing firmly for indigenous land repossession and the self-governance of Yomitan, Yamauchi was aware of one rural municipality's weakness to counteract the state and the U.S. military. So, invoking a tactic of strategic essentialism, he orchestrated a range of cultural and ethical diplomacy and passionately encouraged the villagers to restore indigenous cultural practices and traditions while aiming to renew the sense of pride among Yomitan people. Yamauchi set up spaces and places to produce indigenous textiles and pottery. His actions to promote these indigenous products added recognition and value to them. He also unprecedentedly laid out the village's Master Plan in the local language (Okinawa-ken Yomitan-son 1989; Yamauchi 2014, 132–35). Yamauchi (2014, 132, my translation) noted, "Language is a precious cultural heritage of each place. I think the language used to convey the future of Yomitan, which aims to become a self-sustainable community, should be our language." While physically remaking "indigenous" space through land restoration and development for Yomitan, Yamauchi's cultural promotion expanded the people's sense of belonging and the scales of indigenous identification to fit in a postreversion political structure. Moreover, sketching out Yomitan's landscape and the government plan in the local language, which was once strictly banned by the state, showed the connection between places and indigenous knowledge and opened possibilities of indigenous resurgence that are grounded in and convey their worldviews and value systems.

■ CONCLUSION: RETHINKING OKINAWAN INDIGENEITY

Since the 1990s, Okinawans have increasingly expressed their indigeneity, invoking human rights discourse to seek justice from the continuity of colonial subordination in the form of militarization (United Nations Declaration on the Rights of Indigenous Peoples, for instance) (AIPR 2004; Uemura 2003; Yokota 2015). The promotion of cultural assimilation and the building of Japanese national borders have limited indigenous Ainu and Okinawan social activities and exchanges on the frontier, politically positioning them as "internal others" (Graburn and Ertl 2010, 6; Uemura 2003). Ainu and Okinawans were reductively imagined as an "invisible" and/or "vanishing" population of Japan's geographic peripheries (Graburn and Ertl 2010, 4).

The Japanese government has not yet recognized Okinawans as a distinctive group of people who hold indigenous rights;[13] rather, the government reduced these rights by stressing the ambiguity of the term *Ryūkyū minzoku* (J: Ryukyuan nation) (see also *Ryukyu Shimpō* 2008) and by raising concerns about the disruption of "national and political unity, or territorial integrity" (UN General Assembly Department of Public Information 2007).

While "indigenous" is a relatively new political identity for Okinawans, incorporating transnational solidarities and participation in global social movements (Siddle 2003; Uemura 2003; Yokota 2015), an understanding of Okinawan indigeneity should not be confined to categories of nation or race (i.e., J: *minzoku*), as classified by the Japanese state.[14] Rather, the repossession of the Yomitan Airfield shows when, how, and to what extent "indigeneity" matters in the contemporary land politics of Okinawa. While being "indigenous" has functioned as a mobilizing tool to restore control over one's living space from undesirable occupation and authority, being "indigenous" has also required recognizing "new coalitions and scales of identification" (Clifford 2007, 204). The interactive indigenous place-making process expanded and fostered people's sense of belonging in broader spatial and cultural scales.

An "indigenous" space in Yomitan envisioned with the phoenix has emerged through a discourse of landownership in the villagers' relations to multiple subjectivities. Indigeneity is not only constructed relative to the state and the foreign military but is also assembled on top of the complex relationship between the indigenous landowners and the landless. In the process of dealing with the modern law-governed nation-state, local understandings of "indigenous" space have gradually shifted from a cultural- and genealogical-based sense of belonging and communities to the rights-based membership, entitlement, and management of a community. A rhetoric of governing memberships, rights, authorities, responsibilities, and contributions became relevant for the people in Yomitan to reconceptualize indigeneity by using a contemporary legal framework of land management. Then the discourse of indigeneity emerged from people's efforts to secure "indigenous" living space in a modern political structure and became a voice for Okinawan self-determination.

This article has demonstrated that, rather than just engaging in state-centered and rights-centered discourses, Okinawans have invented and carried out a range of everyday actions and reconceptions of land that are key to indigenous space making for themselves. Historical practices of community governance and land use suggest Okinawan indigeneity be reconfigured with people, land, belonging, and power. As Hathaway (2010, 322) argues, indigeneity is "a process of continuing emergence," and we can see here that various conceptualizations of indigeneity are deeply enmeshed and submerged in rural Okinawan land struggles. Behind the scene of successful Okinawan resistance to the U.S. military occupation, making "indigenous space" meant that conceptions of space, power, and belonging competed throughout the land restoration process. While these entangled knots and conceptual dominance of the land with ownership, entitlement, and membership have pushed some actors to the margins, alternative imaginings of "indigenous" space anchor people's attachment to the land and play an important role in shaping a new political identity and sense of belonging for indigenous Okinawans.

Megumi Chibana holds a PhD in political science (Indigenous politics) from the University of Hawai'i at Mānoa.

■ NOTES

I would like to thank Dr. Michael Hathaway for reviewing an earlier draft of this article and Dr. Noenoe K. Silva for her patience, encouragement, and generous mentorship. This essay also benefited from my participation in the Asian Studies Summer Institute at Pennsylvania State University. I am grateful for comments and extensive knowledge shared by Dr. Pasang Yangjee Sherpa, Dr. Neal Keating, Dr. Charlotte Eubanks, and other participants. Finally, I wish to thank the two anonymous referees and the *Verge* editorial board for their invaluable feedback on this article.

1. Unless otherwise indicated, translations are mine.

2. In support of indigenous language revitalization efforts, I include both Okinawan and Japanese words. When Okinawan- and Japanese-language terms are listed first in the original language, an English translation follows in parentheses. *O* indicates Okinawan language origin, and *J* indicates Japanese language origin. *O/J* indicates the mixed use of Okinawan and Japanese. When English translations are listed first, the original term in romanization follows in parentheses. Romanization of Japanese language is adopted from Barry (1997). Romanization of Okinawan is from the transcription in Sakihara (2006).

3. Indeed, the last line of the poem was changed from "*Mura nu miati* (O: is the guideline of the village)" to "*Ganjuu nu shima* (O: is a healthy community)" in 2008 (Yomitan-son 2013a).

4. I say "diasporically" here because of the history of displacement, endurance, and mobilization of communities from its original homeland. I also imply the fact that Okinawan diasporic communities in the world (especially in Hawai'i) organize subgroups and identify their ancestral connections by village-level or *aza*-level communities.

5. The Okinawan term *shima* has been used equivalently to *aza* and *mura*, while *shima* refers to cultural understandings of a community (Okinawa Daihyakkajiten 1983). In this essay, I use *aza* to highlight its implication of administrative boundaries.

6. For more on *aza* functions, see Nakachi (1989).

7. In both the text and references, Japanese names in Japanese-

language publications are listed following traditional usage (the family name followed by the given name).

8. *Magiri* is a type of administrative district of the Ryukyu Kingdom. Each *magiri* had several villages and was controlled by a local chief, *aji*. After the Japanese government issued the Okinawa Prefectural Islands Municipality Organization Policy (J: *Okinawa-ken tōsho chō-son sei* 沖縄県島嶼町村制) in 1908, a traditional land division and governing unit system *magiri* 間切 (O: *majiri*) became *mura* 村, and the smallest unit *mura* became *aza* 字 (Yomitan-son Yakusho 1969).

9. An Okinawan landowner, Tōyama Seitoku, was fifty-eight years old when he wrote a testifying report in 1977. He claimed that he emigrated to Tinian in 1938 and returned to Okinawa in August 1946 (Shimabukuro 2010, 187).

10. The land area the Japanese Army used does not necessarily coincide precisely with the Yomitan Airfield the U.S. military used (Okinawa-ken Yomitan-son 2005, 7).

11. The Okinawa Development Agency is a cabinet-level administrative agency established by the Prime Minister's Office when Okinawa returned to the Japanese administration in 1972. The agency operates independently from the prefectural government of Okinawa. In 2001, the Prime Minister's Office became the Cabinet Office.

12. The installation of Japanese facilities on the military land was possible based on the Japanese–U.S. Status of Forces Agreement Article II 4 (a), which sets forth, "When facilities and areas are temporarily not being used by the United States armed forces, the Government of Japan may make, or permit Japanese nationals to make, interim use of such facilities and areas provided that it is agreed between the two Governments through the Joint Committee that such use would not be harmful to the purposes for which the facilities and areas are normally used by the United States armed force" (Ministry of Foreign Affairs of Japan 1960).

13. In 2008, the Japanese government passed a resolution to recognize the Ainu as an indigenous people.

14. The Japanese government used "the Japanese national" and "the Japanese race" interchangeably to respond to Okinawan assertions to cultural rights and land rights. For example, see "Comments of the Japanese Government on the Concluding Observations Adopted by the Committee on the Elimination of Racial Discrimination on March 20, 2000, Regarding Initial and Second Periodic Report of the Japanese Government, 1-(2)-a" and "Replies to the List of Questions by the Country Rapporteur in Connection with the Consideration of the Third to Sixth Periodic Report, Question 18, no. 1" (Ministry of Foreign Affairs of Japan 2000, 2010).

More studies are needed to examine translations and uses of the Japanese *minzoku* in relation to Okinawan claims to indigeneity.

■ WORKS CITED

Asato Susumu 安里進, Dana Masayuki 田名真之, Maehira Fusaaki 真栄平房昭, Nishizato Kikou 西里喜行, Takara Kurayoshi 高良倉吉, and Tomiyama Kazuyuki 豊見山和行. 2004. *Okinawaken no rekishi* 沖縄県の歴史 [History of Okinawa prefecture]. Tokyo: Yamakawa Shuppansha.

Association of the Indigenous Peoples of the Ryukyus. 2004. *Q&A Kokusai jinkenhou to Ryukyu/Okinawa* Q&A 国際人権法と琉球・沖縄 [Q&A International human-rights law and Ryukyu/Okinawa]. Okinawa, Japan: Chatan Insatsu.

Baird, Ian G. 2015. "Translocal Assemblages and the Circulation of the Concept of 'Indigenous Peoples' in Laos." *Political Geography* 46: 54–64.

Baird, Ian G. 2016. "Indigeneity in Asia: An Emerging but Contested Concept." *Asian Ethnicity* 17, no. 4: 501–5.

Barry, Randall K, ed. 1997. *ALA-LC Romanization Tables: Transliteration Schemes for Non-Roman Scripts*. Washington, D.C.: Library of Congress Cataloging Distribution Service. http://www.loc.gov/catdir/cpso/romanization/japanese.pdf.

Clifford, James. 2007. "Varieties of Indigenous Experiences: Diasporas, Homelands, Sovereignties." In *Indigenous Experience Today,* edited by Marisol de la Cadena and Orin Star, 197–224. New York: Berg.

Corntassel, Jeff. 2003. "Who Is Indigenous? 'Peoplehood' and Ethnonationalist Approaches to Rearticulating Indigenous Identity." *Nationalism and Ethnic Politics* 9, no. 1: 75–100.

Corntassel, Jeff. 2008. "Toward Sustainable Self-Determination: Rethinking the Contemporary Indigenous-Rights Discourse." *Alternatives: Global, Local, Political* 33, no. 1: 105–32.

Corntassel, Jeff. 2012. "Re-envisioning Resurgence: Indigenous Pathways to Decolonization and Sustainable Self-Determination." *Decolonization: Indigeneity, Education, and Society* 1, no. 1: 86–101.

Elliott, Mark. 2015. "The Case of the Missing Indigene: Debate over a 'Second-Generation' Ethnic Policy." *The Chinese Journal* 73: 186–213.

Erni, Christian, ed. 2008. *The Concept of Indigenous Peoples in Asia: A Resource Book*. Copenhagen, Denmark: International Work Group for Indigenous Affairs.

Graburn, Nelson H., and John Ertl. 2010. "Introduction: Internal Boundaries and Models of Multiculturalism in Contemporary Japan." In *Multiculturalism in the New Japan: Crossing the Boundaries Within,* edited by Nelson H. Graburn, John Ertl, and R. Kenji Tierney, 1–31. New York: Berghan Books.

Gray, Andrew. 1995. "The Indigenous Movement in Asia." In *Indigenous Peoples in Asia,* edited by Robert Harrison Barnes, Andrew Gray, and Benedict Kingsbury, 35–58. Ann Arbor, Mich.: Association of Asian Studies.

Hathaway, Michael. 2010. "The Emergence of Indigeneity: Public Intellectuals and an Indigenous Space in Southwest China." *Cultural Anthropology* 25, no. 2: 301–33.

Keating, Neal B. 2013. "Kuy Alterities: The Struggle to Conceptualise and Claim Indigenous Land Rights in Neoliberal Cambodia." *Asia Pacific Viewpoint* 54, no. 3: 309–22.

Kingsbury, Benedict. 1998. "'Indigenous Peoples' in International Law: A Constructive Approach to the Asian Controversy." *American Journal of International Law* 92, no. 3: 414–57.

Li, Tania Murray. 2010. "Indigeneity, Capitalism, and the Management of Dispossession." *Cultural Anthropology* 51, no. 3: 385–414.

Luo, Yu. 2018. "An Alternative to 'Indigenous' in Early Twenty-First-Century China: Guizhou's Branding of *Yuanshengtai*." *Modern China* 44, no. 1: 68–102.

Matsumura, Wendy. 2015. *The Limits of Okinawa: Japanese Capitalism, Living Labor, and Theorizations of Community.* Durham, N.C.: Duke University Press.

Ministry of Foreign Affairs of Japan. 1960. "Agreement Regarding the Status of United States Armed Forces in Japan, January 19, 1960." Article VI of the Treaty of Mutual Cooperation and Security between Japan and the United States. http://www.mofa.go.jp/region/n-america/us/q&a/ref/2.html.

Ministry of Foreign Affairs of Japan. 2000. "Comments of the Japanese Government on the Concluding Observations Adopted by the Committee on the Elimination of Racial Discrimination on March 20, 2000, Regarding Initial and Second Periodic Report of the Japanese Government." http://www.mofa.go.jp/policy/human/comment0110.html.

Ministry of Foreign Affairs of Japan. 2010. "Replies to the List of Questions by the Country Rapporteur in Connection with the Consideration of the Third to Sixth Periodic Report." http://www.mofa.go.jp/policy/human/pdfs/race_rep4.pdf.

Nakachi Hiroshi 仲地博. 1989. "Zokujinteki jūmin jichi soshiki no ichi kōsatsu: Okinawaken Yomitanson no jirei" 属人的住民自治組織の一考察：沖縄県読谷村の事例 [An examination of an autonomous organization of genealogy-based residents]. In *Saiban to chihōjichi: Wada*

Hideo sensei koki kinen ronbunshū 裁判と地方自治：和田英夫先生古希記念論文集, edited by Wada Hideo sensei koki kinen ronbunshū henshū iinkai, 203–28. Tokyo: Keibundō.

Nakata Minoru 中田実. 2017. *Chihōbunken jidai no chōnaikai, jichikai* 地方分権時代の町内会・自治会 [Neighborhood association and self-governance organizations in the era of decentralization]. Tokyo: Jichitai Kenkyūsha.

Niezen, Ronald. 2003. *The Origins of Indigenism: Human Rights and the Politics of Identity.* Oakland: University of California Press.

Okinawa Daihyakkajiten Kankō Jimukyoku 沖縄大百科事典刊行事務局, ed. 1983. *Okinawa daihyakka jiten* 沖縄大百科事典 [Encyclopedia of Okinawa]. 4 vols. Naha, Japan: Okinawa Taimusu Sha.

Okinawa-ken 沖縄県, ed. (1972) 1977. *Okinawa kenshi: Tsū-shi* 沖縄県史：通史 [Okinawa prefectural history: Overview]. Vol. 1. Tokyo: Gennandō Shoten.

Okinawa-ken Yomitan-son 沖縄県読谷村. 1989. *Yomitan-son dai niji sōgōkeikaku kihon kōsō* 読谷村第2次総合計画基本構想 [The Yomitan village second comprehensive plan]. June. Okinawa.

Okinawa-ken Yomitan-son 沖縄県読谷村. 2005. *Yomitan hojo hikōjō atochi riyō jisshi keikaku* 読谷村補助飛行場跡地利用実施計画 [The implementation plan of the land-use of Yomitan Auxiliary Airfield site, Yomitan village]. March. Okinawa.

Okinawa Prefectural Government. 2016. "U.S. Military Base Issues in Okinawa." Washington, D.C.: OPG Office. http://dc-office.org/basedata.

Ryūkyū Seifu 琉球政府, ed. (1972) 1989. *Okinawa kenshi: Keizai* 沖縄県史：経済 [Okinawa prefectural history: Economy]. Vol. 3. Tokyo: Kokusho Kankōkai.

Ryukyu Shimpō 琉球新報. 2006. "Kokuyū zaisan Okinawan chihōshin, tōkakōkan wo ryōshō Yomitan sonnai no kokuyūchi to sonyūchi de" 国有財産沖縄地方審、等価交換を了承　読谷村内の国有地と村有地で [Okinawa District Court accepts the equivalent exchange of state-owned land and village-owned land in Yomitan]. June 8.

Ryukyu Shimpō 琉球新報. 2008. "'Senjūminzoku' no imi fumeikaku kokurenjinken ikankoku"「先住民族」の意味 不明確　国連人権委勧告 [The ambiguity of the meaning of "Indigenous Peoples"]. December 14, p. 31.

Sakihara, Mitsugu. 2006. *Okinawa–English Wordbook: A Short Lexicon of the Okinawan Language with English Definitions and Japanese Cognates.* Edited by Stewart Curry. Honolulu: University of Hawai'i Press.

Shimabukuro Tsutomu 島袋勉. 2010. *Tatakai no kiroku* たたかいの記録 [The record of the struggle]. Nishihara, Japan: Marumasa Insatsu.

Siddle, Richard. 2003. "Return to Uchinā: The Politics of Identity in Contemporary Okinawa." In *Japan and Okinawa: Structure and Subjectivity,* edited by Glenn D. Hook and Richard Siddle, 133–47. London: Routledge.

Tanji, Miyume. 2006. *Myth, Protest, and Struggle in Okinawa.* London: Routledge.

Uemura, Hideaki. 2003. "The Colonial Annexation of Okinawa and the Logic of International Law: The Formation of an 'Indigenous People' in East Asia." *Japanese Studies* 23, no. 2: 213–22.

United Nations General Assembly Department of Public Information. 2007. "General Assembly Adopts Declaration on Rights of Indigenous Peoples; 'Major Steps Forward' toward Human Rights for All, Says President" (Report GA/10612). https://www.un.org/press/en/2007/ga10612.doc.htm.

Yamauchi Tokushin 山内徳信. 2001. *Kenpō wo jissen suru mura: Okinawa Yomitan sonchō funtō ki* 憲法を実践する村：沖縄読谷村長の奮闘記 [The village practices the constitution: The journal of Yomitan mayor's struggles]. Tokyo: Akashi Shoten.

Yamauchi Tokushin 山内徳信. 2014. *Kaihou wo motomete: Ari no mure raion wo osou* 解放を求めて：アリの群れライオンを襲う [Seeking liberation: A throng of ants attacks a lion]. Naha: Okinawa Taimusu Sha.

Yeh, Emily. 2007. "Tibetan Indigeneity: Translations, Resemblances, and Uptake." In *Indigenous Experience Today,* edited by Marisol de la Cadena and Orin Starn, 33–68. Oxford: Berg.

Yokota, Ryan Masaaki. 2015. "The Okinawan (Uchinānchu) Indigenous Movement and Its Implications for Intentional/International Action." *Amerasia Journal* 41, no. 1: 55–73.

Yomitan Hikōjō Yōchi Shuken Kaifuku Jinushikai 読谷飛行場用地主権回復地主会. 1980. *Dai 4 kai Yomitan hikōjō yōchi shoyūken kaifuku jinushikai sōkai* 第4回読谷飛行場用地所有権回復地主回総会 [Yomitan Airfield Landownership Restitution Working Group meeting agenda]. February 15. Yomitan: Zakimi Kōminkan.

Yomitan-son 読谷村. 1983. *Yomitan hikōjō tenyō keikaku chōsa hōkokusho* 読谷飛行場転用計画調査報告書 [Yomitan Airfield conversion planning report prepared by Chiiki Keikaku Kenkyūsho]. May 15. Okinawa: Yomitan Village Office.

Yomitan-son 読谷村. 1995. *Yomitan-son toshi kihon keikaku* 読谷村都市基本計画 [Yomitan village basic plan]. March. Okinawa: Yomitan Village Office. March.

Yomitan-son 読谷村. 2013a. "Mura zukuri no mokuhyō" 村づくりの目標 [The goal of village building]. Yomitan: Yomitan Village Office.

http://www.vill.yomitan.okinawa.jp/sections/finance2/post-356.html.

Yomitan-son 読谷村. 2013b. "Yomitan hikōjō henkan no hi: 3" 読谷飛行場返還の碑：3 [The monument for the return of the Yomitan Airfield]. http://www.vill.yomitan.okinawa.jp/redevelopment/airfield-return3.html.

Yomitan-son Kyōikuiinkai Bunkasōgōka 読谷村教育委員会文化総合課, ed. 2014. *Aza mappu Uza* 字マップ宇座 [*Aza* map Uza]. March 25. Yomitan, Japan: Aza mappu henshū sagyōhan.

Yomitan-son Yakusho 読谷村役所, ed. 1969. *Yomitan sonshi* 読谷村史 [The Yomitan village history]. Kumamoto, Japan: Shiroki Insatsu.

**CHRISTINE HORN, PATRICIA PHILIP,
AND CLEMENT LANGET SABANG**

Getting Connected: Indigeneity, Information, and Communications Technology Use and Emerging Media Practices in Sarawak

CECILIA LIVES IN A SMALL VILLAGE about an hour's drive from Kuching, Sarawak's state capital. She is Bidayuh, one of several ethnic groups in the region, and she is in her sixties. Most of her children have moved away from the village but often visit the family home and help maintain house and garden. Although Cecilia and her family do not plant much *padi* (rice) anymore, the family still has several orchards, and Cecilia sells fruit and vegetables to middlemen who supply the nearby city. To keep in touch with her large family and to organize sales of produce, Cecilia uses her mobile phone even though she never went to school and does not read or write. She uses speed-dial buttons to store the most important numbers and carries a small notebook where other important numbers are noted, color-coded to help her identify to whom they belong. While mobile phone access in the village is not good, in particular during rainy weather, she knows the places around the house where it is easiest to pick up a signal. The phone, for Cecilia, is a tool for economic engagement and personal empowerment.

Cecilia is the mother of one of the authors, Patricia Philip. Cecilia's engagement with communications technology despite obstacles like the lack of literacy and low levels of access prompted the authors to think more deeply about the impact of information and communication technologies (ICTs) on Indigenous communities in the region. Digital media technologies continue to transform social spaces, interactions, and practices, and even those on the margins of these processes are not exempt

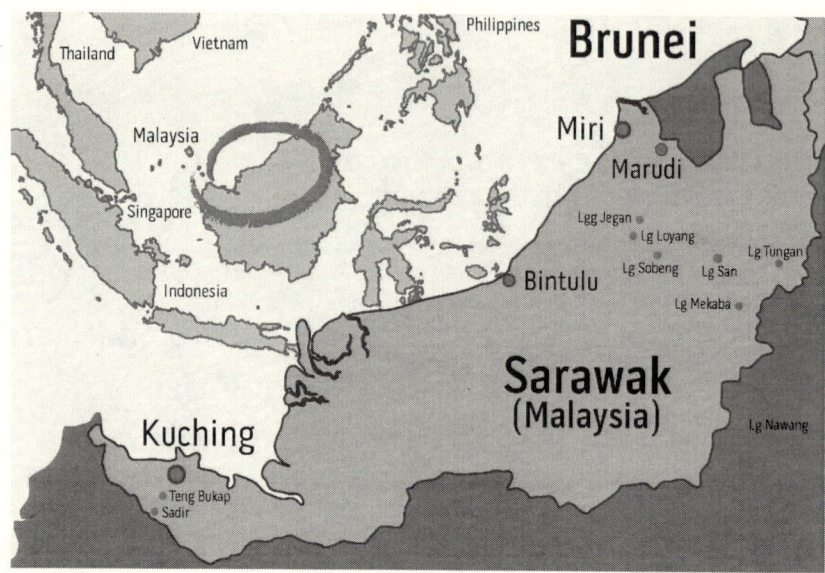

Figure 1. Map of the region.

(Jenkins 2006; Norris and Inglehart 2009; McQuire 2017). The growing ubiquity of ICTs and the internet is often seen as deeply ambivalent, and concerns about the homogenizing effects of globalization on minority culture persist (Holton 2000; Hopper 2007; Pratt 2010; Hershey 2012; O'Sullivan 2012; Stout 2014). Observers point to cultural convergence as a threat to cultural diversity (Tomlinson 1999; Jenkins 2006; Norris and Inglehart 2009; Pieterse 2015). Some suggest that globalization enables the appropriation of Indigenous cultural heritage and that ICTs are a contributing factor (Kraidy 2017). Also, digital inequalities can lead to the marginalization of groups that are already experiencing other kinds of social exclusion (Van Dijk and Hacker 2003; Van Dijk 2006; Zillien and Hargittai 2009; Gilbert 2010; Robinson et al. 2015; van Deursen and Helsper 2015; Hargittai and Jennrich 2016).

All this suggests that a closer look at emerging ICT practices is needed to examine the effects of increasing access in remote areas. In this article, we address some of the explicit and implicit criticisms that have been leveraged against ICT proliferation in Indigenous communities. This critique is valuable, in particular because new practices continue to emerge. A critical approach is also useful to assess the ways in which globalization plays out in socioeconomic and cultural terms (Appadurai 1996; Norris and Inglehart 2009; Hall and Fenelon 2015; Pieterse 2015). However, constructive and emancipatory outcomes of ICT participation necessitate closer scrutiny as well. For instance, where critics are concerned that Indigenous participation and usage of ICTs may have an assimilating effect on cultural minorities (Smith, Burke, and Ward 2000; Smith and Ward 2000), other research suggests that ICTs enable Indigenous people to curate and maintain their heritage, create Indigenous identities, and communicate about social and political issues that concern them (Christensen 2003; Dyson and Underwood 2006; Srinivasan 2006; Ginsburg 2008; Pratt 2010; Dyson 2011; Kral 2011; Carlson 2013; McMahon 2013; Castleton 2014; Owiny, Mehta, and Maretzki 2014; Butet-Roch 2016; Ginsburg 2016; Srinivasan 2017). Another critique is that global media make Indigenous culture available for consumption without granting Indigenous peoples the rights and rewards of authorship (Brown 1998; Smith, Burke, and Ward 2000; Brown and Nicholas 2012; Janke and Iacovino 2012). However, ICTs also enable people to transcribe, collect, and curate elements of their traditional heritage and preserve Indigenous knowledge, for instance, oral history, without the mediation of organizations like libraries, museums, and archives (Nathan and Kelkar 2004; Owiny, Mehta, and Maretzki 2014). ICTs allow individuals to communicate their own lived experiences, which Arjun Appadurai (1996, 33) called people's "imagined worlds." These imaginations allow people "to contest and sometimes even subvert the imagined worlds of the official mind and of the entrepreneurial mentality that surround them" (33). Indigenous representations of culture and heritage can do much to interrogate stereotypical ideas about what it means to identify as a member of an Indigenous group. In addition, ICT practices can help Indigenous groups overcome issues related to socioeconomic inequalities and give voice to Indigenous concerns (Srinivasan 2006; Coleman 2010). Critics point out that digital frameworks of interaction "emerge from the monocultures of Western corporations and cultural institutions" (Srinivasan 2012, 3) and are not always appropriate in other cultural settings. However, many young people with Indigenous backgrounds, as digital natives, are well equipped to unsettle monocultural media landscapes through the production of their own digital content. Apart from the distribution of media content to a global audience, ICTs can be used as a private means of communication between individuals or small groups, for instance, through the use of messaging apps or private groups on social media platforms. Online networks function on local as well as global levels and can help users shape and express individual and communal identities (Christensen 2003; Kral 2011; Carlson 2013).

Assessing the advantages and disadvantages of ICT use becomes more complicated when people live in remote and inaccessible areas with low internet and telephone penetration, which limits participation (Sandvig 2012). To access media platforms and create content, users often need to be literate in nonnative languages and possess the necessary IT and software skills (Hassan et al. 2009). A lack of content in local languages makes it harder for users to engage with the ICTs (Hassan et al. 2010). For low-income groups, acquiring the appropriate technology presents an additional hurdle for digital inclusion. These issues, which contribute to the widening of the "digital divide," the gap between communities with access to an increasing array of media and technology and others who remain outside of the reach of such developments, therefore limit the potential use of media technologies (Van Dijk and Hacker 2003; Srinivasan 2006; Van Dijk 2006; Zillien and Hargittai 2009; Avgerou 2010; Robinson et al. 2015; van Deursen and Helsper 2015; van Deursen et al. 2017). Above all, access to and use of ICTs and the internet are limited by the ability to access ICT infrastructure in rural and remote communities. This criticism raises questions about the underlying structures that enable the use of ICTs—for instance, who can grant or withhold access to mobile telephone networks and the internet for rural communities—and suggests that the state retains a mediating presence with regard to the opportunities for Indigenous groups to engage with ICTs. As we will argue, this is an ongoing issue for some communities included in our research, suggesting that despite the emerging emancipatory potential of ICT use, such practices may not fundamentally change the power dynamics among stakeholders or necessarily lead to more inclusive outcomes. While globalization, in the form of ICTs and the internet, can unsettle some of these power relationships and provide voice and agency to Indigenous communities, it does not provide an automatic route to structural economic, social, or political change (Friedman 1990).

Throughout this text, we use the term *information and communication technology*, or ICT, to refer to the kinds of technology that enable the creation of content, including written texts, digital photographs, digital video, and film. We also include the technologies that make this content available to a local and global audience through the internet, such as computers or smartphones. These technologies are the tools with which people create visual representations, share information and communicate via SMS text messages and instant messaging apps, post on social networks, write emails, or publish articles on blogs and in online news outlets. Our definition of the term excludes broadcast media, such as radio and television. We acknowledge the use of broadcast technologies for remote communities, in particular, community radio and television (Mazzarella 2004; Harris and Harris 2011; Kral 2011; McMahon 2013;

Figure 2. Women looking at pictures on an iPad in Long Luyang, 2016.

Ormond-Parker et al. 2013; Wilson 2015; Ginsburg 2016; Srinivasan 2017). However, our argument in this article focuses on technologies that enable interactive communication and that allow a wide range of users to create and exchange content. We focus on ICTs because they facilitate the production and exchange of content by users in a "many-to-many" model where broadcast media mostly rely on a "one-to-many model" with few selected producers and many consumers (Castells 2007). This difference means that ICTs are more inclusive of content created by a variety of users, often at a low cost and with low barriers to entry.

To ground the academic debate about Indigenous ICT practices in the lived experiences of Indigenous ICT users, we focus on the use of media technology in Sarawak, a state of the federation of Malaysia on the island of Borneo (see Figure 1). This article provides a short introduction to Sarawak and a description of our methods and the processes through which this article came to be. We will also give a brief overview of Malaysia's internet policies with regard to rural communities. We will then discuss three case studies of media usage we observed during our fieldwork and how these practices exemplified the uses of digital media in Indigenous communities.

■ METHODS

The authors collected the data discussed in this article during several years of conversations and discussions with people from Sarawak's rural interior and in the course of extended participant observation. Two of the authors are members of Sarawak's Indigenous groups. Patricia Philip is Bidayuh from the Puncak Borneo area. Clement Langet Sabang is Sebup from the Tinjar River area in central Sarawak. Christine Horn has studied and worked in Sarawak since 2005. Some of the data presented in this article derive from her academic research activities, while other information was collected during loosely structured discussions between the authors and people from Sarawak's Indigenous communities, mostly between 2010 and 2017. Patricia's data were collected in Bidayuh communities in Sarawak's First Division. Clement's work focuses on the Sebup areas along the Tinjar in Sarawak's Fourth Division. Christine's data come from the Baram area, also in Sarawak's Fourth Division, and from Long Nawang in Indonesia. We also held discussions and interviews in Sarawak's capital, Kuching, and in Miri, the second biggest city. The locations of these sites are shown in Figure 1. Each of the three collaborators contributed instances of ICT use among Indigenous communities we felt were relevant to the discussion and illustrated the argument we wanted to make.

In this article, we use the term *ethnic group* to refer to a group of people who identify as belonging to a particular group, such as Bidayuh, Iban, Kayan, or others. These groups often have various subgroups with their own languages and traditions. The term *community* or *community member* refers to people who, even if they live outside their village and longhouse, still identify with a specific group that is often but not always associated with a village or longhouse. These identities are usually historically based and sometimes reflect previous places where people lived in the past. We use the term *community* based on people's self-identification with a particular group even though they may have moved to the city permanently. More information on identity and ethnicity among Sarawak's Indigenous groups is available elsewhere (Tan 1997; Nicolaisen 1997; Winzeler 1997a, 1997b; Metcalf 2010).

When we use the term *Indigenous* or *Indigenous people*, we acknowledge the definition proposed in the Declaration on the Rights of Indigenous Peoples adopted by the United Nations in 2007 (UNDRIP). The UNDRIP definition of Indigenous peoples includes self-identification at the individual and communal levels; links to territories and surrounding natural resources; and distinct social, economic, political systems and language, culture, and beliefs. Malaysia is a signatory to UNDRIP but also uses the name "Bumiputera" (Sons of the Soil) to denote a form of Indigeneity. The term relates to the idea of prior settlement and includes Malays and minority ethnic groups but not Chinese and Indian Malaysians, many of whom migrated to the region during British colonial rule (Balasubramaniam 2007). Bumiputeras are subject to various affirmative action policies, including university access quotas, access to public-sector jobs, business licenses, and government contracts (Balasubramaniam 2007). The government implemented these policies to improve socioeconomic equality among the population (Segawa 2013). However, "Bumiputera" is not synonymous with the term *Indigenous* in the UNDRIP sense, because UNDRIP suggests that Indigenous peoples form nondominant groups of society, and in Malaysia, Malays form the majority of the population and are also the politically dominant group (Balasubramaniam 2007).

Sarawak's Indigenous people use the internet and other digital technologies in much the same way as any other group of people. They connect to friends and family, surf the internet, listen to music, and read the news. However, media technologies offer some additional advantages and benefits to minority groups who share an ethnic background, language, traditions, issues, and concerns. Digital networks provide spaces where community matters can be discussed and where visual content documenting local culture is shared, and they allow Indigenous Sarawakians to connect with community members in Sarawak and overseas. These practices have led to a proliferation of Indigenous websites, forums, blogs, and other types of content (Dyson 2011). However, ICT and internet access are unevenly distributed. Villages near the coast or inland towns have access to landlines as well as mobile phone coverage, but this does not extend to many of the more remote communities. This limits the use of ICT in rural Sarawak despite the improvements in access that the government aims to achieve. For instance, the women in Long Luyang shown in Figure 2 are looking at photographs on an iPad, which they will share with others the next time they travel to the city. People's efforts to engage with ICTs and the obstacles they encounter sometimes become visible in the village environment. Figure 3 shows a little hut in the center of Long San, a village in central Sarawak, the only location in the village at the time with mobile phone coverage. People left their phones in the little holders made from drink cans or plastic bottles if they were expecting a message and picked up the phone after a period of time to check if anything had arrived. The inscription on the right reads, "Di sini ada line telefon!!" (There is telephone reception here!!) The ways in which people in this area engage with ICTs, often against the odds, are the focus of this article. Since the photo was taken, mobile phone infrastructure in Long

Figure 3. Structure indicating the place with mobile phone reception in Long San before the installation of a new tower in the vicinity of the village, 2011.

San has been upgraded, although mobile internet access in the village is still unavailable.

■ MALAYSIA'S DIGITAL DEVELOPMENT

The following section gives an overview of the development of internet infrastructure and practices in Malaysia since the 1990s. The emerging picture is that of a country where internet use and engagement with digital and mobile media have increased rapidly as a result of government strategy. The government's focus on ICTs dates back to 1991, when Malaysia's Prime Minister Mahatir laid out a plan to transform Malaysia from an economy based on manufacturing to a knowledge-based economy. The government "envisaged that by year 2020, all Malaysians would be able to access to information and learning through an info-structure for personal, organizational and national advancement" (Edzan and Saad 2005, 93). Since then, the government has implemented various programs to support the uptake of ICTs among its citizens and to encourage Malaysians to use digital media for education, commerce, and economic development and to access government services. Initially, this strategy was largely driven by urban centers. As internet usage became more widespread, the focus

Figure 4. Mobile phone infrastructure in Long Tungan, 2016.

of government policies increasingly shifted toward rural development. In 2012, Prime Minister Najib Razak stated, "I am determined to do everything possible to bring digital development to our nation's less developed areas and to close the digital divide and I am confident it will not be long before we see kampung [village] and longhouse dwellers posting messages and pictures on social media sites."[1]

The Malaysian government tackles digital inequalities through various programs conceived under the Universal Service Provision (USP), which are administered by the Malaysian Communications and Multimedia Commission, a government body regulating the industry and promoting access and participation (MCMC 2014, 63). Most projects are funded through the Universal Service Funds (USF), which is made up from contributions by telecommunications service providers whose net revenue exceeds RM 2 million. These contributors pay 6 percent of their profits annually into the USF. The money is then reinvested to supply areas where telecommunications services would not otherwise be profitable. Some schemes are aimed at low-income groups, while others are focused on underserved rural and remote areas. For instance, from 2007 onward, MCMC funded more than 650 internet centers in rural communities (MCMC 2015). Other programs under the USP include the distribution of netbooks to schoolchildren from low-income families and the provision of Wi-Fi internet to rural villages (MCMC 2015). In 2009, the MCMC pledged the construction of one thousand telecommunications towers in rural communities, with particular focus on areas with a population of less than eighty inhabitants per square kilometer. By 2013, 699 such towers had been built, 174 of which were located in Sarawak. The scheme is aimed at extending coverage in the country to 97 percent (MCMC 2012).

Despite these efforts, many rural communities in Sarawak still have no ICT infrastructure. Even if they do, it is often prone to disruptions. During a visit in early 2015, several small telecommunication installations in rural villages in the center of the state were out of service due to lightning strikes, flooding, or other technical issues. Some had not been functional for months, or even years, even though the villagers tried to report the problem. The village of Long Tungan was connected to the mobile phone network for several years, before mobile phone connection was suddenly disrupted in 2016. As one respondent explained, "It now only works from 7:00 PM onward, and then only until early in the morning. I don't know why. It was working well and then suddenly it didn't work at all during the daytime" (interview, 2016). Often people in the village find it hard to contact the agencies responsible for maintaining the ICT infrastructure, and the issues remain unresolved. Even though MCMC aims for a proactive and transparent approach in the implementation of USP projects, there is often little information available about specific projects to help the people on the ground get in touch. These issues suggest that much remains to be done despite the government's efforts to supply remote communities with ICT infrastructure.

■ THE CASE STUDIES

Case Study 1: The Impact of Digital Technologies on Minority Languages

In this section, we will take a look at the ways in which ICT use affects local minority languages. Sarawak is linguistically and ethnically diverse, with forty-six different Indigenous languages and dialects by some estimates.[2] Some of these groups comprise only a few hundred speakers. In recent decades, Sarawakians have started to worry about the state of smaller language groups. Our observations suggest that the increased use of ICTs can help preserve minority languages but may also have some unexpected side effects. So far only Iban, the language spoken by the largest Indigenous group in Sarawak, is taught in public schools (Smith 2010). The Bidayuh are another large ethnic group based in the region near the state capital Kuching. Bidayuh speakers are subdivided into subgroups that speak different dialects. The Bidayuh dialects were rarely written down in the past, but the vocabulary and grammar of the language are well documented (Rensch et al. 2006). Bidayuh used to be taught in village schools in the 1960s and 1970s, but this has since ceased (Achoi 2010). Iban and Bidayuh are among the more well-documented languages in Sarawak. The languages of many smaller groups receive less attention, and many have not been transcribed, encoded, or documented systematically. The Sebup and Lepo' Tau, for instance,[3] much less numerous than the Bidayuh, live in the north of the state. They are subgroups of the Kenyah, which is among the groups collectively known as Orang Ulu or "People from Upriver." The Sebup language, like many local languages spoken in Sarawak, includes a variety of sounds that do not correspond to the phonetic systems of either Bahasa Malaysia or English, which made transcription problematic in the past.[4]

ICTs offer a range of other opportunities to engage with literacy. During our work in Sarawak's Indigenous communities, we observed how Iban, Bidayuh, and other minority language speakers increasingly compose text messages with mobile phones or post comments on each other's Facebook profiles in their own languages. According to some, these are the only occasions in which the written forms of the languages are used. For languages such as Sebup, Kenyah Lepo' Tau, or indeed many of the minority languages spoken among Sarawak's Indigenous groups, users make up their own orthography as they go along. As one participant explained in 2016 with regard to Lepo' Tau, people use whichever spelling seems the most appropriate: "At the moment there is nobody determines as to how it should be spelled. . . . But there are some people who now try to write the dictionary for Kenyah, [to tell people] when they spell it, it should be spelled like this, they do make a dictionary like that" (interview, 2016). Thus a side effect of using the minority languages for media interactions is that users establish a written language where none had existed before. Orthography and grammatical structure are systematized through use of written language by the community, and the language is also used more consistently by younger speakers who live in the cities and towns and who might otherwise have little opportunity to speak their native languages.

Not everyone agrees that the use of digital media benefits minority languages. One concern voiced by observers during our research, which speaks to the homogenizing potential of ICTs, was that young users of social media often use a language mix made up of different local languages, including Malay and English, as well as abbreviations and short forms of colloquial expressions. "That is no language at all," commented one participant from Kuching who works in the rural interior. "I can't even understand what they are saying!" (interview, 2013). Another concern voiced by participants was that people would spend all their money on phones and prepaid recharges rather than buying necessary items for their families. "These people go out and buy credit when they should be buying food for their families," criticized one participant while discussing the recently erected telecommunications tower in a small and particularly poor rural community (interview, 2013). Such fears and criticisms of the negative effects of ICT use, seen as "impoverished and antisocial" and implicitly challenging "the moral order" (Thurlow 2006, 688), are not new. Studies suggest, however, that proficiency in variations of language commonly used for digital interactions is not associated with a decline in literacy (Drouin and Davis 2009; Plester and Wood 2009). In fact, being exposed to digital literacy may provide additional engagement with literacy outside of educational environments (Plester and Wood 2009). The girl in Figure 5, for instance, may be among the first generation who uses ICTs to habitually write in Bidayuh when she is messaging her friends or leaving them Facebook posts. Although she may not yet learn the language in school, such practices may help to establish a body of literature that may become useful for language teaching.

People's use of Indigenous languages to communicate online may result in a new kind of vernacular language in which words from other languages are integrated. It nevertheless constitutes a written record of a language that is otherwise mainly spoken. This is not equivalent to the strategic recording and documentation of minority language, but it can help small language groups to create a more permanent record of their language and may prevent the decline experienced by some Indigenous languages. It decreases reliance on outside intervention and can help communities circumvent ethical issues arising in language documentation through outsiders, such as the question of who determines which languages receive attention and which do not (Nambiar and Govindasamy 2010; Gill 2014). Linguists working with endangered languages at times have to rely on limited numbers of accessible participants, or participants from particular regions, which may impact the outcomes of conservation efforts (Dorian 2010). Also, the aims and objectives of linguists documenting Indigenous languages may differ from the reasons why Indigenous communities are seeking to document local languages (Nathan and Fang 2009). The use of digital media technologies benefits linguistic documentation even in cases where outside agencies transcribe local languages collaboratively with the community. As some researchers point out, the use of internet technologies augments the productivity of linguistic research because it

Figure 5. Girl using her mobile phone during rice planting, Kampung Sadir, 2016.

enables researchers to work more collaboratively with source communities (Chin, Yeo, and Musa 2013).

Case Study 2: Presenting Cultural Heritage on the Internet

In this section, we will discuss the ways in which people in Sarawak use ICTs to engage with their cultural heritage, to share and circulate photographs and videos about cultural events, and to discuss related issues online. Many Indigenous Sarawakians who live and work in the cities frequently visit their home villages and the friends and relatives who still live there. Equipped with the necessary technology, these urban Dayak are documenting their home communities through photography, video, and sound recording. They are joined by increasing numbers of ICT users in the villages, as access to mobile networks in remote areas grows.

In 2008, the biggest Sebup community on the Tinjar River, Long Luyang (see Figure 1), celebrated the traditional harvest festival of the Sebup called "So'en."[5] Photographs of the participants, many of whom had traveled from the cities on the coast for the purpose, dressed in their *sunong* (war jackets) made from imitation tiger skin fabric, documented the revival of the traditional festival, which had not been celebrated in several decades (see Figure 6). Traditionally, villages in the region held

Figure 6. Participants from Sarawak on the way to the Long Nawang cultural festival in Indonesia, 2011.

their harvest festival when every family had finished the rice harvest, and so the date of the occasion was subject to change from one year to the next. Different groups had different names and ceremonies for the occasion. In the 1960s, June 1 and 2 became a public holiday in Sarawak called "Gawai." Some of the different groups pragmatically changed former practices to comply with the public holiday. As one member of a small Indigenous group put it during an interview, "Gawai was celebrated by . . . the Iban. But because the Sarawak government is giving us a day off for Gawai, so we might as well celebrate the Gawai together with the Iban" (interview, 2010). However, some Indigenous Sarawakians feel that their own culture was subsumed among a general concept of Indigeneity created by the government administration and are reviving earlier traditions, such as the So'en festival. The Sebup reinvigorated traditional practices, such as the Kelebong ceremonial pole constructed in front of the longhouse (Figure 8a) and the practice of Ketaau, dancing on the rising Kelebong pole (Figure 8d). The festival also included traditional dances like the Datun Julut longdance shown in Figure 8b. Participants created ceremonial attires based on traditional styles and presented them during the festival (Figure 8c). In this instance, digital media technologies supported the localization rather than the homogenization of culture by enabling groups to document revived traditional practices and events.

The localizing potential of ICTs was evident during other local events as well. Long Nawang is a Kenyah Lepo' Tau community in Indonesia that organizes a cultural festival every few years to bring together the numerous different Lepo' Tau communities to hold meetings; discuss issues of cultural, political, and economic concern; and celebrate traditional art forms like music and dance (see Figure 1). Neighboring Kenyah Lepo' Tau people in Malaysia and Indonesia are invited to take part. For the Sarawakian attendants of the Long Nawang cultural festival, the trip involved a three-day journey using buses, boats, and trucks before they finally reached Long Nawang (see Figure 6). For many participants, the trip is a once-in-a-lifetime opportunity to visit their relatives across the border. During the event attended by one of the authors in 2012, spectators brought photo cameras, video cameras, tablets, and mobile phones to record the songs and dances that were presented by various groups, staged photographs with the performers in their traditional costumes, and took pictures to record dance styles and elements of customary attire to re-create them later at home (see Figure 7). One participant from Sarawak explained, "We have our own dance group in Miri, where we come together and practice the Hornbill dance. But here they have all sorts of different styles that I haven't seen" (interview, 2012). The organizers filmed

Figure 7. Audience filming traditional dances of the Lepo' Tau Kenyah in Long Nawang, Indonesia, 2012.

the event and distributed a compilation of the contests to participating groups on a CD. In the weeks after the event, some of these photographs, videos, and sound recordings were posted online on YouTube or private blogs. Many more were consumed and circulated within the community, sent via WhatsApp, or posted on Facebook profiles.

Photos, videos, and sound recordings offer an accessible way to document knowledge that can be fluid, experiential, sensory, and performative (Owiny, Mehta, and Maretzki 2014). These aspects are often lost if such knowledge is formally transcribed, but visual documents can enable viewers to engage with the experiential and performative practices as well (Edwards 2006). For instance, photographs and videos can be used in a social setting to transmit, retell, or perform oral or experiential knowledge. Users can show photographs and videos to each other and discuss the content within the community, online as well as in person. The production and dissemination of digital media are thus associated with alternative methods of transferring knowledge, such as embodied and experiential knowledge (Rice et al. 2016). Often when such documents are shared on the internet, viewers can provide feedback and debate, for instance, where users can leave comments and replies alongside posts, images, or videos. Above all, ICTs enable multiple contributors to describe the world according to their identity and experience, unimpeded by institutionalized ideas about culture or heritage (Healy 2013). These different worldviews are "the ontological keys that unlock the doors to diverse, rich, and incommensurable knowledge communities" (Boast, Bravo, and Srinivasan 2007, 399).

ICTs, digital media, and the internet are often seen as technologies of homogenization that facilitate access to content from anywhere in the world (Tomlinson 1999; Jenkins 2006; Norris and Inglehart 2009). However, ICTs can also be used to communicate on a local level. The same people who interact in online networks may interact in person too, so that online networks constitute extensions of the methods by which families, communities, and other groups of people communicate. Digital media content can be made specifically for local audiences and for friends and family, community members, and others who speak the same language and who share cultural experiences and identities. Users project, document, and construct real identities through online representations, such as photographs, videos, and texts, since "online identities are the product of cultural practices by real social agents" (Carlson 2013, 148). This kind of usage has been termed *inreach,* where content is produced for a specific, limited group of users, as opposed to *outreach,* where producers seek a global audience (Dyson 2011, 259). Indigenous media producers employ both inreach and outreach methods. Media technologies thus play a role for the localization of the global and the globalization or hybridization of the local (Holton 2000; Nathan, Kelkar, and Walter 2004; Pieterse 2015). These processes appear as dynamic, adaptive, and reciprocal engagements that are part of a "complex connectivity" (Tomlinson 1999) that enables communication networks between people with a shared ethnic identity, language, and traditions as well as people and groups in different parts of the world.

Much of the material produced by Indigenous Sarawakians for their own communities and in their own languages or dialects is only accessible to a limited number of native speakers due to the language barrier. Producers of content in social networks, online forums, or blogs negotiate access to written content by using local languages and dialects, Bahasa Malaysia, English, or at times a mixture of the lot, in turn excluding and including various audiences. As Postill points out, literacy can be appropriated to serve various ethnic traditions of oration, social hierarchy, and religious practice (Postill 2003). This is also the case for media literacy and technological capacities. Indigenous media producers are not naive about potential effects of their online activities and strategically use media

Figure 8. Pictures of the So'en festival held in the Sebup communities. One of the authors, Clement Langet Sabang, appears in (c) on the left. Photographs by Clement Langet Sabang.

technology to share information with selected audiences. Photographs, videos, and other documents created with and shared via digital technology function as visual evidence of cultural cohesion and continuity. Digital methods of collecting, collating, and curating Indigenous knowledge allow users to bypass established institutions, such as museums, libraries, and archives, that are not always accessible to rural audiences and may also have agendas that differ from those of the communities (Owiny, Mehta, and Maretzki 2014).

Case Study 3: Civic and Political Participation

The preceding section provided some examples of localized uses of ICTs and the internet. This section concerns the use of ICTs for presenting local concerns to a global public and for political participation. In Malaysia, the importance of the internet as a source of news and political information has grown in recent decades, while subscriptions to newspapers continue to shrink (Tapsell 2013). The Malaysian government exercises direct and indirect control over print media and television (Abbott 2001, 2004; Anuar 2005; Abbott 2011; Gomez and Kaur 2014). Political parties are commercially affiliated with the media sector, in particular, newspaper publishers (Anuar 2005, 2012, 2013). Freedom of speech is enshrined in the Malaysian constitution, but it is curtailed by several laws, such as the

Printing Presses and Publications Act, the Official Secrets Act, the Sedition Act, and the Security Offenses Act (Mohd Sani 2013; Tapsell 2013). These limitations reduce the likelihood of critical reporting on some matters, check freedom of the press, and encourage journalistic self-censorship (Tan 2014). Some news outlets circumvent the Printing Press and Publications Act by publishing news exclusively online. A profusion of websites emerged to give journalists the opportunity to publish critical reporting without being limited by these acts or constrained by the news media's ownership structures. These news sites attract readers because they are often run by professional and well-known journalists, which differentiates them from other sites run by opinionated amateurs, which also proliferate. In addition, Sarawakians increasingly use Facebook, WhatsApp, and other online platforms as news sources. Through these outlets, ICT users express their concerns about development projects, land rights, and other issues concerning Indigenous communities.

In the last few years, one of the main issues causing conflict between remote communities in central Sarawak and the government was the planned construction of a hydroelectric dam on the Baram River. It was one of several projects initiated by the government to produce low-cost energy and attract investors and industry to the state (Sovacool and Bulan 2011, 2012). The dam's reservoir would have flooded more than thirty villages in the region. People in the affected communities protested against the dam's construction by blocking the access road to the dam site to prevent workers from reaching the site. Grassroots organizations campaigned against the dam, rallying support from international non-governmental organizations concerned with the rights of Indigenous peoples. These groups used the internet to publicize their activities along with other protest strategies to raise awareness because, in the words of a protester affiliated with one of these groups, traditional news media are not offering adequate representation to oppositional narratives. "The media in Sarawak, unlike other countries, are all owned by big timber tycoons which are connected to the politicians. . . . They don't say what is going on here. They filter it until it is not recognized, until we are being muted" (interview, 2011).

Videos and photographs of the Baram protests were posted online and shared on Facebook by activists hoping to make their concerns heard by an international audience. Flickr sites were dedicated to the protests, and numerous videos of blockades and demonstrations were uploaded to YouTube. In 2015, late Chief Minister Adenan Satem confirmed that the construction of the dam was put on hold indefinitely.[6] The role ICTs played in this is hard to quantify, but the internet certainly provided a

Figure 9. Children in Long Luyang watching television, 2016.

platform for oppositional discourses that could not be found in more traditional media, such as newspapers or television, in Malaysia.

As a consequence of the limited press freedom in Malaysia, remote communities without ICT access are cut off from the supply of critical information that the internet enables. Many remote longhouses can receive FM radio, and some people also own television sets that they switch on if the family uses a generator (see Figure 9). Without internet access, these are the main news channels available in many villages. This means that people are unable to access information available on the internet about local issues that include critical or oppositional opinions and arguments or to voice their own opinions in this way. This lack of access to critical political reporting can potentially affect people's voting behaviors and thus impact Sarawak's and Malaysia's electoral outcomes, since Malaysia's electoral districts are drawn up in a way that favors rural voters (Pasuni and Liow 2012; Chin 2013; Ostwald 2013; Weiss 2014). In this way, the lack of communication media in many remote villages compounds people's already slim opportunities to take part in political debate and can affect local and federal elections as well.

In recent years, the government is increasingly taking measures against content producers using the Sedition Act (Willnat et al. 2013; Yangyue

Figure 10. Berawan women from Long Jegan dressed up in their traditional costumes, 2011.

2014; FreedomHouse 2015). Some bloggers were arrested, and websites were blocked. The government makes a moral argument for this, "[reminding] the mainstream media of their social responsibility to partner with the government in [the] collective project of nation building" (Anuar 2005, 28). These policies, along with the government's insistence on the media's social responsibility to foster racial harmony, risk discouraging debate around political issues and programs (Anuar 2005). These developments illustrate that even though ICTs have the potential to provide agency and voice to marginalized groups, this remains conditional on governmental approval and support.

■ CONCLUSION

Throughout our work in rural Sarawak, the authors experienced people's engagement with ICTs against odds such as lack of access, literacy, devices, and training. Figure 11 shows a group of children playing with a smartphone in Long Luyang, a village that has no mobile phone access, paved roads, grid electricity, or piped water. Like children in areas with better access, they are keen to engage with the available digital technologies. The use of media technologies by people who are often thought of as beyond

Figure 11. Children in Long Luyang playing games on a smartphone, 2016.

the digital divide, the role of media producers as intermediaries between rural and urban communities, and the relevant and specific functions that ICTs provide reinforce the importance of these technologies for Indigenous communities. Access to ICTs can enable self-directed engagement with traditional culture and promote economic development and political participation for Indigenous communities. However, as Majid Cooke (1997, 219) points out, the recognition of methods and techniques of resistance does not lead to a "reversal to pluralist conceptualisations of power." Dominant and entrenched social, political, and economic frameworks may not be dislodged by critical blogs and Facebook posts. Above all, the prerequisite to ICT use is access, which is dependent on the government's ability and willingness to work toward connecting rural and remote communities to ICT infrastructure. Schools need to provide adequate ICT training for students who may otherwise fall behind urban peers. Our research suggests that despite these limitations and the criticisms of globalization's impact on Indigenous peoples, Indigenous communities in Sarawak use new media technologies to engage with global discussions around issues that concern them, such as language, cultural continuity, economic development, and political participation—provided that access to the technology and infrastructure exists.

Some observers of the processes of cultural globalization argue that access to ICTs can expose Indigenous peoples' cultural heritage to commodification and that ICT access leads to cultural hybridization and loss. We argue that access to ICTs enables creative and self-determined practices that can be used to discuss Indigenous issues and present them to audiences both among Indigenous peoples and in the wider community. These practices are invaluable for people around the world who are historically disenfranchised, who are looking for sustainable socioeconomic development and political participation, but who struggle to make their voices heard.

Christine Horn works as a postdoctoral researcher at Swinburne University of Technology in Melbourne. Her recent research investigates the use of information and communication technologies (ICTs) in remote villages in Sarawak. During her PhD research, she investigated a collection of colonial-era ethnographic photographs taken in the region in collaboration with people from the source communities. She completed her MA at the University of Sarawak, Malaysia, and has lived and worked in the region for several years. Her interest in digital media and ICTs originated from her graduate training and teaching experience in graphic design and communications, which sparked her interest in local digital practices.

Patricia Philip has more than twenty years of experience in applied grassroots research in communities across Sarawak, in the course of which she has visited almost every village in Sarawak. Her professional expertise includes economic assessment of development programs, health, social development, and more. Her personal research focuses on the arts, crafts, and practices of the Bidayuh in the Puncak Borneo region of Sarawak. She has contributed to several books on the topic of local basketry and beads and frequently presents her research at academic conferences. She regularly organizes and facilitates workshops in basketry and other local crafts and owns an extensive collection in artifacts collected around the state. In addition, she acts as a consultant to international researchers and research projects requiring expertise on organizing and managing research in Sarawak.

Clement Langet Sabang is a Sebup from the Baram River in the Miri Division of Sarawak. He holds a master of science degree in human resource development (UNIMAS), a bachelor's degree in business administration (honors) and marketing (UiTM), an advance management program and advance diploma in management (UWA, Australia), a diploma in business studies (marketing) (UiTM), a diploma in training assessment systems (TTI, Australia), and a certificate IV in assessment and workplace training (TTI, Australia). He has lectured at Universiti Putra Malaysia, besides having twenty-five years' working experience as an administrative officer in the Sarawak Civil Service. Currently Clement is the head of marketing and corporate services at the University College of Technology Sarawak. Clement has written lyrics for the first ever Sebup pop songs "Nawai" and "Buwa Upa" as well as a Kenyah song, "Leto Magat," sung by a local artist. He plays the sape, a Kenyah musical instrument, and is a longtime contributor of Sebup-language information to Dewan Bahasa dan Pustaka's project on the Daftar Kata Bahasa Sukuan Sarawak. He has published a dictionary on the Sebup language and has contributed to articles on Sebup and local culture in the *Sarawak Gazette*.

■ NOTES

Christine Horn's PhD was funded through a Swinburne University Postgraduate Research Award. Her current research is funded through Swinburne's Melbourne–Sarawak Research Collaboration Scheme. Ethics approval was granted by the Swinburne University Human Research Ethics Committee. She thanks Ian McShane for advice and critique in writing this article, Ellie Rennie and Sandra M. Gifford for their guidance and support, and the SISR writing group for their feedback and encouragement. Thanks also go to Simpson Njock Lenjau for making the trip to Long Nawang possible and to the organizers and participants at Penn State's Summer Institute on Trans-Asian Indigeneity, who provided invaluable assistance in writing this article.

Clement Langet Sabang's acknowledgments go to his late father, Sabang Chapu, former headman of Lg Luyang, for teaching him the Sebup culture and to Surang Belawing, Suwing Jango, and Pingan Sabang.

1. "PM: Wider Broadband Penetration in Sarawak by Year-End," *Star Online*, April 29, 2012, http:// https://www.thestar.com.my/news/community/2012/04/29/pm-wider-broadband-penetration-in-sarawak-by-yearend/.

2. http://www.archive.ethnologue.com/.

3. The name "Sebup" is also spelled "Sebop" or "Cebop."

4. Clement Langet Sabang, one of the authors, published the first Sebup dictionary in 2015, with a second edition due shortly.

5. "So'en" is the name of the Sebup harvest festival but also of a festival celebrated in the past upon the successful return of a headhunting expedition.

6. "Baram Dam Project Halted Indefinitely," *Borneo Post,* November 19, 2015, http://www.theborneopost.com/.

■ WORKS CITED

Abbott, Jason P. 2001. "Democracy@internet.asia? The Challenges to the Emancipatory Potential of the Net: Lessons from China and Malaysia." *Third World Quarterly* 22, no. 1: 99–114.

Abbott, Jason P. 2004. "The Internet, Reformasi and Democratisation in Malaysia." In *The State of Malaysia: Ethnicity, Equity, and Reform,* edited by Edmund Terence Gomez, 79–104. London: Routledge Curzon.

Abbott, Jason P. 2011. "Electoral Authoritarianism and the Print Media in Malaysia: Measuring Political Bias and Analyzing Its Cause." *Asian Affairs: An American Review* 38, no. 1: 1–38.

Achoi, Jacob. 2010. "Bid to Revive Bidayuh Language in Schools." *Borneo Post,* November 28.

Anuar, Mustafa K. 2005. "Politics and the Media in Malaysia." *Kasarinlan: Philippine Journal of Third World Studies* 20, no. 1: 25–47.

Anuar, Mustafa K. 2012. "Reporting the Environment Human Rights, Development and Journalism in Malaysia." *Asia Pacific Media Educator* 22, no. 2: 253–62.

Anuar, Mustafa K. 2013. "Seeking Democracy in Malaysia." In *Democracy, Media, and Law in Malaysia and Singapore: A Space for Speech,* edited by Andrew T. Kenyon, Tim Marjoribanks, and Amanda Whiting, 83–105. New York: Routledge.

Appadurai, Arjun. 1996. *Modernity at Large: Cultural Dimensions of Globalization.* Minneapolis: University of Minnesota Press.

Avgerou, Chrisanthi. 2010. "Interdisciplinary Agendas in Visual Research: Re-situating Visual Anthropology." *Information Technologies and International Development* 6: 1–18.

Balasubramaniam, Vejai. 2007. "A Divided Nation: Malay Political Dominance, Bumiputera Material Advancement and National Identity in Malaysia." *National Identities* 9, no. 1: 35–48.

Boast, Robin, Michael Bravo, and Ramesh Srinivasan. 2007. "Return to Babel: Emergent Diversity, Digital Resources, and Local Knowledge." *The Information Society* 23: 395–403.

Brown, D., and G. Nicholas. 2012. "Protecting Indigenous Cultural Property in the Age of Digital Democracy: Institutional and Communal Responses to Canadian First Nations and Maori Heritage Concerns." *Journal of Material Culture* 17: 307–24.

Brown, Michael F. 1998. "Can Culture Be Copyrighted?" *Current Anthropology* 39, no. 2: 193–222.

Butet-Roch, Laurence. 2016. "Virtual Aamjiwnaang: Indigenous Interactive Storytelling." MA thesis, Ryerson University, Toronto.

Carlson, Bronwyn. 2013. "The 'New Frontier': Emergent Indigenous Identities and Social Media." In *The Politics of Identity: Emerging Indigeneity,* edited by M. Harris, M. Nakata, and B. Carlson, 147–68. Sydney: University of Technology Sydney.

Castells, Manuel. 2007. "Communication, Power and Counter-power in the Network Society." *International Journal of Communication* 1, no. 1: 238–66.

Castleton, Alexander. 2014. "Inuit Identity and Technology: An Exploration of the Use of Facebook by Inuit Youth." MA thesis, Carleton University, Ottawa.

Chin, James. 2013. "So Close and Yet So Far: Strategies in the 13th Malaysian Elections." *The Round Table* 102, no. 6: 533–40.

Chin, Sook-Kuan, Alvin W. Yeo, and Nadiantra Musa. 2013. "An Online Collaborative Framework for Orthography System Development." *International Journal of Computer Science* 10: 312–15.

Christensen, Neil Blair. 2003. *Inuit in Cyberspace: Embedding Offline, Identities Online.* Copenhagen: Museum Tusculanum Press.

Coleman, E. G. 2010. "Ethnographic Approaches to Digital Media." *Annual Review of Anthropology* 39: 487–505.

Cooke, Fadzilah Majid. 1997. "The Politics of 'Sustainability' in Sarawak." *Journal of Contemporary Asia* 27, no. 2: 217–41.

Dorian, Nancy C. 2010. "Documentation and Responsibility." *Language and Communication* 30, no. 3: 179–85.

Drouin, Michelle, and Claire Davis. 2009. "R u txting? Is the Use of Text Speak Hurting Your Literacy?" *Journal of Literacy Research* 41, no. 1: 46–67.

Dyson, Laurel. 2011. "Indigenous Peoples on the Internet." In *The Handbook of Internet Studies,* vol. 11, edited by Robert Burnett, Mia Consalvo, and Charles Ess, 251–69. Malden, Mass.: Wiley Blackwell.

Dyson, Laurel Evelyn, and Jim Underwood. 2006. "Indigenous People on the Web." *Journal of Theoretical and Applied Electronic Commerce Research* 1, no. 1: 65–76.

Edwards, Elizabeth. 2006. "Photographs and the Sound of History." *Visual Anthropology Review* 21: 27–46.

Edzan, N. N., and Mohd Sharif Mohd Saad. 2005. "NILA-A National Information Literacy Agenda for Malaysia." *Malaysian Journal of Library and Information Science* 10, no. 1: 91–103.

FreedomHouse. 2015. "Freedom on the Net Malaysia." http:// https:// freedomhouse.org/sites/default/files/FOTN%202015%20Full%20 Report.pdf.

Friedman, Jonathan. 1990. "Being in the World: Globalization and Localization." *Theory, Culture, and Society* 7, no. 2: 311–28.

Gilbert, Melissa. 2010. "Theorizing Digital and Urban Inequalities: Critical Geographies of 'Race,' Gender and Technological Capital." *Information, Communication, and Society* 13, no. 7: 1000–1018.

Gill, Saran Kaur. 2014. "Drastic Change in the Medium of Instruction: From Bahasa Malaysia to English." In *Language Policy Challenges in Multi-ethnic Malaysia*, 55–69. Dordrecht, Netherlands: Springer.

Ginsburg, Faye. 2008. "Rethinking the Digital Age." In *The Media and Social Theory*, edited by David Hesmondhalgh and Jason Toynbee, 127–44. Abingdon, U.K.: Routledge.

Ginsburg, Faye. 2016. "Indigenous Media from U-Matic to YouTube: Media Sovereignty in the Digital Age." *Sociologia and Antropologia* 6, no. 3: 581–99.

Gomez, Edmund Terence, and Surinder Kaur. 2014. "Struggling for Power: Policies, Coalition Politics and Elections in Malaysia." Paper presented at the Conference on Dominant Party Systems, University of Michigan, Ann Arbor, May 9–10.

Hall, Thomas D., and James V. Fenelon. 2015. *Indigenous Peoples and Globalization: Resistance and Revitalization*. Abingdon, U.K.: Routledge.

Hargittai, Eszter, and Kaitlin Jennrich. 2016. "The Online Participation Divide." In *The Communication Crisis in America, and How to Fix It*, edited by Mark Lloyd and Lewis A. Friedland, 199–213. New York: Palgrave Macmillan.

Harris, Charlotte A., and Roger W. Harris. 2011. "Information and Communication Technologies for Cultural Transmission among Indigenous Peoples." *The Electronic Journal of Information Systems in Developing Countries* 45, no. 1: 1–19.

Hassan, M. S., M. Shaffril, H. Azril, and J. L. D'Silva. 2009. "Problems and Obstacles in Using Information and Communication Technology (ICT) among Malaysian Agro-Based Entrepreneurs." *European Journal of Scientific Research* 36, no. 1: 93–101.

Hassan, Salleh, Hayrol Azril Mohamed Shaffril, Sham Shahkat Ali Ali, and Nor Sabila Ramil. 2010. "Agriculture Agency, Mass Media and Farmers: A Combination for Creating Knowledgeable Agriculture Community." *African Journal of Agricultural Research* 5, no. 24: 3500–3513.

Healy, Jessica De Largy. 2013. "Yolngu Zorba Meets Superman: Australian Aboriginal People, Mediated Publicness and the Culture of Sharing on the Internet." *Anthrovision* 1, no. 1.

Hershey, Robert. 2012. "'Paradigm Wars' Revisited: New Eyes on Indigenous Peoples' Resistance to Globalization." Arizona Legal Studies Discussion Paper 12-19.

Holton, Robert. 2000. "Globalization's Cultural Consequences." *Annals of the American Academy of Political and Social Science* 570, no. 1: 140–52.

Hopper, Paul. 2007. *Understanding Cultural Globalization.* Cambridge: Polity.

Janke, Terri, and Livia Iacovino. 2012. "Keeping Cultures Alive: Archives and Indigenous Cultural and Intellectual Property Rights." *Archival Science* 12: 151–71.

Jenkins, Henry. 2006. *Convergence Culture: Where Old and New Media Collide.* New York: NYU Press.

Kraidy, Marwan. 2017. *Hybridity, or the Cultural Logic of Globalization.* Philadelphia: Temple University Press.

Kral, Inge. 2011. "Youth Media as Cultural Practice: Remote Indigenous Youth Speaking Out Loud." *Australian Aboriginal Studies* 1: 4–16.

Mazzarella, William. 2004. "Culture, Globalization, Mediation." *Annual Review of Anthropology* 33: 345–67.

McMahon, Rob. 2013. "Digital Self-Determination: Aboriginal Peoples and the Network Society in Canada." PhD diss., Simon Fraser University, Vancouver.

MCMC. 2012. *Universal Service Provision Annual Report.* Cyberjaya, Selangor: Suruhanjaya Komunikasi dan Multimedia Malaysia/Malaysian Communications and Multimedia Commission.

MCMC. 2014. *Universal Service Provision Annual Report.* Cyberjaya, Selangor: Suruhanjaya Komunikasi dan Multimedia Malaysia/Malaysian Communications and Multimedia Commission.

MCMC. 2015. *Universal Service Provision Annual Report.* Cyberjaya, Selangor: Suruhanjaya Komunikasi dan Multimedia Malaysia/Malaysian Communications and Multimedia Commission.

McQuire, Scott. 2017. *Geomedia, Networked Cities, and the Politics of Urban Space: Networked Cities and the Future of Public Space.* Chichester, U.K.: Polity Press.

Metcalf, Peter. 2010. *The Life of the Longhouse: An Archaeology of Ethnicity.* Cambridge: Cambridge University Press.

Mohd Sani, Mohd Azizuddin. 2013. "Balancing Freedom of Speech and National Security in Malaysia." *Asian Politics and Policy* 5, no. 4: 585–607.

Nambiar, Mohana Kumari, and Subramaniam Govindasamy. 2010. "Documenting the Languages of the Orang Asli of Malaysia: Some Ethical Concerns." *Language and Communication* 30: 171–78.

Nathan, David, and Meili Fang. 2009. "Language Documentation and Pedagogy for Endangered Languages: A Mutual Revitalisation." *Language Documentation and Description* 6: 132–60.

Nathan, Dev, Govind Kelkar, and Pierre Walter. 2004. *Globalization and Indigenous Peoples in Asia: Changing the Local–Global Interface.* London: Sage.

Nicolaisen, Ida. 1997. "Timber, Culture, and Ethnicity: The Concept of Power and the Politicization of Ethnic Identity among the Punan Bah of Sarawak." In *Indigenous Peoples and the State,* edited by Robert L. Winzeler, 228–60. New Haven, Conn.: Yale University Southeast Asia Studies.

Norris, Pippa, and Ronald Inglehart. 2009. *Cosmopolitan Communications: Cultural Diversity in a Globalized World.* Cambridge: Cambridge University Press.

Ormond-Parker, Lyndon, Aaron Corn, Cressida Fforde, Kazuko Obata, and Sandy O'Sullivan. 2013. *Information Technology and Indigenous Communities.* Canberra: Australian Institute of Aboriginal and Torres Strait Islander Studies.

Ostwald, Kai. 2013. "How to Win a Lost Election: Malapportionment and Malaysia's 2013 General Election." *The Round Table* 102, no. 6: 521–32.

O'Sullivan, Dominic. 2012. "Globalization and the Politics of Indigeneity." *Globalizations* 9: 637–50.

Owiny, Sylvia A., Khanjan Mehta, and Audrey N. Maretzki. 2014. "The Use of Social Media Technologies to Create, Preserve, and Disseminate Indigenous Knowledge and Skills to Communities in East Africa." *International Journal of Communication* 8: 234–47.

Pasuni, Afif, and Joseph Chinyong Liow. 2012. "Malaysia: Sign of the Times: Election Fever, Recurring Themes, and Political Malaise." *Southeast Asian Affairs* 2012, no. 1: 171–84.

Pieterse, Jan Nederveen. 2015. *Globalization and Culture: Global Mélange.* New York: Rowman and Littlefield.

Plester, Beverly, and Clare Wood. 2009. "Exploring Relationships between Traditional and New Media Literacies: British Preteen Texters at School." *Journal of Computer-Mediated Communication* 14, no. 4: 1108–29.

Postill, John. 2003. "Knowledge, Literacy and Media among the Iban of Sarawak: A Reply to Maurice Bloch." *Social Anthropology* 11: 79–100.

Pratt, Yvonne Poitras. 2010. "Merging New Media with Old Traditions." *Native Studies Review* 19, no. 1: 1–27.

Rensch, Calvin R., Carolyn M. Rensch, Jonas Noeb, and Robert Sulis Ridu. 2006. *The Bidayuh Language: Yesterday, Today, and Tomorrow.* Kuching: SIL International/Dayak Bidayuh National Association.

Rice, Emma S., Emma Haynes, Paul Royce, and Sandra C. Thompson. 2016. "Social Media and Digital Technology Use among Indigenous

Young People in Australia: A Literature Review." *International Journal for Equity in Health* 15, no. 1: 81–97.

Robinson, Laura, Shelia R. Cotten, Hiroshi Ono, Anabel Quan-Haase, Gustavo Mesch, Wenhong Chen, Jeremy Schulz, Timothy M. Hale, and Michael J. Stern. 2015. "Digital Inequalities and Why They Matter." *Information, Communication, and Society* 18, no. 5: 569–82.

Sandvig, Christian. 2012. "Connection at Ewiiaapaayp Mountain: Indigenous Internet Infrastructure." In *Race after the Internet,* edited by Lisa Nakamura and Peter Chow-White, 168–200. New York: Routledge.

Segawa, Noriyuki. 2013. "Affirmative Action and Nation Building in Malaysia: The Future of Malay Preferential Policies." *African and Asian Studies* 12, no. 3: 189–214.

Smith, Claire, Heather Burke, and Graeme K. Ward. 2000. "Globalisation and Indigenous Peoples: Threat or Empowerment?" In *Indigenous Cultures in an Interconnected World,* edited by Claire Smith and Graeme Ward, 1–24. Vancouver: University of British Columbia Press.

Smith, Claire, and Graeme Ward, eds. 2000. *Indigenous Cultures in an Interconnected World.* Vancouver: University of British Columbia Press.

Smith, Karla J. 2010. "Minority Language Education in Malaysia: Four Ethnic Communities' Experiences." *International Journal of Bilingual Education and Bilingualism* 6, no. 1: 52–65.

Sovacool, Benjamin K., and L. C. Bulan. 2011. "Behind an Ambitious Megaproject in Asia: The History and Implications of the Bakun Hydroelectric Dam in Borneo." *Energy Policy* 39, no. 9: 4842–59.

Sovacool, Benjamin K., and L. C. Bulan. 2012. "Energy Security and Hydropower Development in Malaysia: The Drivers and Challenges Facing the Sarawak Corridor of Renewable Energy (SCORE)." *Renewable Energy* 40, no. 1: 113–29.

Srinivasan, Ramesh. 2006. "Indigenous, Ethnic and Cultural Articulations of New Media." *International Journal of Cultural Studies* 9: 497–518.

Srinivasan, R. 2012. "Re-thinking the Cultural Codes of New Media: The Question Concerning Ontology." *New Media and Society* 15: 203–23.

Srinivasan, Ramesh. 2017. *Whose Global Village? Rethinking How Technology Shapes Our World.* New York: NYU Press.

Stout, Noelle. 2014. "Bootlegged: Unauthorized Circulation and the Dilemmas of Collaboration in the Digital Age." *Visual Anthropology Review* 30, no. 2: 177–87.

Tan, Chee-beng. 1997. "Indigenous People, the State and Ethnogenesis: A Study of the Communal Associations of the 'Dayak' Communities in Sarawak, Malaysia." *Journal of Southeast Asian Studies* 28: 263–74.

Tan, Jeff. 2014. "Rent-Seeking and Money Politics in Malaysia." In *Rout-*

ledge Handbook of Contemporary Malaysia, 200–213. New York: Routledge.

Tapsell, Ross. 2013. "The Media Freedom Movement in Malaysia and the Electoral Authoritarian Regime." *Journal of Contemporary Asia* 43, no. 4: 613–35.

Thurlow, Crispin. 2006. "From Statistical Panic to Moral Panic: The Metadiscursive Construction and Popular Exaggeration of New Media Language in the Print Media." *Journal of Computer-Mediated Communication* 11, no. 3: 667–701.

Tomlinson, John. 1999. *Globalization and Culture.* Chicago: University of Chicago Press.

van Deursen, Alexander J. A. M., and Ellen J. Helsper. 2015. "The Third-Level Digital Divide: Who Benefits Most from Being Online?" In *Communication and Information Technologies Annual,* 29–52. https://doi.org/10.1108/S2050-206020150000010002.

van Deursen, Alexander, Ellen Helsper, Rebecca Eynon, and Jan van Dijk. 2017. "The Compoundness and Sequentiality of Digital Inequality." *International Journal of Communication* 11: 452–73.

Van Dijk, Jan A. G. M. 2006. "Digital Divide Research, Achievements and Shortcomings." *Poetics* 34, no. 4–5: 221–35.

Van Dijk, Jan, and Kenneth Hacker. 2003. "The Digital Divide as a Complex and Dynamic Phenomenon." *The Information Society* 19, no. 4: 315–26.

Weiss, Meredith L. 2014. "New Media, New Activism: Trends and Trajectories in Malaysia, Singapore and Indonesia." *International Development Planning Review* 36, no. 1: 91–109.

Willnat, Lars, W. Joann Wong, Ezhar Tamam, and Annette Aw. 2013. "Online Media and Political Participation: The Case of Malaysia." *Mass Communication and Society* 16, no. 4: 557–85.

Wilson, Pamela. 2015. "Indigenous Media: Linking the Local, Translocal, Global and Virtual." In *Mediated Geographies and Geographies of Media,* 367–83. New York: Springer.

Winzeler, Robert L., ed. 1997a. *Indigenous Peoples and the State.* New Haven, Conn.: Yale University Southeast Asia Studies.

Winzeler, Robert L. 1997b. "Modern Bidayuh Ethnicity and the Politics of Culture in Sarawak." In *Indigenous Peoples and the State,* edited by Robert L. Winzeler, 201–27. New Haven, Conn.: Yale University Southeast Asia Studies.

Yangyue, Liu. 2014. "Controlling Cyberspace in Malaysia: Motivations and Constraints." *Asian Survey* 54, no. 4: 801–23.

Zillien, Nicole, and Eszter Hargittai. 2009. "Digital Distinction: Status-Specific Types of Internet Usage." *Social Science Quarterly* 90, no. 2: 274–91.

  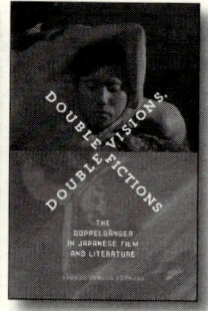